Speak Chinese with Millions

The Language of Everyday Conversation

P. C. T'ung
Hugh D. R. Baker

The Commercial Press

Library of Congress Cataloging-in-Publication Data
Tong, Bingzheng.
    Speak Chinese with millions : The Language of Everyday Conversation
P. C. T'ung and Hugh D. R. Baker.
        p. cm.
    Includes index.
    ISBN 978-0-9821816-9-0 (pbk.)
    1. Chinese language -- Conversation and phrase books -- English. 2. Chinese
language -- Spoken Chinese. I. Baker, Hugh D. R. II. Title.

    PL1125. E6T66 2009
    495. 1'83421 -- dc22

2009006441

Speak Chinese with Millions : The Language of Everyday Conversation

Authors :	© 2010 P. C. T'ung and Hugh D. R. Baker
Executive Editor :	K. L. Wong
Published by :	The Commercial Press (U.S.) Ltd.
	The Corporation, 2nd Floor New York, NY10013
	http://www.commercialpress.com.hk
Printed by :	Elegance Printing & Book Binding Co. Ltd.,
	Block A, 4/F, Hoi Bun Industrial Building, Hong Kong
Edition :	First edition, 2010
	© 2010 The Commercial Press (U.S.) Ltd.
	ISBN 978 098 21 8169 0
	Printed in Hong Kong.

For our wives
Yih and Sue

(We didn't do it alone)

PREFACE

Fifteen years ago we published *Chinese in Three Months* in the Hugo's Language Books series, revising it for a new edition in 1998. The book has been out of print for some time, but there is still a demand for it from individuals and from institutions, so we decided to make a thorough-going revision, updating vocabulary, re-ordering the presentation, writing new dialogues, and adding nearly thirty new exercises. In many respects this is a new work, and we have given it a new title to reflect that.

Our principal aim has been to make the book clear and accessible to self-learners. For them especially, the large number of exercises will help to reinforce what has been learned, and will allow self-testing as a check that it has been understood correctly. Careful attention to the recordings that accompany the book should enable the student to become accustomed to the sound of Chinese and to acquire accurate pronunciation. The format has also proved to work well in the classroom, and we have had very positive feedback from teachers in institutions that have been using it as a textbook. We know that they will welcome the updated version.

Chinese is an exciting language to learn, and we have again done our best to show that and to make the process an enjoyable one.

P. C. T'ung

Hugh D. R. Baker

London, February 2010

CONTENTS

⌒ This symbol indicates the track number of the recording.

INTRODUCTION

There are scores of Chinese dialects, and although all of them are related, many sound so different that a speaker of one cannot understand the speaker of another — they are really separate languages. This is a problem for communication and unity nationwide, so since the early 20th century Chinese governments have been encouraging their people to speak and understand one standard, universal Chinese language.

In the West this language is usually called 'Mandarin'. Some Chinese names for it are **Guānhuà** 'Officials' Language', **Guóyǔ** 'National Language', and **Pǔtōnghuà** 'Universal Language' (by which name it is now officially known in mainland China). It is this language, based on the speech of Beijing itself, that we set out to teach here. We shall refer to it quite simply as 'Chinese'.

Our aim is to help you teach yourself a tongue which will let you communicate in real life, whether your purpose is to do business, to travel, or just to study out of interest. The language we use here is as 'everyday' as we can make it, and we have tried to present it in scenes which are common and natural in China today.

Naturally, you are the one who has to do the work. We can only make your job as interesting and as much fun as possible, we cannot actually learn Chinese for you. But by way of encouragement, we can let you into a secret: it is not a particularly difficult language! Of course those who haven't tried it don't know that and they will be full of admiration for your brilliance in learning some, however elementary. Only you and other brave souls like you will know that the admiration is very cheaply won. So treat yourself — learn it and be smug!

For a start you can throw away quite a lot of the ideas which you have acquired about other languages. Don't look for tenses — there aren't any; don't ask how verbs conjugate — they don't; don't worry about gender; don't think about case — nominative, genitive, accusative and all the rest of their friends don't exist in modern Chinese; say goodbye to irregular verbs, strong and weak nouns, agreements, subjunctives, singulars and plurals, declensions, ...

Having emptied your mind by this turn-out, you should be able to find room for some new ideas. There are 'measures', 'particles', and a series of 'word orders' which are really like mathematical formulae into which you fit your vocabulary. Sentences usually begin with a 'topic' rather than a grammatical subject; conditions are always set out before the main business; and logical order is required (in Chinese it is impossible to go to Shanghai from Beijing, you can only go from Beijing to Shanghai). In matters of time and place the larger always comes before the smaller (year before month before day; country before city before street before house number).

None of these is very frightening, and we have tried to present them in a 'user-friendly' way. In fact, Chinese is simple enough not to need lots of grammatical jargon, so we cannot claim too much credit if we have succeeded in avoiding technicalities. Sometimes what seems to be a grammatical problem is actually a matter of cultural difference, and you will find that some of our 'grammar notes' seem more like explanations of Chinese culture.

What often alarms the beginner most is the fact that Chinese sings its sounds in four different tones. There isn't any reason to be scared, it's a problem soon overcome; but tones are important because Chinese has a very restricted sound range (only about 400 different sounds) and having tones increases the number of possible distinct ones. Even so, the limited number means that many words have to share a sound. English, with a much larger sound range, does not escape the problem entirely — think of **to**, **too**, and **two**, or **pare**, **pair**, and **pear** — but Chinese rarely has the luxury of only three 'homophones'. As an extreme example, one elementary dictionary of Chinese has no fewer than 80 words pronounced **yi**, but by combining them with other sounds to make words of more than one syllable misunderstanding is avoided.

You may have been told that Chinese is 'a monosyllabic language'. Well, it is and it isn't. It is true that each Chinese written character represents one syllable and that each character has its own meaning, but in speech, as we have just explained, it is impossible always to tell which of the many characters that share a pronunciation is meant, so the spoken language frequently puts two or more syllables together to make **compound words** that are more easily identified and understood by the listener. For this reason, it usually takes more syllables to say something than to write it, and what is 'monosyllabic' in script is 'polysyllabic' in speech.

The written language is the one major area that we have not covered in detail in this book. To learn Chinese characters is a time-consuming and arduous business because they are not directly connected with speech. English spelling is often ridiculed for being only a poor representation of the sounds of the spoken language ('fish', it is claimed, could be spelled **ghoti**, using the **gh** of 'enough', the **o** of 'women', and the **ti** of 'nation'), but the Chinese writing system in some cases does not even pretend to represent the sounds of the language. It uses symbols to represent the **ideas** being spoken as much as the **sounds** by which those ideas are expressed. The snag is that while English only uses 26 letters to be able to write everything, Chinese needs a different symbol for every idea it has to convey. There are over 50,000 Chinese characters in existence: no-one knows them all and somewhere about 4,000 of them are enough for literacy, but to learn even that many would enlarge the scope of this book beyond reason. In Chapter Twenty we explain characters more fully and give some common ones which might come in handy in China.

It goes without saying that sooner or later the student of Chinese will have to get down to learning characters, but meanwhile the **spoken language** can be learned perfectly adequately through the medium of an alphabetised (usually called 'romanised') system. Many ways of romanising Chinese have been invented over the years, but we shall be using the official Beijing government system called **Hànyǔ pīnyīn**. **Hànyǔ pīnyīn** spells the sound and adds a mark over the main vowel to represent the tone, and this gives all the information needed to pronounce the word correctly. **The sounds of Chinese** section which follows sets out the system in detail. If you think about it, Chinese people learn their language in the same way as you are doing — they learn to speak before they learn reading and writing. And there is an additional advantage to learning through **Hànyǔ pīnyīn**: each Chinese character is written separately and pronounced as a single syllable, and if you learn your language that way, there is a strong tendency to speak in single separate syllables, stiltedly, without stress or emotional expression, and that of course is not what ordinary speech should sound like. The romanisation helps you to identify which syllables belong together as a word and what the stress on particular syllables should be, and it is then easier to learn how to speak in a natural-sounding way.

Each chapter of this book is organised around a particular theme. The heart of the material consists of conversations, four short or three long ones to a chapter. New words and grammar notes are placed before the conversations, but you will certainly need to refer back to them to understand fully what you are reading. There are lots of exercises, designed to reinforce the learning process by making you think about what you have learned, and the answers are at the back of the book to give you confirmation that you were right.

How you use this book is up to you, but you should try to set aside a certain amount of time each day and 'keep taking the medicine regularly'. Spend a few minutes working back over the material you studied last. Then read the notes and list of new words that are placed before each new conversation you come to. Listen to the recording as you read the conversation so that you get the sound and flow of it in your head. As soon as you can, try to listen to it without the text in front of you, concentrating hard, and forcing yourself to understand what is being said, listening over and over until it makes sense.

As you progress you will certainly find that you need to go back over material you have already studied but need to be reminded about. The Index at the back of the book is a useful tool for this: it refers you to the grammar notes, and to categories like 'adverbs', 'colours', 'health', 'negatives', and 'comparison' so that you can get a broad overview of them. The Chinese-English Word-list will also help you as a reference tool.

Read the material, listen to the recordings, try to think and understand even while you are mechanically repeating sounds. You are about to become one of that tiny minority in the world who can converse with that vast majority of people who are Chinese! This medicine is not nasty, we promise. Here goes ... !

⌢₁ A. *The sounds of Chinese*

Very few of the sounds of Chinese are difficult for a native speaker of English to make. The **Hànyǔ pīnyīn** system is on the whole easy to read and sensible in its spellings, with just a few oddities which need to be learned. To help you make sense of the list of sounds we have given some pronunciation guides, and you can use them as a rough model while you listen closely to the recording for the polished version which you need to copy if you are to acquire a good accent.

A1. The initial consonants.

With two exceptions (**-n** and **-ng**) consonants do not appear at the end of syllables, they occur at the beginning, which explains why they are called 'initial consonants'. So while Chinese does have words like the English *bin* and *bang* it does not have words ending with other consonants like *of* or *as* or *ash* or *it* or *up* or *east* or *leg* or *kick*. Here is the complete list of initial consonants, with pronunciation guides and an example of each to read while listening to the recording:

b-	much as in *bath*	**bā**
p-	as in *puff*	**pā**
m-	as in *man*	**mā**
f-	as in *fun*	**fā**
d-	much as in *dig*	**dā**
t-	as in *tickle*	**tā**
n-	as in *nasty*	**nā**
l-	as in *large*	**lā**
z-	as in *adze*	**zā**
c-	as in *cats*	**cā**
s-	as in *sat*	**sā**
zh-	as in *ajar*	**zhā**
ch-	as in *char*	**chā**
sh-	as in *shout*	**shā**
r-	as in *run*	**rāng**
j-	as in *jeans*	**jī**

q-	as in _cheek_	qī
x-	something like _hiss ye_	xī
g-	much as in _gun_	gā
k-	as in _king_	kā
h-	as in _huh!_	hā

In English some words (like 'owe' and 'eat') do not have an initial consonant at all, and the same is true of Chinese. Where such words would begin with an **i** or a **ü**, **Hànyǔ pīnyīn** prefers to use a **y**: so **i** becomes **yi**, **iao** becomes **yao**, **iong** becomes **yong**, **ü** becomes **yu**, and **üe** becomes **yue**. Similarly **w** is used where words might otherwise begin with a **u**: so **u** becomes **wu**, **uang** becomes **wang**, and **uo** becomes **wo**.

A2. The vowels and final consonants.

a	as in _father_	mā	chā			
o	as in _saw_	bō	mō			
e	much as in _her_	hē	kē			
er	much as in _err_	fēr	gēr			
u	much as in _shoe_	pū	chū			
ü	as in the French _tu_	jū	qū	xū	yū	lǜ

Note the difference between **u** and **ü**. The **ü** sound only appears after **n- l- j- q- x-** or on its own. The **u** sound appears after all initial consonants except **j- q- x- y-**. So it is only after **n- l-** that there can be any confusion between them, and it is only after **n- l-** that the **umlaut ü** actually needs to be used.

| i | as in _bee_ | dī | jī | qī | xī | yī |

BUT beware that after **z- c- s-** the **i** is pronounced more like the noise a bee makes (a buzzing behind the teeth) than a full vowel

| | | zī | cī | sī |

AND after **zh- ch- sh- r-** the **i** stands for a buzzing between the curled-back tongue and the roof of the mouth

| | | zhī | chī | shī | rì |

| ai | as in _sky_ | pāi | kāi |
| ei | as in _day_ | fēi | bēi |

ao	as in _no<u>w</u>_	**cāo**	**dāo**
ou	as in _<u>owe</u>_	**gōu**	**tōu**
an	much as in _<u>fun</u>_	**sān**	**kān**
en	as in _brok<u>en</u>_	**fēn**	**shēn**
ang	as in _b<u>ung</u>_	**bāng**	**zāng**
eng	try saying _<u>erng</u>_	**pēng**	**zhēng**
ong	try saying _<u>oong</u>_	**kōng**	**sōng**
ia	as in _<u>yah</u>_	**qiā**	**xiā**
iao	as in _<u>miaow</u>_	**piāo**	**liāo**
ie	as in _<u>ye</u>s_	**diē**	**tiē**
iou	as in _<u>ye</u>oman_	**jiū**	**qiū**
ian	as in _<u>yen</u>_	**biān**	**yān**

Note how **an** changes sound after **i** or **y**.

in	midway between _<u>sin</u>_ and _<u>seen</u>_	**qīn**	**yīn**
iang	much as in _<u>young</u>_	**yāng**	**xiāng**
ing	as in _<u>England</u>_	**tīng**	**jīng**
iong	try saying _<u>yoong</u>_	**xiōng**	**yōng**
ua	as in _n<u>ow</u> argue_	**guā**	**zhuā**
uo	as in _<u>do or</u> die_	**tuō**	**suō**
uai	much as in _<u>why</u>_	**wāi**	**shuāi**
uei	midway between _<u>way</u>_ and _<u>we</u>_	**duī**	**cuī**
uan	as in _<u>one</u>_	**kuān**	**chuān**
uen	as in _<u>sow 'n</u> reap_	**hūn**	**wēn**
uang	as in _<u>wonky</u>_ (but no <u>k</u>)	**huāng**	**guāng**
üe	rather as in _<u>you ate</u>_	**yuē**	**quē**
üan	between _<u>U.N.</u>_ and _<u>you anger</u>_	**juān**	**yuān**
ün	much as in _<u>United</u>_	**xūn**	**yūn**

In Beijing dialect the **ér** sound is added to the end of many words, making the language sound rather like an exaggerated stage version of West Country English. To some extent this is found in standard Chinese too, and here and there in the book you will find an **r** added to a syllable to indicate that this happens. If you listen carefully to the recording at such points you should be able to hear the effect and to notice that in some cases it changes the pronunciation very markedly.

You will notice from time to time that an apostrophe has crept into a spelling, as with **Xī'ān** for example. The purpose of the apostrophe is to separate out the syllables — if we had spelled the word **Xiān** you might have assumed that it was the single syllable **xiān** rather than two syllables **xī** and **ān**.

⌢²⌣ *B. The tones.*

Don't be alarmed if this section seems difficult at first. Read it and understand as much as you can, but don't be put off if it doesn't immediately make sense to you. You can always come back later to read it as often as you like, and as you go on with the book you will find that the mystery resolves itself. The four tones are:

Tone 1.   A high level tone
Tone 2.   A high rising tone
Tone 3.   A low dipping and rising tone
Tone 4.   A high falling tone

Their patterns can be shown diagrammatically on a scale rising from a low pitch [1] to a high pitch [5]:

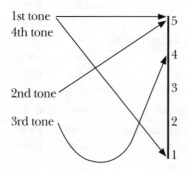

They are represented in **Hànyǔ pīnyīn** by marks placed over the main vowel:

Tone 1.	**mā**	**jiā**	**shēn**	**xiē**	**chuāng**
Tone 2.	**má**	**jiá**	**shén**	**xié**	**chuáng**
Tone 3.	**mǎ**	**jiǎ**	**shěn**	**xiě**	**chuǎng**
Tone 4.	**mà**	**jià**	**shèn**	**xiè**	**chuàng**

In the text you will see that not all syllables are given a tone mark. This is because (1) grammatical particles do not have a tone, taking their pitch from the words which come before them (2) in two-syllable words the second syllable may be so little stressed as virtually not to have a tone or (3) a few single syllable words, notably **shi** 'to be', **lai** 'to come', and **qu** 'to go', are commonly used without stressed tone in certain contexts. In such cases no tone mark is used. The vast majority of syllables, though, do have tone, and it is necessary to learn the correct tone for every word as it is encountered. The difference between saying 'buy' and 'sell' is the difference between **mǎi** and **mài**, so beware!

Tone can be heard very clearly when a word is pronounced in isolation, though it is to some extent modified when spoken in a sentence. There are cases where tones are very much changed by the tone of the following syllable. The clearest example of this is where two Third Tone words come together — the first of them changes into a Second Tone. So **kěkǒu** is pronounced as **kékǒu**, and **wǒ hǎo** is said **wó hǎo**. (But note that you will not find this automatic tone change reflected in the tone-marking in the text — the **Hànyǔ pīnyīn** system does not show the change.)

Two words of Chinese have their own tone rules. **Yi**, meaning 'one', is pronounced in the First Tone when it is said in isolation, in the Second Tone before a Fourth Tone word, and in the Fourth Tone in front of a First, Second or Third Tone word. **Bu**, meaning 'not', is also pronounced in the Second Tone before a Fourth Tone word and in the Fourth Tone in front of any other tone, and in some contexts it is given no tone at all. You will find that they have been marked accordingly in the text.

Here and there in the book you will find an asterisk (*) beside a new word. This has nothing to do with pronunciation, it is a warning that the word is not to be used on its own, it always appears as part of what we called above a **compound word** (a fixed two or three syllable expression). It is rather like the English words 'socio-' or 'Anglo-', which are completely meaningful but are only ever used as part of fuller expressions. We use the asterisk to try to stop you from saying something in Chinese that would sound as silly as 'That is a socio problem' or 'My home is in the Anglo city of Manchester'.

The spelling and the tone mark can give you an accurate indication of how to pronounce a syllable, but a little more is needed to get the expression into it so that it sounds as though it were spoken by Chinese lips. Musical notation is not just a matter of writing down the long and short notes in the right order, and composers add in further instructions to be loud or soft, to slow down or speed up, to play joyfully or plaintively, etc. Chinese really needs such additional aids, particularly with regard to the stress on the different syllables of compound words, but **Hànyǔ pīnyīn** can only show stress by the rather crude device of leaving the tone mark off certain syllables. You should pay particular attention to the recordings in order to pick up the nuances of stress which make all the difference between speaking like a bookworm robot and speaking like a native.

C. Pronunciation practice.

C1. The four tones.

mā	má	mǎ	mà
bā	bá	bǎ	bà
yī	yí	yǐ	yì
wū	wú	wǔ	wù
yū	yú	yǔ	yù
zhōng	huá	yǔ	diào
yīn	yáng	shǎng	qù

C2. Two-syllable words.

Běijīng	Beijing (Peking)
Shànghǎi	Shanghai
Guǎngzhōu	Guangzhou (Canton)
Chóngqìng	Chongqing (Chungking)
Yúnnán	Yunnan
kòutóu	kowtow
chǎomiàn	chowmein
zásuì	chop-suey
gōngfu	kungfu
táifēng	typhoon

C3. Three-syllable words.

Máo Zédōng	Mao Tse-tung
Zhōu Ēnlái	Chou En-lai
Dèng Xiǎopíng	Teng Hsiao-ping
Hú Jǐntāo	Hu Jintao
Wēn Jiābǎo	Wen Jiabao

C4. Neutral tones.

zhuō + zǐ	zhuōzi	table
yǐ + zǐ	yǐzi	chair
qián + tóu	qiántou	in front
hòu + tóu	hòutou	behind
tīng + tīng	tīngting	listen
kàn + kàn	kànkan	look
péng + yǒu	péngyou	friend
dōng + xī	dōngxi	thing
huí + lái	huílai	come back
dòu + fǔ	dòufu	bean-curd

Note how a change from full tone to neutral tone can transform the meaning of certain words:

dàyì	=	gist	BUT	dàyi	= careless
dìdào	=	tunnel	BUT	dìdao	= genuine
dōng-xī	=	east & west	BUT	dōngxi	= thing

C5. Tone changes.

Listen carefully to the recording to hear how the tones change when they are used in combination with other tones:

3 + 1	mǎ + chē	mǎchē	cart
3 + 2	mǎ + dá	mǎdá	motor
3 + 4	mǎ + lì	mǎlì	horsepower
3 + 0	mǎ + hu	mǎhu	casual
3 + 3	mǎ + biǎo	mǎbiǎo	stopwatch
3 + 3 + 3	zhǎn + lǎn + guǎn	zhǎnlǎnguǎn	exhibition centre
4 + 4	zài + jiàn	zàijiàn	goodbye

C6. The er ending.

Here are some examples of the **er** ending added to other sounds. Listen carefully to the recording — some of the resulting sounds are not what you might expect from the spellings!

gē + er	=	gēr
hàomǎ + er	=	hàomǎr

pái + er	=	**páir**
yíkuài + er	=	**yíkuàir**
běn + er	=	**běnr**
yìdiǎn + er	=	**yìdiǎnr**
líng + er	=	**língr**
diànyǐng + er	=	**diànyǐngr**

Chapter 1

SOME ESSENTIAL PHRASES

Chinese has many set expressions which may not make logical sense but which have become part of everyday language. These expressions should just be learned and understood without bothering to try to fit them into the normal rules of grammar. Here are a few. Some of them you will meet all the time; some of them we hope you will never need to use, but you should learn them just in case. Listen carefully to the recording and practice them often — you will need to be really fluent with these, and the practice will help your pronunciation of everything else too.

⌕4 1.1 Hello

Typical greeting between a Chinese and a foreigner at any time:

A : **Nǐ hǎo!** [lit: You well]   Hello!
B : **Nǐ hǎo!**   Hello to you!

⌕5 1.2 Morning greeting

A : **Zǎo!** [lit: Early]   (Good) morning!
B : **Nǐ zǎo!**   (Good) morning to you!

In more formal situations, such as when a television newsreader starts a programme or a public speaker begins to speak, you may hear the following:

Zǎoshang hǎo!   Good morning!
Wǎnshang hǎo!   Good evening!

⌕6 1.3 Answering the phone

A : **Wéi, nǐ hǎo!**   Hello!
B : **Nǐ hǎo!**   Hello!

(7) 1.4   A thanks B for an offering

A : **Xièxie, xièxie.**　　　　Thank you.

B : **Búxiè.** [not thank]　　　Don't mention it.

(8) 1.5   A thanks B for help

A : **Xièxie.**　　　　　　　　Thank you.

B : **Méi guānxi.** [no relevance]　Not at all;
　　or **Méi shìr.** [no matter]　it's nothing.

(9) 1.6   A apologizes to B

A : **Duìbuqǐ.**　　　　　　　(I'm) sorry.

　　or **Bù hǎo yìsi.**　　　　[I'm embarrassed] Sorry.

B : **Méi guānxi.** *or* **Méi shìr.**　It doesn't matter.

(10) 1.7   Welcoming a guest

A : **Huānyíng, huānyíng!**　　Welcome!

B : **Xièxie, xièxie!**　　　　　Thank you.

(11) 1.8   Welcoming customers

At a shop, restaurant, hotel etc.

　　Huānyíng guānglín!　　Welcome! [Literally: Welcome the
　　　　　　　　　　　　　　light of your presence]

(12) 1.9   After you

A : **Qǐng.** [please]　　　　　After you.

B : **Nín qǐng.** [You please]　　After you.

(13) 1.10 *Please be seated*

Qǐng zuò, qǐng zuò.   Please take a seat.

(14) 1.11 *At dinner*

Host A and Guest of Honour B:

A : **Qǐng, qǐng.**   Please, do start.
B : **Hǎo, hǎo. Dàjiā qǐng.**   Yes, everybody please start.
[OK, everybody please]

(15) 1.12 *A toast*

A : **Gānbēi!** [dry glass]   Bottoms up!
B : **Gānbēi!**   Cheers!

(16) 1.13 *Congratulations!*

Gōngxǐ, gōngxǐ!   Congratulations!
or **Zhùhè nǐ!**   Congratulations to you!

(17) 1.14 *Happy New Year!*

Xīnnián hǎo!   Happy New Year!
or **Gōngxǐ fācái!**

Literally **Gōngxǐ fācái!** means 'Congratulations and get wealthy'. Many people in the West will know it as **Kung hay fat choy!** which is how it is said by Cantonese-speaking overseas Chinese.

(18) 1.15 *Come on!*

Jiā yóu! [add fuel]   Come on! Play up!

This is how you encourage your favourite team or athlete.

(19) *1.16   Staccato speech*

In Chinese, as in English, people quite commonly use brief phrases rather than long full sentences. The following exchange could be heard any day in China, it has not been kept especially short and simple in order to help beginners.

There is a knock at the door ....

A : **Shéi?**	Who (is it)?
B : **Wǒ.**	(It's) me.

Here as everywhere in this book you will only be taught correct Chinese, there will be no need to 'un-learn' anything later.

(20) *1.17   Look out!*

Xiǎoxīn! [Focus mind]   Take care! Watch out! Be careful!

(21) *1.18   If there is a fire*

Zháo huǒ la! [caught fire]   Fire!

(22) *1.19   When in danger*

Jiùmìng a! [save life]   Help!

(23) *1.20   Parting company*

A : **Zàijiàn.** [again see]	See you again.
B : **Zàijiàn.**	Goodbye.

Chapter 2

INTRODUCTIONS

In this chapter you will learn how to get started when meeting new people, how to address them without giving offence, how to find out about them and how to tell them about yourself.

Chinese culture has always stressed the importance of getting the names of people and things right, and in traditional times there were extremely complicated terms for all the different relatives that you might meet in the large extended families and clans. Even today, when things are much simpler, there is no one word which is the equivalent of 'uncle'. Instead there is one word for 'Father's elder brother', one for Father's younger brother', one for 'Mother's brother', and one for 'Father's sister's husband'. You will not be learning all these, but you will find that Chinese people appreciate careful attention to how you address them. After all, no-one likes to be called 'Oy, you!' even in English.

First of all you need to learn a few words so that you have something to work with ...

2.1 *Pronouns*

Singular:	**wǒ**	I, me
	nǐ	you (singular)
	nín	you (polite form)
	tā	he, him, she, her

Note that there is no difference between nominative and accusative cases (I and me, she and her) or between the sexes (he and she).

Plural:	**wǒmen**	we, us
	nǐmen	you (plural)
	tāmen	they, them

It is tempting to conclude from this list of pronouns that **–men** makes plurals, but BEWARE that **–men** only works this way for the pronouns and a very small handful of exceptional 'human' nouns. Never use **–men** with any noun unless you have heard a Chinese person say it.

2.2 Names

Chinese people always put their surname before their personal names, so that in the names Mao Zedong and Zhou Nan **Máo** and **Zhōu** are the surnames. If English did the same **John Henry Smith** would become **Smith John Henry.** To ask someone's surname you say **Nín guì xìng?** which literally means 'Your honourable surname?' The answer is **Wǒ xìng...** 'I am surnamed...'.

Surname

There are thousands of Chinese surnames, including a few 'double-barrelled' ones, but no more than a few dozen are common, and the twenty most common probably account for well over half the population. By contrast there is an unlimited number of personal names, some consisting of one Chinese character, some of two. Each character is one syllable, so there are three characters in Mao's name (**máo** 毛, **zé** 泽 and **dōng** 东) and two in Zhou's (**zhōu** 周 and **nán** 南).

2.3 Nations and nationality

Guó means 'country', and **Zhōngguó** means 'China' (literally: Central country). In most foreign country names, the sound of the foreign word is imitated by the Chinese word. Some have **guó** added to an appropriate sound with a good meaning:

Yīngguó	Britain (**Yīng** imitates <u>Eng</u>land and means 'hero')
Měiguó	U.S.A. (**Měi** imitates <u>Ame</u>rica and means 'beautiful')
Fǎguó	France (**Fǎ** imitates <u>Fra</u>nce and means 'law')
Déguó	Germany (**Dé** imitates <u>Deut</u>sch and means 'virtue')
wàiguó	foreign country (**wài** means 'outside')

Where there is already more than one syllable in the name, **guó** is not used:

Yìdàlì	Italy
Xībānyá	Spain
Jiānádà	Canada
Rìběn	Japan
Àodàlìyà	Australia

Rén means 'person'. It can be added to the names of countries or places to show that that is where a person comes from:

Zhōngguó rén	a Chinese person

Yīngguó rén	a British person
wàiguó rén	a foreigner
Běijīng rén	a person from Beijing
Lúndūn rén	a Londoner

Exercise 1
Can you identify the following countries?

1. **Hélán**	2. **Dānmài**	3. **Yìndù**
4. **Ài'ěrlán**	5. **Mòxīgē**	6. **Mǎláixīyà**
7. **Sūgélán**	8. **Éluósī**	

* Answers to all exercises are between pp. 267-292.

(26) 2.4 *Verbs*

a) Chinese verbs only have one form. So where English has lots of forms of the verb 'to be' (am, are, is, was, were, will be, would have been, etc.), Chinese only has **shì**. Note that unless special emphasis is required **shì** is pronounced in neutral tone **shi**:

Wǒ shi Běijīng rén.	I'm from Beijing.
Nǐ shi Běijīng rén.	You're from Beijing.
Tā shi Běijīng rén.	He/she's from Beijing.
Wǒmen shi Běijīng rén.	We're from Beijing.
Nǐmen shi Běijīng rén.	You (pl.) are from Beijing.
Tāmen shi Běijīng rén.	They're from Beijing.

b) The verb **xìng** means 'to be surnamed':

Wǒ xìng Wáng.	I am surnamed Wang.

But if the full name is given, **xìng** cannot logically be used (it would sound silly to say 'I am surnamed John Henry Smith' in English too), and then it is **shi** which is used:

Wǒ shi Wáng Hànshēng.	I am Wang Hansheng.

c) The verb **jiào** means 'to call' or 'to be called', so **Wǒ jiào Wáng Hànshēng** could mean either 'I call Wang Hansheng' or 'I am called Wang Hansheng'. Usually it is obvious which one is meant, but to avoid ambiguity **míngzi** 'name' is added in. **Wǒ míngzi jiào Wáng Hànshēng** can only mean 'I am called Wang Hansheng'.

2.5 Nouns

Nouns only have one form, like verbs. So **Běijīng rén** means 'person from Beijing' or 'persons from Beijing', man or men, woman or women, child or children. It is the same with all other nouns — car/cars, mouse/mice, tree/trees, the Chinese word is the same regardless of whether the noun is singular or plural. The exceptions mentioned in **2.1** above are so few that you can afford to ignore them until such time as they pop up, by which time you will be advanced enough not to find them a problem.

Exercise 2
True or false?

1. **Máo Zédōng shi Zhōngguó rén.**
2. **Zhōu Ēnlái shi Shànghǎi rén.**
3. **Mǎgē Bōluó** (Marco Polo) **shi Yìdàlì rén.**
4. **Xiāo Bónà** (George Bernard Shaw) **shi Lúndūn rén.**
5. **Bìjiāsuǒ** (Pablo Picasso) **shi Fǎguó rén.**

(27) CONVERSATION 2A

Wang Hansheng introduces himself:

Wǒ shi Wáng Hànshēng.	I am Wang Hansheng.
Wǒ xìng Wáng, míngzi jiào Hànshēng.	My surname is Wang. My personal name is Hansheng.
Wǒ shi Zhōngguó rén.	I am a Chinese.
Wǒ shi Běijīng rén.	I'm from Beijing.

And who's this?

Tā shi Lǐ Dàwěi.	He's David Lee.
Tā xìng Lǐ, míngzi jiào Dàwěi.	His surname is Lee, and his personal name is David.
Tā shi Yīngguó rén.	He is British.
Tā shi Lúndūn rén.	He's from London.

(28) 2.6 Titles

Chinese people always put their names before their title, so that:

Mr Smith would become *Smith Mr.*

Mr John Henry Smith becomes *Smith John Henry Mr.*

The word for 'Mr.' is **xiānsheng**, so *Mr David Lee* is **Lǐ Dàwěi xiānsheng**.

Among groups of people who know each other well, it is common for older members to be addressed by their surname with **lǎo** 'old' in front. They would address younger and junior people by putting **xiǎo** 'little', 'young' in front of the surname:

Lǎo Zhāng.	Old Zhang.
Xiǎo Lǐ.	Young Lee.

It is usually better for non-Chinese to stick to the polite forms of address, such as **Wáng xiānsheng** (Mr Wang), **Wáng xiǎojie** (Miss Wang), and **Wáng fūren** (Mrs Wang).

Exercise 3
Introduce yourself in Chinese:

1. I am (your full name).
2. My surname is (___), my first name is (___).
3. I am (your nationality).
4. I'm from (your home town).

(29) 2.7 Final particles 'ma' and 'ba'

All particles have neutral tone. The particle **ma** at the end of a sentence changes a statement into a question:

Tā shi Běijīng rén.	He's from Beijing.
Tā shi Běijīng rén ma?	Is he from Beijing?

The particle **ba** at the end of a sentence also asks a question, but it asks it in such a way that it shows that the questioner expects the answer 'Yes':

Tā shi Běijīng rén ba?	He's from Beijing, right?

Of course the questioner may be contradicted.

Ba is also used when trying to encourage someone to do something:

    Nǐ jiào wǒ Lǎo Lǐ ba.   Just call me Old Lee.

Exercise 4
Change these statements into questions:

1. **Tā shi Běijīng rén.**   2. **Tā shi Ài' ěrlán rén.**
3. **Tā xìng Lǐ.**   4. **Tā jiào Wáng Zhōng.**

(30) 2.8   *Yes and No*

Bu is placed in front of verbs to make them negative:

    Wǒ bú shi Běijīng rén.   I'm not from Beijing.

There is no need in Chinese to say 'Yes' or 'No' in answering questions. In general the verb of the question is used to give a yes or no answer:

A : **Nǐ shi Měiguó rén ma?**   Are you American?
B : **Shì.** *or*   Yes.
    Bú shi.   No.

[Remember that **bù** becomes a Second Tone before a Fourth Tone word, even when that Fourth Tone word is unstressed, as here. See *The sounds of Chinese* in the Introduction.]

(31) 2.9   *This and that*

Zhè means 'this'. Its opposite word is **nà** 'that':

    Zhè shi Lǐ xiáojie.   This is Miss Lee.
    Nà shi Wáng xiānsheng.   That's Mr Wang.

Exercise 5
Say it in Chinese:

1. Say that you're from Canada.   2. That you're not from London.
3. That your name is not Tony.   4. That this is Mr **Zhōu Jūn**.

⌒₃₂ *CONVERSATION 2B*

Ms Wang introduces Miss Lee to her colleague Mr Zhang.

W:	**Lǎo Zhāng, zhè shi Lǐ xiáojie.**	Old Zhang, this is Miss Lee.
Z :	**Lǐ xiáojie, nǐ hǎo!**	Hello! Miss Lee.
L :	**Nǐ hǎo!**	Hello!
Z :	**Lǐ xiáojie shi Měiguó rén ba?**	You're from America?
L :	**Bú shi, wǒ shi Jiānádà rén. Zhāng xiānsheng shi Běijīng rén ma?**	No, I'm not. I'm Canadian. Are you from Beijing?
Z :	**Bú shi, wǒ shi Shànghǎi rén. Xiǎo Wáng shi Běijīng rén.**	No, I'm from Shanghai. Young Wang is from Beijing.

⌒₃₃ *New words*

dōu	all, both
hǎo	good, fine, well, nice, OK
péngyou	friend
yě	also

⌒₃₄ *2.10 Possessive*

Later in this chapter you will learn the formal way to show the possessive, but with close personal relationships nothing more is required than to put the possessor and the possessed together as in:

wǒ péngyou	my friend
nǐ fūren	your wife

⌒₃₅ *2.11 Adverbs*

There is a golden rule for using adverbs like **dōu**, which means 'all' or 'both'. They always sit right in front of a verb:

> **Tāmen dōu xìng Wáng.**   Both of them are called Wang.

Yě, meaning 'also', is another of these adverbs, and like **dōu**, it comes right before a verb:

> **Wǒ yě shi Fǎguó rén.**   I'm French too.

Exercise 6

Read aloud and translate into English:

1. **Wǒmen dōu shi péngyou.**
2. **Tāmen dōu xìng Wáng.**
3. **Nǐ yě shi Déguó rén ma?**
4. **Wǒ shi Yīngguó rén, tāmen yě dōu shi Yīngguó rén.**

(36) *CONVERSATION 2C*

American student Mary Stones and her friend John Woods run into Mary's Chinese friend He Ping.

M: **Ēi, Xiǎo Hé, nǐ hǎo!**	Hey, young He, How are you?
H: **Nǐhǎo!**	Hello!
M: **Zhè shi wǒ péngyou** John Woods.	This is my friend John Woods.
H: **Nǐ hǎo!**	Hello !
J : **Nǐ hǎo. Zhōngguó péngyou dōu jiào wǒ Wú Qiáng. Nǐ yě jiào wǒ Wú Qiáng ba.**	Hello. Chinese friends all call me Wu Qiang. You can call me Wu Qiang too.
H: **Hǎo. Wú Qiáng, nǐ yě shi Měiguó rén ma?**	Fine. Wu Qiang, are you also from America?
J : **Wǒ bú shi Měiguó rén, wǒ shi Àodàlìyà rén.**	No, I'm not, I'm from Australia.

2.12   Names can be confusing

There are different ways of romanising the sounds of Chinese and different ways of writing Chinese names. You may have been puzzled by seeing a previous Chinese leader's name appear as **Deng Xiaoping, Teng Hsiao-p'ing, Teng Hsiao P'ing**, or even **Hsiao-p'ing Teng**. In this book we shall use the standard form adopted by Beijing, writing the surname first and putting the personal name (whether of one or two characters) as one word after it. You will find only **Dèng Xiǎopíng** here, not a sign of a **Hsiao-p'ing Teng**.

Beijing has adopted a standard way of writing foreigners' names in Chinese, using syllables which more or less give the sound of the names, and dividing Christian names from surnames with a dot. For example:

Alistair Cook is written **Ālǐsītài'ěr·Kùkè.**
John Masefield is **Yuēhàn·Màisīfēi'ěrdé.**

But sometimes foreigners are given Chinese names which look like Chinese names while still sounding something like the original foreign name (with the surname first):

Lǐ Yuēsè for Joseph Needham
Xiāo Bónà for George Bernard Shaw
Wú Qiáng for John Woods, as we have seen

(37) 2.13 *Possessive again*

The standard way to show the possessive is by using the particle **de**, which works just like the *'s* in English:

Lǐ Dàwěi de míngpiàn   David Lee's namecard
wǒ de míngpiàn   my namecard

Namecards

Namecards (**míngpiàn**) are an important means of telling people what your position is and therefore how you would like to be addressed. They aren't just for boasting, they help people to remember your name and give them a record of your contact details. The ritual of exchanging cards when you first meet someone is well established, and you will find it very useful. Anyone who is anyone (and almost everyone who isn't anyone too) has a supply of name cards ready to hand at all times. Most foreigners have their cards printed either in Chinese on one side and their own language on the other, or with the two mixed on one side only. When handing out your card and when receiving someone else's you should do it **with both hands** — using one hand only seems casual and impolite to a Chinese. The same is true for giving and receiving anything.

Exercise 7
Say it in Chinese.

1. That is my wife.
2. This is not my name.
3. This is my friend David Lee.
4. That is his namecard.

(38) *CONVERSATION 2D*

David Lee and his wife meet a Chinese official at a formal reception.

D : **Nín hǎo!**	Hello! How do you do?
O : **Nǐmen hǎo! Nín guì xìng?**	How do you do? May I ask your (sur)name?
D : **Wǒ xìng Lǐ. Wǒ jiào Lǐ Dàwěi. Zhè shi wǒ fūren.**	My name is Lee, David Lee. This is my wife.
O : **Lǐ fūren hǎo!**	How do you do, Mrs Lee?
W: **Nín hǎo!**	How do you do?
O : **Wǒ xìng Wáng. Zhè shi wǒ de míngpiàn.**	My name is Wang. This is my card.
D : **Xièxie.** *[Reads the card]* **Wáng xiānsheng de míngzi jiào Wáng Jiàn ma?**	Thank you ... Mr Wang, is your name Wang Jian?
O : **Bú jiào Wáng Jiàn. Wǒ jiào Wáng Jí'ān.**	No, I'm not called Wang Jian. I'm called Wang Ji'an.
D : **Duìbuqǐ! Duìbuqǐ!**	So sorry!
O : **Méi guānxi.**	That's alright.

(39) *Exercise 8*
Pronunciation practice:

1. **Wǒ xìng Wáng, bú xìng Wāng.**
2. **Tā xìng Liú, bú xìng Liǔ.**
3. **Tā jiào Wáng Guāng, bú jiào Wáng Guǎng.**
4. **Tā jiào Lí Tiānzhòng, bú jiào Lǐ Tiánzhōng.**

Exercise 9
Translate into Chinese:

1. My name is Lee. I'm from England.
2. Are you from Beijing?
3. We all call him Old Wang.
4. His wife is from America too.
5. This is not my namecard.
6. All his friends are from Hong Kong [**Xiānggǎng**].

Chapter 3

FINDING OUT

When people or things are lost you need to be able to ask questions to get them back. In **3.1** we suggest that you think of what the answer would be as a way of checking that you have phrased the question correctly. That seems silly, but the 'fault' lies with English, which changes word orders between questions and answers. The Chinese is more logical, and doesn't change the order. So you will need to overcome the urge to translate word-for-word from English into Chinese.

Using the telephone is daunting for learners of any new language, but we can't do without it, and the mobile phone is now very much part of life in China. You will discover here that phoning is actually quite straightforward, and of course it is wonderful number practice. Numbers are something you need to be familiar with as soon as possible.

(40) *3.1   Question words*

shéi?	who?
shéi de?	whose?
shénme?	what? what kind of?
něi?	which?

All these words are used in the same part of the sentence as their answer words come. So:

'Who is he?' is **Tā shi <u>shéi?</u>** and the answer is **Tā shi <u>Wáng xiānsheng</u>**.

'Whose passport?' is **<u>Shéi de</u> hùzhào?** and the answer is **<u>Wǒ de</u> hùzhào.** [**hùzhào** = passport]

'What nationality is he?' is **Tā shi <u>něi</u> guó rén?** and the answer is **Tā shi <u>Yīngguó</u> rén.**

Exercise 10

Using a question word to replace the underlined words, make up questions for the following answers:

1. **Tā xìng <u>Wáng</u>.**
2. **Tā jiào <u>Wáng Píng</u>.**
3. **Tā shi <u>Zhōngguó</u> rén.**
4. **Nà shi <u>wǒ de hùzhào</u>.**
5. **Tā shi <u>wǒ péngyou de péngyou</u>.**

3.2 Leaving out the topic

Once the topic under discussion has been established, or when it is very obvious, there is no need to mention it. In Conversation 3A, **Jiào shénme míngzi?** (What's your first name?) and **Něi guó rén?** (What nationality?) may not seem 'grammatical', but they are perfectly alright in the context.

Exercise 11

Ask in Chinese:

1. What is this?
2. Who is he?
3. Whose friend is she?
4. What nationality is he?/ Which country is he from?

⁽⁴¹⁾ CONVERSATION 3A

David Lee is sitting in the departure lounge of Beijing Airport. Suddenly he hears someone shouting.

S : **Zhè shi shéi de hùzhào?**   Whose passport is this?
    Zhè shi shéi de hùzhào?

    [He checks and realises that his own passport is missing]

D : **Shì wǒ de ba.**   It's mine, I think.

S : **Nǐ xìng shénme?**   What's your surname?

D : **Wǒ xìng Lee.**   My surname is Lee.

S : **Jiào shénme míngzi?**	What's your first name?
D : David, David Lee.	David, David Lee.
S : **Něi guó rén?**	What nationality?
D : **Yīngguó rén.**	British.
S : **Zhè shi nǐ de hùzhào ma?**	Is this your passport?
D : **Shì, shì. Xièxie, xièxie.**	Yes it is. Thank you very much.

Be polite

Traditionally it was polite to 'talk up' other people and their qualities, and to be excessively modest about oneself. So it was quite normal to refer to 'your mansion on high' (your house) but 'my wretched hovel' (my house), to 'your great one' (your wife) but 'my miserable thorn' (my wife), and so on. Aggressive equality and modern impatience have done away with most of these rather quaint expressions, but here and there one has survived. In Conversation 2D, the official used the polite and formal term **Nín guì xìng**, which literally means '(what is) your honourable surname?' The correct response in the old days was **Xiǎo xìng Wáng** '(My) little surname is Wang' or **Bì xìng Wáng** '(My) humble surname is Wang', but most people would respond now in the same way as David Lee did: **Wǒ xìng ...** In Conversation 3A you can see that there is no attempt to be over-polite on the part of the person who has found the passport. Could it be that she is an official, slightly irritated at the carelessness of the public?

3.3 Language or literature?

Zhōngwén means 'Chinese literature' or 'written Chinese', and you no doubt recognise **Zhōng** as the 'Central' bit of **Zhōngguó**, the Central Country, China. Quite often though, **Zhōngwén** is used loosely to mean 'Chinese language', and it is alright to say that someone 'speaks **Zhōngwén**'. In the next conversation you will meet **Zhōngwén míngzi** 'Chinese name', 'name in Chinese'. In the same way it is possible to say that you speak **Yīngwén** 'English' or **Déwén** 'German'.

3.4 Final particle 'a'

Like the particles **ma** and **ba**, the particle **a** appears at the end of a sentence. It does not make a question out of a statement, but it does help to reinforce a question word such as **shéi?** that has been used earlier in the sentence, and it makes the question sound less abrupt. The second time it occurs in Conversation 3B it is used slightly differently, and rather than backing up a previous question word it expresses mild surprise, something like 'Oh, is that who it is?!'

3.5 Negative questions

Chinese has negative questions in the same way that English does. It forms these questions, logically enough, by using the negative form of the verb with the particle **ma** added at the end of the sentence:

Tā bú shi Yīngguó rén ma?   Isn't he British?

(42) 3.6 The overseas Chinese

People who are ethnically Chinese but who live outside China are usually known as 'overseas Chinese' in English, and as **Huáqiáo** in Chinese. So a Chinese living in Germany is called a **Déguó Huáqiáo**. Other words using **qiáo** 'to live abroad' are:

Yīngqiáo	British expatriates
Měiqiáo	American expatriates
wàiqiáo	aliens, foreigners

Exercise 12
Ask in Chinese:

1. Is he an Australian overseas Chinese?
2. Isn't she your friend?
3. Isn't this your passport?
4. Aren't they all British?

3.7   The adverb 'jiù'

Jiù has a number of different meanings, one of which is 'just'. So **Jiù shi tā** means 'That's exactly who he is', 'That's the chap'.

3.8   The verb 'rènshi'

Rènshi means 'to recognise', 'to know', 'to get to know'. It is mostly used with people ('I know him') or Chinese characters ('I don't recognise that character'):

> **Wǒ rènshi tā, kěshi bú**   I know him, but I don't know his wife.
> **rènshi tā fūren.**

Exercise 13

Fill in the blanks with appropriate adverbs:

1. **Tā ____ shi Lúndūn rén.** (She is also a Londoner)

2. **Wǒ fūren ____ xìng Zhāng.** (My wife's name is Zhang too)

3. **Tāmen ____ shi Mǎláixīyà Huáqiáo.** (They are all Malaysian Overseas Chinese)

4. **Tā ____ shi Lǐ Huá.** (She is the person called Li Hua)

5. **Nǐmen ____ ____ shi Wáng xiānsheng de péngyou ma?** (Are you all Mr Wang's friends too?)

(43) *New words*

fùqin	father
kěshi	but
mǔqin	mother
Òu!	Oh!

(44) *CONVERSATION 3B*

Wang loves classical music and has a poster of a cellist on his wall. His friend Jones, a student of Chinese, looks at this poster.

J :	**Zhè shi shéi a?**	Who is this?
W :	**Mǎ Yǒuyǒu.**	**Mǎ Yǒuyǒu.**
J :	**Mǎ Yǒuyǒu? Òu, zhè shi** Yo-yo Ma **a?**	**Mǎ Yǒuyǒu?** Oh, it's Yo-yo Ma?
W :	**Shì, jiù shi tā. Mǎ Yǒuyǒu shi tā de Zhōngwén míngzi.**	Yes, that's him. **Mǎ Yǒuyǒu** is his Chinese name.
J :	**Tā bú shi Měiguó rén ma?**	Isn't he American?
W :	**Tā shi Měiguó rén, kěshi tā fùqin, mǔqin dōu shi Huáqiáo.**	He's an American, but his father and mother are both overseas Chinese.
J :	**Nǐ rènshi tā ma?**	Do you know him?
W :	**Wǒ rènshi tā, kěshi tā bú rènshi wǒ.**	Yes, I do, but he doesn't know me.

(45) 3.9 *The numbers 0 – 10*

0 =	**líng**	6 =	**liù**
1 =	**yī**	7 =	**qī**
2 =	**èr**	8 =	**bā**
3 =	**sān**	9 =	**jiǔ**
4 =	**sì**	10 =	**shí**
5 =	**wǔ**		

On the telephone and in other circumstances where it is necessary to be clearly understood (such as with bus numbers or room numbers) the word for 'one' is usually pronounced **yāo** instead of **yī**. Telephone numbers are given just as in English, so **5601** is **wǔ-liù-líng-yāo**.

Exercise 14

Read these telephone numbers aloud in Chinese:

1. 104
2. 999
3. 01328 756261
4. 020 7234 5689
5. 01865 533 6472

3.10 Ages

Suì means 'year of age', and, in the conversation below, Billy Wood's reply **shí suì** means that he is 'ten years old'.

(46) 3.11 More question words

Jǐ? means 'How many?'. **Duōshao?** can mean either 'How many?' or 'How much?'. Generally **Jǐ?** expects a small number as its answer, perhaps no more than ten or so: and if a larger number is expected, **duōshao?** is used.

A: **Nǐ jǐ suì?**   B: **Wǒ jiǔ suì.**   A: How old are you? B: I'm nine.

A: **Tā duōshao suì?** B: **Tā sìshibā suì.** A: How old is he? B: He's 48.

(47) *New words*

bàba	dad, daddy, father
diànhuà	telephone
diàn	electricity, electric
huà	speech
hàomǎ	number
diànhuà hàomǎ	phone number
hùzhào hàomǎ	passport number
jiā	home, family
māma	mum, mummy, mother
shǒujī	mobile phone, cell-phone
shǒujī hàomǎ	mobile number
Wéi!	Hello! (on the phone)

Exercise 15
Say it in Chinese:

1. What's your house (home) number?

2. His father is 53 years old.

3. What's your passport number?

4. My mobile phone number is 0798 591 8392.

(48) CONVERSATION 3C

Billy Wood, a ten-year old American boy, loses his way in the suburbs of Beijing and has been led to the police station.

P :	**Nǐ jiào shénme míngzi?**	What's your name?
B :	**Wǒ jiào** Billy Wood.	My name is Billy Wood.
P :	**Jǐ suì?**	How old are you?
B :	**Shí suì.**	Ten years old.
P :	**Nǐ shi něi guó rén?**	Where are you from?
B :	**Wǒ shi Měiguó rén.**	I'm American.
P :	**Nǐ jiā de diànhuà hàomǎ shi duōshao?**	What's your home phone number?
B :	**Yāo-sān-jiǔ-líng èr-wǔ-liù sì-yāo-qī-bā.**	1390 256 4178.
P :	**Zhè shi shǒujī hàomǎ a?**	Isn't that a mobile number?
B :	**Shì, shi wǒ bàba de shǒujī.**	Yes, it's my dad's mobile.
P :	*[Rings the number]* **Wéi. Nǐ hǎo. Shi** Wood **xiānsheng ma?**	Hello, is that Mr Wood?

(49) 3.12 The verb 'zhīdao'

While **rènshi**, as we have seen, means 'to know a person', **zhīdao** means 'to know a fact':

Nǐ zhīdao <u>tā de diànhuà hàomǎ</u> ma?   Do you know his phone number?

Nǐ zhīdao <u>tā shi něi guó rén</u> ma?   Do you know what nationality he is?

Notice that the Chinese of the second example shows very clearly how there are really two questions here, one embedded within the other:

1.	**Nǐ zhīdao ma?**	Do you know?
2.	**Tā shi něi guó rén?**	What nationality is he?

(50) *New words*

fàndiàn	hotel
fángjiān	a room
gōngsī	company

jiē	to connect
jīnglǐ	manager (can be used as a title too)
Qǐng	Please; Will you please …

Exercise 16
Say it in Chinese:

1. Say that you don't know.
2. That you don't know who she is.
3. That you know Mr Wang's mobile phone number.
4. Ask the switchboard to connect you to Room 1046.

(51) *CONVERSATION 3D*

Mr Laker asks his Chinese assistant for a telephone number.

L : **Wáng xiáojie, nǐ zhīdao Běi-jīng Fàndiàn de diànhuà ma?**
Miss Wang, do you know the phone number for the Beijing Hotel?

W : **Zhīdao. Liù-wǔ-yāo-sān qī-qī-liù-liù.**
Yes, I do. (It's) 6513-7766.

L : **Dàxīn Gōngsī de fángjiān hàomǎ shi duōshao?**
What's the room number for The Daxin Company?

W : **Sì-èr-bā-jiǔ.**
4289.

[Laker dials]

O : **Nǐ hǎo. Běijīng Fàndiàn.**
Hello. Beijing Hotel.

L : **Qǐng jiē sì-èr-bā-jiǔ.**
Connect me to 4289, please.

Z : **Nǐ hǎo. Dàxīn Gōngsī.**
Hello. Daxin Company.

L : **Wéi, shi Zhāng jīnglǐ ma? Wǒ shi Léikè.**
Is that Manager Zhang? I'm Laker.

Z : **Òu, Léikè xiānsheng, nǐ hǎo!**
Oh, Mr Laker, how are you?

Exercise 17

Pronunciation practice:

1. **Yī èr sān**
2. **Sān èr yī**
3. **Yī èr sān sì wǔ liù qī**
4. **Qī liù wǔ sì sān èr yī**

Exercise 18

Translate into Chinese:

1. A: What's his surname?
   B: His name is Wang.

2. A: What's your phone number?
   B: 0121-486 5739.

3. A: Whose passport is this?
   B: It's my friend's.

4. A: Do you know what nationality she is?
   B: Yes, I do. She's French.

5. A: Is Manager Wang from Shanghai?
   B: No, he is an Overseas Chinese from Japan.

6. A: Hello, is that Mr Zhang?
   B: Yes, speaking. You're ...?

Chapter 4

MAKING REQUESTS

In this chapter you will meet another interesting way to ask questions.

What you do is to give a choice of possible answers, and then all the other person has to do is to pick one of them. Once you've grasped the beautiful simplicity of the idea you will start to feel sorry for those who have to cope with learning English, twisting their minds into knots as they struggle to turn their statements inside out in order to make them into questions. Chinese grammar really is quite simple.

And even when there are irregularities they tend to be minor ones. So here you will meet the verb 'to have' which has an irregular negative — but it is the only verb which is odd like this, so it doesn't take a lot of learning.

(53) *4.1   The verb 'yǒu'*

Yǒu means 'to have'. It has one distinctive feature in that unlike all other verbs its negative is formed with **méi** not with **bù**:

> **Wǒ méi yǒu míngpiàn.**   I have no name card.

(54) *New words*

chá	tea
fáng	a room
dānrénfáng	single room
shuāngrénfáng	double room
tián biǎo	to fill in a form
wèishēngjiān	bathroom
yào	to want

4.2   Choice-type questions

Chinese can ask questions simply by offering a choice of answers:

> **Nǐ shi Yīngguó rén shi Měiguó rén?**   Are you British or American?

You will see that this is actually two contradictory statements (*You are British* and *You are American*), and you are being asked to choose one of them, so it works as a question. In the Conversation, the receptionist does the same by offering a choice to John White:

Nín yào dānrénfáng, yào shuāngrénfáng?   Do you want a single room or a double room?

⁵⁵ *4.3 Measure words*

Whenever Chinese counts nouns it counts them with special measure words. **Bēi** is 'a cup', and 'three cups of tea' is **sān bēi chá.** Here it is clear that **bēi** is measuring the amount of tea, just as 'cups' is in the English version. The same principle applies, though, even when there is no obvious appropriate measure in English. 'Three men', 'five name cards', 'ten bicycles' have no measures in English, but in Chinese they do. The most common measure word is **gè**. It is used (generally with neutral tone) for people and for many other things:

    sì ge rén   four people

Other measures are:

    wèi   for people to whom you wish to be polite
    jiān   for rooms
    píng   a bottle of

Three things to note:

First,   when you count nouns with a measure word, the noun itself never changes to show whether it is singular or plural. We said in **2.1** that, exceptionally, some nouns have a plural form, but even they do not change. So although **péngyou** 'friend' does have a plural form **péngyoumen** 'friends', still 'three friends' is **sān ge péngyou**, just as 'one friend' is **yí ge péngyou**.

Second,   **suì** (year of age), **nián** (year), and **tiān** (day) are unusual in that they are nouns which carry with them their own measuring function. So it is correct to say **shí suì** (ten years old), **liù nián** (six years), and **wǔ tiān** (five days).

Third,   in front of measure words the number 'two' is **liǎng** not **èr**. It's as if in English we always insisted on saying 'a couple of' instead of 'two': so 'two people' is **liǎng ge rén**, and 'two years' is **liǎng nián**.

Exercise 19

Fill in the blanks where necessary:

1. **yí ____ rén** (one person)
2. **liǎng ____ chá** (two cups of tea)
3. **sān ____ dānrénfáng** (three single rooms)
4. **sì ____ suì** (four years old)
5. **wǔ ____ Zhōngguó péngyou** (five Chinese friends)

4.4 Making a contrast

Yǒu shuāngrénfáng says quite simply 'We have a double room', but changing the order to **shuāngrénfáng yǒu** points to a contrast and conveys the meaning 'As to a <u>double room</u>, that we have (but if you'd asked for a <u>single room</u> now ...)'.

4.5 The verb 'dài'

Dài basically means 'to bring with', 'to lead', or 'to carry'. In the conversation it is translated as 'with', but that should be understood as a short way of saying 'come with':

    Dài wèishēngjiān ma?   Does it come with bathroom?

4.6 The verb 'zhù'

Zhù means 'to live' or 'to dwell', but it will also translate 'to stay' in the sense of 'to stay overnight'.

4.7 The adverb 'xiān'

Xiān means 'first'. Like **yě**, **dōu** and **jiù** it comes right in front of the verb:

    Xiān tián biǎo.   First fill in the form.

Exercise 20

Say it in Chinese:

1. Say that we all have passports.
2. That she doesn't have a mobile phone.
3. That we want to stay for two days.
4. Ask if that is the bathroom?

56 *CONVERSATION 4A*

A tourist and his friend talk to the hotel receptionist.

R :	**Nǐ hǎo!**	Hello!
T :	**Nǐ hǎo! Yǒu fángjiān ma?**	Hello! Do you have any rooms?
R :	**Nín yào dānrénfáng, yào shuāngrénfáng?**	Do you want single rooms or a double room?
T :	**Wǒmen yào yì jiān shuāngrén fáng.**	We want a double room.
R :	**Shuāngrénfáng yǒu.**	We have a double room.
T :	**Dài wèishēngjiān ma?**	With bathroom?
R :	**Dài. Nǐmen zhù jǐ tiān?**	Yes. How many days will you be staying?
T :	**Sān tiān.**	Three.
R :	**Hǎo. Qǐng xiān tián biǎo.**	Fine. Please fill in the form first.

4.8 Here and there

Nàr means 'there' and **zhèr** means 'here'. If you think of them as meaning 'that place' and 'this place' you will probably be reminded of another pair of words (**nà** 'that' and **zhè** 'this') which we met in Chapter Two. Clearly they are connected.

In the same way, when 'me' means 'here where I am' (as in 'come to me'), the Chinese is not just **wǒ** but **wǒ zhèr**, and when 'you' means 'there where you are', the Chinese is **nǐ nàr**.

4.9 Is that O.K.?

Kěyǐ means 'may', 'can' or 'it is possible that'. It is often tagged onto the end of a sentence with the particle **ma** (**... kěyǐ ma?**) to give the meaning 'Is that O.K.?' 'Do you agree?' Another 'question tag' which is used in the same way is **hǎo ma?**

4.10 The verb 'xiǎng'

Xiǎng literally means 'to think', but when it appears in front of other verbs it means 'would like to':

    Wǒ xiǎng zhù wǔ tiān.   I'd like to stay for five days.

Exercise 21
    Change the following into negatives:

1. **Wǒ xiǎng zhù Běijīng Fàndiàn.**
2. **Tāmen dōu yǒu hùzhào.**
3. **Nǐmen yào shuāngrénfáng ma?**
4. **Nín yǒu míngpiàn ma?**
5. **Wǒmen de fángjiān dōu dài wèishēngjiān.**

4.11 The colour of tea

In Chinese, tea is classified as 'red' (**hóng**) for fermented varieties, and 'green' for unfermented. **Hóng** is translated as 'black' in the Conversation, because in English the two types are normally known as 'black' and 'green' rather than 'red' and 'green'.

4.12 The adverb 'zhǐ'

Zhǐ 'only' is another adverb like **yě, dōu, jiù** and **xiān**, and it therefore must come immediately in front of a verb.

(57) *New words*

chī	to eat
diǎnxin	pastries, snacks
hē	to drink
jiǔ	alcoholic drink
píjiǔ	beer
kāfēi	coffee
Kěkǒu Kělè	Coca Cola
niúnǎi	(cow's) milk
táng	sugar
zuò	to sit

(58) CONVERSATION 4B

A tourist and three friends are in a hotel coffee shop. A waitress meets them at the door.

W :	**Nǐ hǎo! Jǐ wèi?**	Hello! How many?
T :	**Wǒmen sì ge rén. Zuò nàr kěyǐ ma?**	Four of us. Can we sit over there?
W :	**Kěyǐ...Nǐmen xiǎng hē shénme?**	Yes...What would you like to drink?
T :	**Yǒu hóngchá ma?**	Do you have black tea?
W :	**Méi yǒu. Yǒu kāfēi.**	No. We have got coffee.
T :	**Yǒu píjiǔ ma?**	Do you have any beer?
W :	**Yǒu.**	Yes.
T :	**Hǎo. Wǒmen yào liǎng bēi kāfēi, yì píng píjiǔ, yí ge Kěkǒu Kělè.**	Good. We want two cups of coffee, a bottle of beer, and a Coca Cola.
W :	**Kāfēi yào táng ma?**	Do you need sugar for the coffee?
T :	**Zhǐ yào niúnǎi, bú yào táng.**	Just milk, no sugar.
W :	**Chī diǎnxin ma?**	Do you want some pastries?
T :	**Bú yào, xièxie.**	No, thank you.

Exercise 22
> *At the café:*
>
> 1. Ask your friend to sit down.
> 2. Find out what your friend would like to drink.
> 3. Order two cups of black tea.
> 4. Ask the waitress if they have any pastries.

4.13 Floors

Lóu means 'a storeyed building' or 'a floor'. The Chinese count their storeys in the same way as the Americans, that is with the ground floor as the first floor. **Èr lóu** is the floor above the ground floor, the one which the British call 'the first floor', **sān lóu** is the British 'second floor', and so on. But in this book we will translate **èr lóu** as 'second floor', **sān lóu** as 'third floor', etc.

(59) 4.14 To be or not to be?

Chǎo means 'noisy' or 'to be noisy'; **rè** means 'hot' or 'to be hot'. And so it is with all adjectives (big, beautiful, difficult, etc.), and we will sometimes refer to them as 'adjectival verbs' to remind you of it. So, normally there is no question of translating the verb 'to be' when it comes before an adjective:

> **Niúnǎi bú rè.**   The milk is not hot.
> **Wǒ hěn hǎo.** [**hěn** = 'very']   I'm very well.

But just occasionally you may wish to give particularly strong emphasis to an adjective, and then Chinese does make use of the verb 'to be' (**shì**):

> **Yìdàlì kāfēi shì hěn hǎo.**   Italian coffee <u>is</u> very good.

and in the conversation there is another example:

> **Èr lóu shì hěn chǎo.**   The second floor is indeed very noisy.

(60) *4.15   Too much!*

'To be too noisy' is **tài chǎo le**. **Tài** means 'too much', and **le** is a particle which shows that something is excessive or 'over the top'. So:

Tài rè le!	It's too hot!
Tài hǎo le!	Great! Fantastic!

(61) *4.16   The verb 'yǒu' again*

As we have seen in **4.1** above, **yǒu** means 'to have':

Nǐ yǒu diànhuà ma?   Have you got a phone?

But after place words ('here', 'on the table' etc.) **yǒu** is used like 'there is', 'there are' in English:

Èr lóu yǒu wèishēngjiān ma? Is there a bathroom on the second floor?

4.17   Measure v. noun

Hàomǎ is a noun meaning 'number', as we have seen. **Hào** is a measure word also meaning 'number', and it is used where in English we might abbreviate to 'No.'. Compare the following examples:

nǐ de diànhuà hàomǎ	your telephone number
Sān hào fáng(jiān)	Room No.3

Exercise 23
What do they mean?

1. **Wǒ de fángjiān méi yǒu diànhuà.**
2. **Sān lóu yǒu liǎng ge wèishēngjiān.**
3. **Lúndūn yǒu Zhōngguó gōngsī ma?**
4. **Tāmen nàr yǒu chá, yě yǒu kāfēi.**

(62) *New words*

bǐjiào	rather, quite, comparatively
diàntī	lift, elevator

huàn	to change, exchange
pà	to fear, be afraid of
shì	business, matter, affair

⟨63⟩ *CONVERSATION 4C*

A tourist complains to the hotel receptionist about his room.

R :	**Nín yǒu shénme shì?**	Can I help you?
T :	**Wǒ de fángjiān tài chǎo le.** **Kěyǐ huàn yì jiān ma?**	My room is too noisy. Can I change it?
R :	**Nín zhù jǐ hào fáng?**	What's your room number?
T :	**Èr lóu, èr-yāo-bā.**	Second floor. 218.
R :	**Èr lóu shì hěn chǎo. Liù lóu kěyǐ ma?**	The second floor is indeed very noisy. Will the sixth floor do?
T :	**Kěyǐ.**	Yes.
R :	**Kěshì liù lóu bǐjiào rè.**	But it's rather hot on the sixth floor.
T :	**Wǒ bú pà rè.**	I'm not afraid of heat.
R :	**Wǒmen zhèr méi yǒu diàntī.**	There isn't a lift here.
T :	**Méi guānxi.**	That doesn't matter.

⟨64⟩ *4.18 Doubling up*

It is quite common for Chinese to double words for emphasis:

Kěyǐ, kěyǐ!   Of course that's OK!

With some verbs, such as **xiūxi** 'to rest', doubling up gives a sense of 'having a little go at':

Xiūxi xiūxi ba!   Have a little rest!

⟨65⟩ *4.19 Measure words again*

When the object of a verb is in the singular, it is quite common to omit the word **yi** 'one'. For instance, **yì bēi kāfēi** is 'a cup of coffee' and **yì zhī yān** is 'a cigarette', but:

Hē (yì) bēi kāfēi ba!	Have a cup of coffee!
Chōu (yì) zhī yān ba!	Have a cigarette! (**chōu yān** 'to smoke' [literally: to drag smoke])

(66) 4.20   *Choice-type questions again*

As we have seen, one way of asking straightforward questions is to add **ma?** to a statement:

Kāfēi rè ma?	Is the coffee hot?

Another way of making questions is by using the positive and negative forms of a verb together, effectively giving a choice of two answers from which to pick:

Kāfēi rè bu rè?	Is the coffee hot?
Nǐ hē bu hē chá?	Will you have some tea?
Nǐ xiǎng bu xiǎng xiūxi?	Do you want to rest?
Wǒ kě (yǐ) bu kěyǐ chōu yān?	May I smoke?
Nǐ zhī (dao) bu zhīdao ... ?	Do you know that ... ?

You will probably find this pattern very similar to pattern **4.2** above, and indeed they work on the same principle. And in case you are puzzled about why 'hot' is a verb, check back to **4.14**.

Exercise 24
Make choice-type questions out of the following:

1. **Tā shi Běijīng rén.**
2. **Tā yǒu Zhōngguó péngyou.**
3. **Tā xiǎng hē hóngchá.**
4. **Tā bú rènshi Dèng Xiǎopíng.**
5. **Nàr bú rè.**

(67) 4.21   *Final particles 'a' and 'ba'*

The particle **a** has an additional use, which is to make mild rhetorical questions of the 'Oh, so that's how it is, is it?' type:

Òu, tā shi Zhōngguó rén a?	Oh really, he's Chinese?
Bù kěyǐ chōu yān a?	So we can't smoke?

You may like to note that after an **–n** (as with the above two examples) the **a** sounds more like **na**: it seems to be easier to say.

Ba, you will remember, is used to express encouragement:

Nǐ hē ba!   Go ahead and drink!

(68) *4.22   Don't!*

Bié is short for **bú yào**, and either of them can be used to give negative commands — 'Don't!' So, both **Bié zuò nàr!** and **Bú yào zuò nàr!** mean 'Don't sit there!'

Bié chǎo!   Quiet!

Exercise 25
Ask for permission in Chinese:

1. May I smoke?
2. May I sit here?
3. May I have a beer?
4. May I have a little rest?

(69) *New words*

fēngjǐng	scenery
kuàngquánshuǐ	mineral water
shuǐ	water
piàoliang	(to be) beautiful
yān	smoke; a cigarette
zhào xiàng	to take a photograph
zhī	measure for stick-like things
zhǔn	to permit, be permitted

(70) *CONVERSATION 4D*

A foreign student and his Chinese travelling companion enter a pavilion on top of a scenic mountain.

S : **Zhèr fēngjǐng tài piàoliang le!**　　The scenery here is fantastic!

C : **Zuò zhèr xiūxi xiūxi ba.**　　Sit here and take a rest.

S : **Hǎo. Chōu (yì) zhī yān ba.**　　Good. Have a cigarette.

C : **Duìbuqǐ . Zhèr bù zhǔn chōu yān.**　　Sorry. No smoking allowed here.

S : **Òu, bù zhǔn chōu yān a?**　　Oh, so there's no smoking?

C : **Hē bu hē shuǐ? Wǒ zhèr yǒu Kělè, yě yǒu kuàngquánshuǐ.**　　Do you want a drink? There's some Coke here, and some mineral water.

S : **Tài hǎo le! Wǒ hē kuàngquánshuǐ. Zhèr zhǔn bu zhǔn zhào xiàng?**　　Great! I'll have mineral water. Is it alright to take photos here?

C : **Zhǔn. Nǐ zhào ba. Kěshi bié zhào wǒ!**　　Yes. Go ahead and take. But don't go taking me!

Exercise 26
Pronunciation practice:

1. **Yān, jiǔ, wǒ dōu yǒu.**
2. **Nǐ yào chōu yān, qǐng chōu yān.**
3. **Nǐ yào hē jiǔ, qǐng hē jiǔ.**

Exercise 27
Translate into Chinese:

1. A: Have you got two single rooms?
   B: No, we only have one double room.

2. A: How many days will you be staying?
   B: Five.

3. A: What would you like to drink?
   B: Two teas and one coffee.

4. A: Our room is too hot.
   B: Do you want to change it?

5. A: Is drinking allowed here?
   B: No, I'm sorry. Neither drinking nor smoking is allowed.

6. A: Is the scenery there beautiful?
   B: Yes, and the people there are also beautiful.

Chapter 5

LOCATIONS

Here you will learn how to place one thing in relation to another, and how to handle compass directions. The Chinese discovered the properties of the magnetised needle before anyone else did, and the fact that it was an independent discovery is shown by the fact that they call it the 'south-pointing needle', while other cultures think of it as pointing north. Of course both views are correct, but it is interesting that the intermediate directions (northeast, southeast, southwest, northwest) are also 'back-to-front' in Chinese, as you will find out in **5.15**.

The Chinese developed grid-plan cities very early on, and much of Beijing is laid out with north-south, east-west main streets. When you get directions from people in Beijing and some other cities, they will usually say "Turn north" rather than "Turn left", so it is well worth learning the directions carefully.

5.1 *Politeness*

Qǐng wèn literally means 'please may I ask...' (**wèn** is 'to ask [a question]'), and it is used as a polite lead-in to asking questions, especially of strangers:

    Qǐng wèn nín guì xìng?   May I ask your name?

(72) 5.2 *Location (1)*

Zài means 'to be there, to be in':

    A: **Wáng xiānsheng zài ma?**   Is Mr Wang there?
    B: **Tā bú zài.**   He's not in.

In front of place words **zài** means 'to be at/in/on' and is used to show the location of things:

    zài jiā   at home
    zài èr lóu   on the second floor
    zài zhèr   here, at this place

zài nàr	there, at that place
zài nǎr?	where? at which place?
A: **Wáng jīnglǐ zài nǎr?**	Where is Manager Wang?
B: **Tā zài Xiānggǎng.**	He's in Hong Kong.

(73) *5.3   Full sets*

Note that we now have two parallel sets of similar words:

zhè (this)	**zhèr** (this place, here)
nà (that)	**nàr** (that place, there)
něi? (which?)	**nǎr?** (which place? where?)

Exercise 28
Say it in Chinese:

1. Ask your friend where his home is.
2. Tell your friend that your room is on the fourth floor, not the tenth.
3. Ask him if Miss Wang is in Shanghai?
4. Tell your friend that you don't know where his mobile phone is.

(74) *5.4   More doubling up*

We saw in **4.18** that doubling the verb **xiūxi** gave it the meaning 'have a little rest!' When single syllable verbs are doubled, they can appear either as *verb*-**yi**-*verb* [**yi** = one] or as *verb-verb*:

wèn 'to ask': **wèn-yi-wèn** or **wènwen**	to make an enquiry
kàn 'to look at': **kàn-yi-kàn** or **kànkan**	to have a look at
Qǐng nǐ wènwen Lǎo Wáng zài bu zài.	Please ask if old Wang is in.
Qǐng nǐ kàn-yi-kàn zhè shi shénme.	Please see what this is.

(75) *5.5   The verb 'yǒu'*

The negative of **yǒu**, remember, is **méi yǒu**. When **méi yǒu** is followed by an object it is often shortened just to **méi**:

Wǒ méi hùzhào.	I haven't got a passport.
Méi rén jiē.	No-one's answering the phone.
Tā jiā méi (yǒu) diànhuà.	There's no phone in his home.

(76) *New words*

dìxià	basement, lower ground floor
kāfēitīng	café
kěnéng	maybe
qù	to go
yàoshi	a key
yīnggāi	ought to, should
yóuyǒngchí	swimming-pool
yóuyǒng	to swim

(77) CONVERSATION 5A

A visitor goes to the hotel to look for Miss Laker.

V :	**Qǐng wèn Léikè xiáojie zài ma?**	Excuse me, is Miss Laker in?
R :	**Tā zhù jǐ hào fáng?**	What's her room number?
V :	**Sān líng jiǔ yāo.**	3091.
R :	**Wǒ kànkan.** *[Checks keys]* **Yàoshi bú zài, rén yīnggāi zài.**	Let me see. The key isn't here; she should be in.

[Rings 3091, but there is no answer]

	Méi rén jiē. Kěnéng zài kāfēitīng, yě kěnéng zài yóuyǒngchí.	No answer. Maybe she's in the café, or maybe in the swimming-pool.
V :	**Kāfēitīng zài nǎr?**	Where's the café?
R :	**Zài èr lóu. Yóuyǒngchí zài dìxià. Nín qù kànkan ba.**	On the second floor. The pool's in the basement. You can go and have a look.
V :	**Hǎo. Xièxie nǐ.**	OK. Thank you.
R :	**Méi shìr.**	Not at all.

(78) 5.6 Location (2)

Some common place words which go with **zài** are:

zài qiántou	in front
zài hòutou	behind
zài shàngtou	on top, over, above
zài xiàtou	below, under
zài zuǒbianr	on the left
zài yòubianr	on the right
zài lǐtou	inside
zài wàitou	outside
Wáng xiáojie zài wàitou.	Miss Wang is outside.
Kāfēitīng zài yòubianr.	The café is on the right.

Remember that when the Beijing dialect **-er** *ending is added to words ending in* **-n***, the* **-n** *sound is lost, so that* **-bianr** *is pronounced as if it were spelled* **biar***.*

Exercise 29
Say it in Chinese:

1. Is Mr. Li in?
2. Is Miss Wang at home?
3. The bathroom is on the 1st floor.
4. She is inside.
5. The café is on the left.
6. Beijing Hotel is just up ahead.

(79) 5.7 Money

Qián 'money' is measured in units of currency. In China the basic units are called **kuài** or **yuán**, and they are divided into ten **máo** (i.e. a **máo** is ten cents, 'a dime'), which in turn are divided into ten **fēn**:

duōshao qián?	How much?
shí kuài	10 yuan
jiǔ kuài sān (máo qián)	9 yuan 30 cents
bā kuài qī máo wǔ	8 yuan 75 cents

Just as in English we say 'two pounds ten' rather than 'two pounds ten pence', so Chinese can leave off obvious units, as in **jiǔ kuài sān** above.

(80) *New words*

cèsuǒ	the toilet, washroom
fùjìn	nearby
jiǎo fèi	to pay fees, pay charges
jiē	street
jìn	near, close
yuǎn	far, distant

> ### Yuán
>
> **Yuán** is the formal word for the basic currency unit, and that is what is printed on the banknotes, for instance. But in ordinary speech most people say **kuài** rather than **yuán**. It's something like saying 'quid' instead of 'pounds', or 'bucks' instead of 'dollars', except that **kuài** is not a slang word, it is fully acceptable as educated literate language.

(81) ## CONVERSATION 5B

After a meal, a tourist asks the waiter for the toilet.

T : **Qǐng wèn, cèsuǒ zài nǎr?**	Excuse me, where's the toilet?
W : **Duìbuqǐ, wǒmen zhèr méi cèsuǒ.**	Sorry, we don't have one here.
T : **Méi cèsuǒ?! Fùjìn yǒu ma?**	No toilet?! Is there one nearby?
W : **Dōnghuá Jiē yǒu yí ge.**	There's one on Donghua Street.
T : **Yuǎn ma?**	Is it far?
W : **Hěn jìn. Jiù zài qiántou.**	Very close. Just up ahead.

[The tourist finds the place but is stopped by an attendant]

A : **Èi, xiān jiǎo fèi!**	Hey, pay up first!
T : **Shénme? Yào qián? Duōshao?**	What? There's a charge? How much?
A : **Wǔ máo.**	Fifty cents.

(82) 5.8 Buying and selling

Be very careful! The only difference in Chinese between buying and selling is in the tones:

mǎi	to buy
mài	to sell

5.9 Measure words

We saw in Chapter Four that whenever a noun was counted, the appropriate measure word had to be used. Measure words are also used when a noun is specified with 'this', 'that', or 'which?':

Něi ge rén?	Which person?

In front of numbers and measure words **zhè** is often pronounced **zhèi** and **nà** is often prounounced **nèi**:

nèi ge rén	that person
zhèi píng píjiǔ	this bottle of beer
nèi sān bēi kāfēi	those three cups of coffee

When it is clear which noun is meant, it is possible to leave it out, but still the measure word is used:

A: **Něi wèi xiáojie?**	Which young lady?
B: **Zhèi wèi.**	This one.

5.10 Place words as adjectives

Place words like **qiántou** and **yòubianr** can be used as adjectives:

qiántou (de) nèi ge rén	the person in front
yòubianr (de) nèi ge	the one on the right

(83) 5.11 The numbers 11 – 99

In Chapter Three we counted only as far as ten. Eleven is 'ten and one', twelve is 'ten and two', and so on up to nineteen. Twenty is 'two tens', twenty-one is 'two tens and one'...up to ninety-nine:

11 **shíyī**	12 **shí'èr**	13 **shísān**	14 **shísì**	15 **shíwǔ**
16 **shíliù**	17 **shíqī**	18 **shíbā**	19 **shíjiǔ**	20 **èrshí**
21 **èrshiyī**	22 **èrshi'èr**	23 **èrshisān**	24 **èrshisì**	25 **èrshiwǔ**
26 **èrshiliù**	27 **èrshiqī**	28 **èrshibā**	29 **èrshijiǔ**	30 **sānshí**
40 **sìshí**	50 **wǔshí**	60 **liùshí**	70 **qīshí**	80 **bāshí**
90 **jiǔshí**	91 **jiǔshiyī**	95 **jiǔshiwǔ**	99 **jiǔshijiǔ**	

Exercise 30
Tell the prices:

1. ¥ 0.50
2. ¥ 1.20
3. ¥ 18.00
4. ¥ 45.50
5. ¥ 67.30
6. ¥ 99.99

5.12   Final particle 'ne'

Ne added to the end of a phrase or sentence has the effect of asking a question with the minimum number of words. Often it will translate as 'And how about...?' Note the economy of effort in the following:

A: **Nǐ hǎo ma?**   How are you?
B: **Wǒ hěn hǎo. Nǐ ne?**   I'm very well. How about you?

Exercise 31
Fill in the blanks with question words:

1. **Qǐng wèn nèi ge rén shi ____ ?**
2. **Qǐng wèn Lǐ xiānsheng zhù ____ hào fáng?**
3. **Qǐng wèn kāfēitīng zài ____ ?**
4. **Qǐng wèn nèi wèi xiáojie xìng ____ ?**
5. **Qǐng wèn zhèi ge ____ qián?**
6. **Qǐng wèn ____ yǒu cèsuǒ?**

(84) *New words*

| **bíyānhú** | snuff bottle |
| **dōngxi** | thing |

| guì | expensive |
| xǐhuan | to like, be fond of |

(85) *CONVERSATION 5C*

A tourist wants to buy snuff bottles at a department store. He is met by the courtesy staff at the door.

CS: **Huānyíng guānglín.**	Welcome, sir.
T : **Nǐmen zhèr mài bíyānhú ma?**	Do you sell snuff bottles?
CS: **Mài. Zài sì lóu.**	Yes. On the fourth floor.

[On the fourth floor]

T : **Xiáojie, wǒ kànkan zhèi ge bíyānhú kěyǐ ma?**	Miss, can I have a look at this snuff bottle?
S : **Něi ge? Zhèi ge ma?**	Which one? This one?
T : **Bú shi. Shì hòutou nèi ge. Duōshao qián?**	No, the one behind. How much is it?
S : **Jiǔshíwǔ kuài.**	95 yuan.
T : **Nèi ge ne? Zuǒbianr nèi ge?**	How about that one? The one on the left?
S : **Zhèi ge bāshí kuài. Nín xǐhuan něi ge?**	This one is 80 yuan. Which one do you prefer?
T : **Dōu tài guì le.**	They're both too expensive.
S : **Kěshi dōngxi hǎo. Nín mǎi yí ge ba!**	But they are good quality. You should buy one!
T : **Hǎo, jiù mǎi zhèi ge.**	OK, I'll just buy this one.

5.13 Shīfu

Shīfu is a term of respect for master craftsmen, such as kungfu masters, chefs or jade-carvers, but it is also now commonly used as a form of address to anyone (male or female) who is serving you, rather as English uses 'boss', 'captain', 'guv'nor', 'chief', 'maestro', 'chef', 'driver', etc.

5.14   More on 'de'

We met the little word **de** in its role as the possessive marker (**wǒ de míngpiàn** 'my card'). It has another important role as the link word joining adjectives to nouns. Simple single-syllable adjectives like **hǎo** 'good' go straight in front of nouns just as in English:

hǎo rén	a good chap
rè chá	hot tea

but when an adjective has more than one syllable or is modified by an adverb it is normally linked with the noun it refers to by **de**:

piàoliang de xiáojie	a beautiful girl
hěn rè de chá	very hot tea

(86) 5.15   Compass points

The four cardinal directions are:

dōng	east
nán	south
xī	west
běi	north

and they are generally given in that order. To make place words out of them it is only necessary to add **-bianr** ('side'), to give **dōngbianr** 'the east', **nánbianr** 'the south', etc. The intermediate directions NE, SE, SW, and NW are always expressed in reverse order from English, so SE actually becomes ES (**dōngnán**), NE becomes EN (**dōngběi**), and so on.

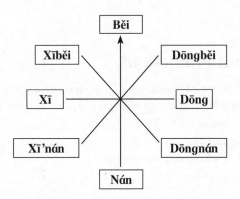

5.16 Rhetorical questions

Questions showing great surprise or assuming the agreement of the listener in advance are expressed with **bú shì ... ma?!**

Nà bú shi Lǐ xiānsheng ma?!   Isn't that Mr Li?!

5.17 Location (3)

The little word **zài** introduces place words, as we have seen with such phrases as **zài nàr** 'over there', **zài lǐtou** 'inside' and **zài Běijīng** 'in Beijing'. We can extend its use now to deal with phrases like 'behind Mr Wang' (**zài Wáng xiānsheng (de) hòutou**) and 'on the right of that person' (**zài nèi ge rén (de) yòubianr**). So the pattern is:

zài - noun - (de) - place word

zài wǒ (de) hòutou   behind me
zài Běijīng Fàndiàn (de) yòubianr   on the right of Beijing Hotel

---

Exercise 32

Give their relative locations:

1. **Ài'ěrlán zài Yīngguó (de)** _____
2. **Rìběn zài Zhōngguó (de)** _____
3. **Xībānyá zài Fǎguó (de)** _____
4. **Jiānádà zài Měiguó (de)** _____
5. **Shànghǎi zài Běijīng (de)** _____

5.18 Final Particle 'a'

We have seen that **a** reinforces a question word coming earlier in the sentence. It also can be used to stress the obviousness of a fact. So if you were to ask "Why is his English so fluent?", the answer might be:

Tā shi Yīngguó rén a!
(Because) he's English (of course!).

(87) *New words*

bǎihuò dàlóu/gōngsī	department store
dìfang	a place, a location
gōngyuán	a park
gǔdǒng	antiques
hǎowánr	good fun, enjoyable, amusing, 'fun'
lǚyóu	tourism; to tour
lǚyóutú	tourist map
dìtú	a map
shìchǎng	a market

The City God

In traditional times **Chénghuáng**, the City God, had a temple (**miào**) in every administrative city of the Chinese empire. When a new chief official was posted to the city, his first duty was to report his arrival to **Chénghuáng** by worshipping him and seeking his spiritual help in the work of ruling. Some City God temples still survive in China, where they have become tourist attractions for Chinese and foreigners alike.

(88) *CONVERSATION 5D*

A tourist asks an old newspaper seller about local places of interest.

T :	**Shīfu, yǒu Yīngwén lǚyóutú ma?**	Do you have a tourist map in English, chief?
S :	**Méi yǒu.**	No.
T :	**Qǐng wèn zhèr fùjìn yǒu hǎowánr de dìfang ma?**	Are there any interesting places nearby?
S :	**Yǒu. Nǐ kàn, dōngbianr jiù shi gōngyuán, xībianr yǒu ge gǔdǒng shìchǎng.**	Yes. Look, the park's there to the east, and to the west there's an antique market.
T :	**Chénghuáng Miào zài běibianr ma?**	Is the City God Temple north of here?
S :	**Bù, zài nánbianr.**	No, it's south.
T :	**Yuǎn ma?**	Is it far?
S :	**Bù yuǎn. Nǐ kàn, nà bú shi bǎihuò dàlóu ma? Jiù zài bǎihuò dàlóu hòutou.**	No. Look, isn't that the department store? It's just behind that.

T : **Chénghuáng Miào lǐtou yǒu shénme?** What's inside the temple?

S : **Yǒu shénme? Yǒu Chénghuáng a!** Inside? The City God, of course!

Exercise 33
Pronunciation practice:

1. **chǎng, shìchǎng, gǔdǒng shìchǎng**
2. **lóu, dàlóu, bǎihuò dàlóu**
3. **diàn, fàndiàn, Běijīng Fàndiàn**
4. **yuán, gōngyuán, Tiāntán Gōngyuán**

Exercise 34
Translate into Chinese:

1. A: Hello, is Mr. Wang there?
   B: Sorry, he's not in.

2. A: Where are they?
   B: They're all in the café.

3. A: Excuse me, where is the toilet?
   B: On the 2nd floor.

4. A: How much is this tea pot [**cháhú**]?
   B: ¥16.50.

5. A: Where's his house?
   B: It's on the east of the park.

6. A: Can I have a look at your tourist map?
   B: Yes, go ahead.

Chapter 6

DIRECTIONS

Public transport is not always easy in China. There are so many people who need to move around that almost every kind of transport is overcrowded, and traffic congestion in the cities and on the major highways is a headache for all. We can tell you how to take a bus and how to ask for a ticket, but we apologise that we cannot guarantee you a seat. Of course you can always resort to a taxi, but make sure that you ask for your destination clearly and that the driver knows where it is. The example of Miss A in Conversation 6D is meant to be part of your education!

6.1   How to go?

Zěnme? means 'how?'. **Zǒu** basically means 'to walk' but it also has many of the same meanings as the English word 'go', such as when we say that a watch 'goes', or 'he's going' (leaving).

> **Zěnme zǒu?** asks which direction to go in order to get somewhere.
>
> **Zěnme qù?** asks by what means to get somewhere, that is, whether by bus, by train, on foot, etc.

6.2   Travel by

Zuò means 'to sit' or 'to sit on'. It also means 'to travel by'. **Chē** means 'a wheeled vehicle' and can refer to a car, a bus, a train or whatever according to context.

Zuò chē	to travel by vehicle
Zuò diàntī	to ride in a lift

6.3   For preference

Háishi means 'or would it be?' and is used in questions where the answer requires a choice, such as "Are you Japanese or Chinese?" **Nǐ shi Rìběn rén háishi Zhōngguó rén?** The answer simply requires the choosing of one of the two alternatives **Wǒ shi Rìběn rén** or **Wǒ shi Zhōngguó rén.**

6.4   Go west, young man

Wǎng means 'towards' and **guǎi** means 'to turn'. **Wǎng xī guǎi** literally means 'towards the west turn', so 'turn to the west'.

Exercise 35
Give directions in Chinese:

1. Go forward.
2. Turn east.
3. Turn left.
4. No right turn ahead.
5. Go to the park.

6.5   Final particle 'le'

Le is a sentence particle which is used in many different ways. It indicates completion and shows that a new state of affairs has come about:

Tā zhīdao le.	He knows now.
Tā zǒu le.	She's left.
Tā dào le.	He has arrived. [**dào** = to arrive at, to reach]

Exercise 36
'A taste of le'. Translate:

1. **Tā qù Shànghǎi le.**
2. **Lǐ xiáojie dào Běijīng le.**
3. **Tāmen dōu zhīdao le.**
4. **Tā qù gōngyuán le.**
5. **Nǐ kàn lǚyóutú le ma?**

New words

cóng	from
dà	big
dàlù	main road
kèqi	polite
bú kèqi	impolite; don't be polite (= don't mention it)
Tiān'ānmén	Tiananmen
tiáo	(measure for long flexible things)
yìzhí	direct(ly), straight
zǒu lù	to walk

⟨92⟩ *CONVERSATION 6A*

A tourist asks a policeman the way.

T : **Tóngzhì, qǐng wèn, qù Tiān'ānmén zěnme zǒu?** — How do I get to Tiananmen, comrade, please?

P : **Zuò chē háishi zǒu lù?** — By bus or on foot?

T : **Wǒ xǐhuan zǒu lù.** — I prefer to walk.

P : **Hǎo, dào qiántou nèi tiáo dàlù wǎng xī guǎi, yìzhí zǒu, jiù dào le.** — OK, turn west when you get to the main road ahead, then just keep going and you'll get there.

T : **Wǎng xī guǎi? Něi bianr shi xī a?** — Turn west? Which way is west?

P : **Cóng nán wǎng běi, wǎng xī guǎi jiùshi wǎng zuǒ guǎi.** — You are going from south to north, and turning west means turning to the left.

T : **À, zhīdao le! Xièxie.** — Oh, got it! Thank you.

P : **Bú kèqi.** — Not at all.

6.6 All change!

Dǎo chē means 'to change buses or trains'. You may also hear people say **huàn chē** with the same meaning.

6.7 Bus routes

Lù literally means 'a road', 'a way' but is also used for 'a bus route', so **jiǔ lù** is 'a number 9 bus'. Up to a number 99, the routes are counted in a straightforward manner (**èrshi'èr lù**, **bāshiliù lù**, etc), but three figure bus numbers are generally 'spelled out' as **sān-sān-yāo** (331), **yāo-liù-bā** (168), and so on.

6.8 Measure words

The correct measure word for a bus ticket and other objects of flat, sheet-like appearance is **zhāng**, but when asking for 'two tickets' on a bus it is usual to

Comrade

Tóngzhì 'comrade' was the common way to address everyone in the early decades of the Communist revolution, but in the 21st century it has tended to be reduced in usage to addressing officials, such as Communist Party members, policemen, and members of the People's Liberation Army (PLA).

ask for **liǎng ge** and not **liǎng zhāng**, perhaps indicating that the speaker is thinking of the number of persons travelling rather than the number of tickets for them.

Exercise 37

Practice with measure words:

1. **yí** _____ **tóngzhì** (one comrade)
2. **liǎng** _____ **cèsuǒ** (two toilets)
3. **sān** _____ **kāfēi** (three cups of coffee)
4. **sì** _____ **lù** (four roads)
5. **wǔ** _____ **dìtú** (five maps)
6. **liùshíbā** _____ **wǔ** (¥68.50)

6.9 Giving change

When giving change, the verb **zhǎo** (which literally means 'to look for') is used:

Zhǎo nǐ bā máo.   80 cents change for you.

6.10 The adverb 'hái'

Hái means 'in addition', 'still', or 'yet'. It comes, like other adverbs, before the verb:

Nǐ hái yǒu qián ma?   Do you still have some money?

6.11 The adverb 'jiù'

Jiù we met before (**3.7**) meaning 'just', 'exactly'. It has another meaning of 'immediately', 'at once':

Wǒ jiù qù.   I'm going at once.

(93) *New words*

děi	must; require
piào	ticket

rénmín	the people
zhàn	station, stop, stand
Zhōngshān	Sun Yat-sen

Zhōngshān

You may be wondering how **Zhōngshān** comes to be translated as Sun Yat-sen. Dr. Sun was a revolutionary who was in the forefront of the overthrow of the Manchu Qing dynasty (1644-1911) and he was later made President of the new Republic of China. For many years before the revolution succeeded he found sanctuary in Japan, where he assumed the Japanese surname 'Nakayama' 中山. That surname translates literally as 'Central Mountain', and he adopted it as one of his Chinese personal names for the rest of his life. 'Central Mountain' in Chinese is **Zhōngshān**, and in China many streets, parks and public buildings are named in his memory. Even his native place, **Xiāngshān** in Guangdong province, is now called **Zhōngshān**.

CONVERSATION 6B

Two tourists want to go to the People's Park, but the conductor tells them they're on the wrong bus.

T : **Qǐng wèn, zhèi chē dào Rénmín Gōngyuán ma?**
Excuse me, does this bus go to the People's Park?

C : **Bú dào. Děi zài Zhōngshān Lù dǎo chē.**
No, you'll have to change at Zhongshan Road.

T : **Dǎo jǐ lù?**
To what number?

C : **Jiǔ lù… Zhōngshān Lù dào le. Nǐmen jiù zài zhèr dǎo chē.**
A number 9…This is Zhongshan Road. You change here now.

T : **Xièxie.**
Thank you.

[On the Number 9 bus]

C : **Piào, piào, mǎi piào!**
Tickets, tickets, get your tickets!

T : **Rénmín Gōngyuán, liǎng ge.**
Two to the People's Park.

C : **Yí kuài.**
One yuan.

T : **Zhè shi wǔ kuài.**   Here's five yuan.

C : **Zhǎo nín sì kuài.**   ... and four yuan change.

T : **Rénmín Gōngyuán hái yǒu jǐ**   How many more stops to the Park?
    zhàn?

C : **Sān zhàn.**   Three.

Exercise 38
'Like' and 'would like to'

Select appropriate words from A and B and put them into the pattern
Wǒ xǐhuan ... , wǒ xiǎng qù ... *to make four meaningful sentences:*

A. 1. **mǎi dōngxi**   B. 1. **Xībānyá**

   2. **hē chá**   2. **Guìlín**

   3. **rè de dìfang**   3. **kāfēitīng**

   4. **kàn fēngjǐng**   4. **bǎihuò dàlóu**

---

(95) 6.12   *More on 'de'*

In **5.14** you learned how **de** could be used to link an adjective to a noun, as in
hěn rè de chá 'very hot tea'. When the adjective is a more complex one, for
instance when it is composed of a verb and a noun, the same pattern applies.
So in the next conversation you meet 'a place to change money' **huàn qián de
dìfang.** If you are puzzled by this, try re-translating the English of **hěn rè de chá**
as 'tea which is very hot', and then look at the following examples and work
out how they all achieve the linking of a description (that's what an adjective is
after all) with a noun, and they all use the same *adjective-de-noun* pattern, even
though English finds different ways of doing it.

hěn hǎo *de* chá	tea *that* is very nice
huàn qián *de* dìfang	a place *where* to change money
nǐ xǐhuan *de* xiáojie	the girl *whom* you like
wǒ xiǎng qù *de* Chénghuáng Miào	the City God Temple *that* I want to go to
tā xǐhuan hē *de* píjiǔ	the beer *which* he likes drinking

Exercise 39

Translate into Chinese:

1. people who drink tea
2. places which sell snuff bottles
3. the park he wants to go to
4. buses which go to Tiananmen
5. people who travel by car

(96) 6.13 Choice of transport

Just as a matter of convenience we list here some transport which you can **zuò** 'sit on', 'travel by':

chē	any wheeled vehicle (and **chēzhàn** can be a station or a stop or a stand depending what **chē** means in the context)
chūzū(qì)chē	a taxi
diàntī	a lift, elevator
dìtiě	the subway, underground, metro
fēijī	an aircraft, plane
gōnggòngqìchē	a bus, coach
huǒchē	a railway train
qìchē	a car, automobile

> ### RMB
>
> **Rénmínbì** is the name of the Chinese currency. It means 'People's currency' and is often abbreviated to **RMB.**, with the **yuán** shown by the symbol **¥**. 'Pounds Sterling' is **Yīngbàng** 'British pounds' and 'American dollars' are quite simply 'American dollars' **Měiyuán**, while the Euro is **Ōuyuán** 'European dollars'.

(97) 6.14 Once, twice, three times

Here are a few examples of things you can do with **cì**, the measure word for 'occasion', 'occurrence', 'time' which you will meet in the conversation below:

zhèi cì	this time
yí cì	once
liǎng cì	twice
shàng cì	last time
xià cì	next time

(98) *New words*

huàn qián	to change money
Nà	Well then… ; In that case…
xiànjīn	cash, ready money
yínháng	bank
zhīpiào	a cheque
lǚxíng zhīpiào	travellers cheque

(99) *CONVERSATION 6C*

A tourist wants to find a bank to change some money. He asks the way from a passer-by.

T : **Qǐng wèn zhèr fùjìn yǒu méi you huàn qián de dìfang?**
Excuse me, is there a place near here where I can change money?

P : **Méi yǒu. Nǐ děi qù huǒchēzhàn qiántou de Zhōngguó Yínháng.**
No. You'll have to go to the Bank of China in front of the railway station.

T : **Hǔochēzhàn? Yuǎn ma?**
The railway station? Is it far?

P : **Hěn yuǎn. Zhèr méi dìtiě, zuò gōnggòngqìchē děi dǎo liǎng cì chē.**
It's a long way. There's no subway here; you have to change buses twice.

T : **Nà wǒ zuò chūzūqìchē qu ba.**
In that case I'll go by taxi.

[At the bank counter he speaks to the clerk]

T : **Zhèr kěyǐ huàn qián ma? Měiyuán huàn Rénmínbì.**
Can I change money here? US dollars to Renminbi.

C : **Kěyǐ. Shì xiànjīn háishi lǚxíng zhīpiào?**
You can. Cash or travellers cheques?

T : **Lǚxíng zhīpiào. Zhè shi wǒ de hùzhào.**
Travellers cheques. Here's my passport.

C : **Hǎo. Qǐng xiān tián biǎo.**
Fine. Please first fill in the form.

Exercise 40

Give the Chinese equivalents of the following:

1. The coffee they drink is very expensive.
2. This is not the tourist map I want to buy.
3. The place he wants to go to is very far.
4. There are too many people who would like to go to China.

6.15 Build-up words

Chinese is very clever at piling up words to make new ones. Here are three sets of build-ups with the literal meanings in brackets:

1. **chē**   vehicle
   huǒchē   railway train [fire vehicle]
   huǒchēzhàn   railway station [fire vehicle stop]

2. **chē**   vehicle
   qìchē   motor vehicle [steam vehicle]
   gōnggòngqìchē   bus [public together steam vehicle]
   gōnggòngqìchēzhàn   bus stop [public together steam vehicle stop]

3. **piào**   ticket
   zhīpiào   cheque [payment ticket]
   lǚxíng zhīpiào   travellers cheque [travel payment ticket]

4. **lóu**   building
   dàlóu   large building
   bǎihuò dàlóu   department store
   Běijīng Bǎihuò Dàlóu   Beijing Department Store

6.16 In order to

You have already met **qù** meaning 'to go' in Chapter Five. It also means 'to go to' as in **Wǒ qù Rìběn.** 'I'm going to Japan.' Its opposite partner is **lái** 'to come' or 'to come to'. In English, 'come to' and 'go to' often convey a sense of purpose (like 'in order to'): think for example of "He's come to read the gas meter". **Lái** and **qù** work much the same in Chinese:

Wǒ yào qù kàn péngyou.	I will go to see friends.
Tā lái mǎi dìtú.	He's come to buy a map.

Exercise 41

Practise the sentences and translate into English:

1. **Wǒ yào qù bǎihuò dàlóu mǎi dōngxi.**
2. **Tā xiǎng lái Yīngguó lǚxíng.**
3. **Wǒ xiǎng qù běibianr kàn péngyou.**
4. **Nǐ xiǎng bu xiǎng qù gōngyuán wánr?**
5. **Wǒ xiǎng qù gǔdǒng shìchǎng kànkan.**

6.17 Boarding and disembarking

Qù and **lái** are opposites, and so are **shàng** 'to ascend' and **xià** 'to descend'. To embark on a train, ship, aircraft, bus, car etc is **shàng** and to disembark is **xià**. So in the next conversation the taxi driver invites Miss A to get in the cab by saying **Qǐng shàng chē.**

6.18 To drive

You will meet the verb **kāi** again later, but in this chapter it means 'to drive' or 'to pilot', depending on what mode of transport it refers to:

kāi chūzūqìchē	to drive a taxi
kāi fēijī	to fly an aircraft.

What follows **kāi** is usually a noun, as in the two examples above, but there are other possibilities, and in the next conversation Miss A asks **Nǐ kāidào nǎr le?** 'Where have you brought us to?'. You will recognise **dào** as the verb 'to arrive at' acting here as the equivalent of 'to':

A: **Tā yào kāidào nǎr qu?**   Where is he driving to?
B: **Shànghǎi.**   To Shanghai.

Exercise 42

Guesswork: use the vocabulary you know to make new words to translate the following into Chinese:

1. hot water
2. West Station
3. Far East Company
4. car key
5. Sun Yat-sen Gate
6. No market for snuff bottles

(101) ## 6.19   It is the case that ...

The verb **shì** 'to be' has to work very hard. One of its regular meanings is 'it is the case that', a much more emphatic way of saying that something 'is':

Tā shì bù xǐhuan hē píjiǔ.   He really does not like beer.

Wǒ bú shì yào qù zuò fēijī.   It's not the case that I am going to catch a plane.

As might be expected **shì** carries full tone value in this function.

6.20   The adverbs 'jiù' and 'mǎshang'

Jiù means 'just', 'exactly', and has the additional meaning 'immediately', 'at once'. **Mǎshang** literally means 'on horseback', but it also means 'immediately', 'at once'. Sometimes it combines with **jiù** as **mǎshang jiù**, but the meaning of the two together is still the same. Like other adverbs we have met, both of these come just before the verb:

Wǒ mǎshang jiù kàn.   I'll look at it immediately.

(102) *New words*

diàotóu	to turn around
duì	correct
(fēi)jīchǎng	airport
huàjù	a play
jùchǎng	a theatre
shǒudū	capital city (of a country)

(103) ## CONVERSATION 6D

Miss A calls a taxi to go to the Capital Theatre to see a play.

T : **Qù nǎr, xiáojie?**   Where to, miss?

A : **Shǒudū Jùchǎng.**   The Capital Theatre.

T : **Hǎo, qǐng shàng chē.**   OK. Please get in.

[On the way]

A : **Shīfu, zhè lù bú duì ba?**   Driver, surely this isn't the right way,
    Nǐ kāidào nǎr le?   is it? Where have you brought us to?

T : **Nín bú shi yào qù Shǒudū**   Didn't you want the Capital
    Jīchǎng ma?   Airport?

A : **Bú shi, bú shi. Wǒ yào qù**   No, no, I want the Capital Theatre.
    Shǒudū Jùchǎng.

T : **Shénme? Shǒudū Jùchǎng?!**   What? The Capital Theatre?

A : **Shì a. Wǒ yào qù kàn huàjù,**   Yes, I'm going to see a play, not
    bú shi yào qù zuò fēijī.   to catch a plane.

T : **Duìbuqǐ, duìbuqǐ. Wǒ**   Sorry, sorry. I'll turn round at once.
    mǎshang diàotóu.

Exercise 43
Pronunciation practice:

1. **Qìchē, qìchē, wǒ yào zuò chūzūqìchē.**

2. **Kělè, Kělè, wǒ yào hē Kěkǒu Kělè.**

3. **Zuò qìchē, hē Kělè.**

4. **Wǒ, wǒ, wǒ ... nǎr yǒu cèsuǒ?**

Exercise 44
Translate into Chinese:

1. A: Excuse me, where's the train station?

    B: Look, it's over there. Just behind that big hotel.

2. A: Comrade, how do I get to the antiques market, please?

    B: It's a long way. I don't know how to get there either.

3. A: Excuse me, does this bus go to Tiananmen?

    B: Yes, it does. Two more stops.

4. A: Have they all gone to China?

    B: Yes, they have.

5. A: Is there a bank nearby?

    B: Yes, there is. It's just inside that building.

6. A: I'm going to the airport.

    B: Are you going by bus or by taxi?

Chapter 7

TIME

In traditional times the Chinese day was divided into twelve two-hour periods starting at 11 p.m. Each period had a name: the one which ran from 11 a.m. to 1 p.m was called **wǔ** and noon was known as **zhōngwǔ** 'the middle of **wǔ**'. The Western concept of the hour came to be called a 'little period', a **xiǎoshí**, and, as we shall see, **xiǎoshí** is the word for an hour today.

There was no seven-day week — though a ten-day lunar week was used for some purposes — but when it became necessary to accommodate the idea, the Chinese adopted a very sensible approach. The sun and the moon were already in use for telling the years and the months, so they decided to use the stars for the weeks, calling the week a **xīngqī** 'star period' and starting the week on Monday with **xīngqīyī** 'star period one'.

In this chapter you will meet these words and the rest of the modern way of telling the time. You'll be pleased to know that it is all quite straightforward.

(105) 7.1   Time goes by

For convenience we list here two sets of important time words:

qiántiān	the day before yesterday	**qiánnián**	the year before last
zuótiān	yesterday	**qùnián**	last year
jīntiān	today	**jīnnián**	this year
míngtiān	tomorrow	**míngnián**	next year
hòutiān	the day after tomorrow	**hòunián**	the year after next

(106) 7.2   Dates

Chinese generally prefers to list the general before the particular, and with dates this means that the year (**nián**) is shown before the month (**yuè**) and the month before the day (**hào**, the colloquial word, or **rì**, the more formal term).

The year is spoken as a straightforward series of digits:

1984 is	**yì-jiǔ-bā-sì nián**
2012 is	**èr-líng-yī-èr nián**

The months are simply numbered from one to twelve:

January is	**Yí yuè**,
February is	**Èr yuè**,
March is	**Sān yuè**, and so on down to
December	**Shí'èr yuè**.

The days are also simply numbered from one to thirty-one:

The first is **Yí hào** or **Yí rì**

The second is **Èr hào** or **Èr rì**, and

The thirty-first is **Sānshiyī hào** or **Sānshiyī rì**.

Remembering the year-month-day order, we can now translate:

7th July	**Qī yuè qī hào/rì**
1st October 1949	**Yì-jiǔ-sì-jiǔ nián shí yuè yí hào/rì**

Exercise 45
Say it in Chinese:

1. 28th April 1842
2. 10th October 1911
3. 11th September 2001
4. 8th August 2008
5. 31st January 2025

7.3 The final particle 'le' again

With **yǐjing** 'already' the particle **le** shows that something has happened and a new state of affairs has already come into being:

Tā yǐjing yǒu le.	He's already got it.
Wǒmen yǐjing méi yǒu le.	We've run out (of it) already.

Exercise 46
Put into English:

1. **Tā yǐjing qù Zhōngguó le.**
2. **Nèi ge dōngxi wǒ yǐjing mǎi le.**
3. **Wǒmen yǐjing rènshi le.**
4. **Huǒchē yǐjing dào le.**
5. **Jīntiān yǐjing wǔ hào le.**

(107) *7.4 More question words*

We saw at **3.1** that **shénme** means 'what' or 'what kind of'. It combines with **shíhou** ('time'), **dìfang** ('place'), **rén** ('person'), and **shì** ('matter') to make other questions:

shénme shíhou?	what time? when?
shénme dìfang?	what place? where?
shénme rén?	what person? who?
shénme shì?	what matter? what's up?

And similarly it combines with **wèi** 'on account of':

wèishénme?	on account of what? why?

(108) *New words*

chūshēng	to be born
dàoqī	to expire, to reach time limit
dǎsuan	to intend to, to plan to
qiānzhèng	a visa
wèntí	a question, a problem

(109) *CONVERSATION 7A*

A tourist checks in at hotel reception.

R : **Nǐ hǎo!**
Hello!

T : **Nǐ hǎo. Yǒu fángjiān ma?**
Hello. Have you a room?

R : **Yǒu. Nín dǎsuan zhù jǐ tiān?**
Yes. How long are you planning to stay?

T : **Sì tiān. Jīntiān shi wǔ yuè bā hào ba?**
Four days. Today is the 8th May, isn't it?

R : **Bù, jīntiān shi wǔ yuè jiǔ hào.**
No, it's the 9th.

T : **Òu, yǐjing jiǔ hào le. Nà wǒ zhǐ néng zhù sān tiān le.**
Oh, it's the 9th already. In that case I can only stay three days.

R : **Qǐng nín xiān tián zhèi zhāng biǎo.**
Please first fill in this form.

[The receptionist examines the form]

R : **Xiānsheng, nín de chūshēng nián-yuè-rì bú duì ba?**
Sir, your date of birth isn't correct, is it?

T : **Wèishénme?**
Why is that?

R : **Nín kàn**, **èr-líng-yī-líng nián wǔ yuè jiǔ rì. Zhè bú shi jīntiān ma?**	Look, 9th May 2010. Isn't that today?
T : **Duìbuqǐ, bù hǎo yìsi! Yīnggāi shi yī-jiǔ-qī-bā nián shí'èr yuè sānshí rì.**	I'm so sorry, how embarrassing! It ought to be 30th December 1978.
R : **Méi guānxi. Qǐng wèn nín de qiānzhèng shénme shíhou dàoqī?**	That's alright. May I ask when your visa expires?
T : **Wǒ kànkan … liù yuè shíwǔ rì.**	Let me see … 15th June.
R : **Hǎo, nà méi wèntí.**	Good, then there's no problem.

(110) *7.5 A reminder about 'de'*

In **5.14** we met **de** used to join adjectives to nouns, as with **piàoliang de xiáojie** 'a beautiful girl', and in **6.12** we saw that **de** will join adjectical clauses to nouns in the same way. Here are a few more examples to drive the point home:

hǎowánr de dìfang	a place where it is good fun
zuò huǒchē de rén	people who travel by train
mǎi kāfēi de qián	money for buying coffee
lái Zhōngguó de Àodàlìyà rén	Australians coming to China
qù Shànghǎi de piào	a ticket for Shanghai

Exercise 47
Translate into Chinese:

1. All beautiful things are expensive.
2. This is not the way to the airport.
3. Is there a bank for money exchange nearby?
4. I have lots of friends who like drinking alcohol.

7.6 The express

A fast train is called a **kuàichē**. **Tèkuài** is an express and is short for **tèbié kuàichē** 'especially fast train'.

7.7   The question word 'něi?'

Něi? 'which?' is normally followed by a measure word as we saw in **5.9**. So 'which bottle of beer?' is **Něi píng píjiǔ?** Note that **nián** 'year', **tiān** 'day', and **suì** 'year of age' act as measure words, so that **Něi tiān?** means 'which day?' and **Něi nián?** means 'which year?' Unlike these words, **yuè** can occur with or without the measure word **ge**: so either **Něi yuè?** or **Něi ge yuè?** will translate 'Which month?'

(111) 7.8   Days of the week

Xīngqī (literally: 'star period') means 'week'. 'One week' is either **yì xīngqī** or **yí ge xīngqī**. 'Two weeks' is **liǎng ge xīngqī**, 'three weeks' is **sān ge xīngqī**, and so on.

'Sunday' is **Xīngqītiān** or **Xīngqīrì**, and the other days of the week are simply counted starting from Monday:

Xīngqīyī	Monday
Xīngqī'èr	Tuesday
Xīngqīliù	Saturday.

To ask 'Which day of the week?' the question word **jǐ?** 'how many?' is used:

Jīntiān (shi) xīngqījǐ?	What day of the week is it today?

Exercise 48
Give a quick answer:

1. **Jīntiān wǔ hào, míngtiān jǐ hào?**
2. **Zuótiān xīngqīsān, jīntiān xīngqījǐ?**
3. **Jīntiān èrshiyī hào, hòutiān èrshijǐ hào?**
4. **Qiántiān jiǔ yuè sānshí hào, jīntiān jǐ yuè jǐ hào?**

7.9   Yet more on 'de'

We have seen that **de** either makes the possessive or links adjectives and adjectival clauses to nouns. Quite often the noun can be omitted if it is clear what is meant:

Zhèi bēi kāfēi shi wǒ de, nèi bēi shi nǐ de.	This cup of coffee is mine, that one is yours.

Qù Běijīng de piào yǒu, qù Shànghǎi de méi yǒu.	There are tickets for Beijing, but none for Shanghai.

(112) *New words*

chēcì	train number
Chéngdū	Chengdu (capital of Sichuan province)
Chóngqìng	Chongqing (Chinese WWII capital on the Yangtse)
chū wèntí	to develop a problem
wèntí	a question, problem
diànnǎo	computer
fù	to pay
shuākǎ	swipe-card, credit card, 'plastic'
wǎn	late

(113) CONVERSATION 7B

A tourist buys a railway ticket at the travel agent in Chongqing.

T :	**Nǐ hǎo. Wǒ xiǎng mǎi zhāng qù Chéngdū de tèkuài.**	Hello, I'd like a ticket for the express to Chengdu.
C :	**Něi tiān zǒu?**	Which day will you be travelling?
T :	**Hòutiān, xīngqīliù.**	The day after tomorrow, Saturday.
C :	**Shì sì yuè yí hào ma? Něi ge chēcì?**	Is that April 1st? Which number train?
T :	**Bā-jiǔ-líng cì tèkuài.**	Express No.890.
C :	**Bā-jiǔ-líng de piào méi yǒu le. Bā-jiǔ-bā kěyǐ ma?**	There are no tickets for No.890 left. Is No.898 OK?
T :	**Bā-jiǔ-bā dào Chéngdū tài wǎn le. Xīngqītiān de Bā-jiǔ-líng hái yǒu piào ma?**	898 gets into Chengdu too late. Are there still any tickets for No.890 on Sunday?
C :	**Sì yuè èr hào de hái yǒu.**	Yes, there are for April 2nd.
T :	**Nà wǒ mǎi zhāng sì yuè èr hào de.**	Then I'll buy one for April 2nd.
C :	**Hǎo, qīshibā kuài.**	Fine, that's 78 yuan.
T :	**Shuākǎ kěyǐ ma?**	Is a card OK?
C :	**Duìbuqǐ, diànnǎo chū wèntí le; nín děi fù xiànjīn.**	I'm sorry, the computer has developed a problem; you'll have to pay cash.

(114) *7.10 Clock time*

To cope with clock time you need the following words:

zhōng	a clock
diǎn	a dot [used for 'an hour']
fēn	a minute
bàn	half
kè	a notch [used for 'a quarter']

'One o'clock' is **yì diǎn zhōng** [literally: one dot on the clock]

'Six o'clock' is **liù diǎn zhōng** [six dots on the clock]

When it is clearly understood that you are talking about time, you can leave out the **zhōng**, so 'six o'clock' can also be **liù diǎn**, and when the minutes are mentioned **zhōng** is almost never used. The time is told quite logically:

6 o'clock	**liù diǎn (zhōng)**
6.15	**liù diǎn yí kè** [six dots and one notch]
6.30	**liù diǎn bàn**
6.45	**liù diǎn sān kè** [six dots and three notches]
6.25	**liù diǎn èrshiwǔ**
6.37	**liù diǎn sānshiqī**
6.05	**liù diǎn líng wǔ (fēn)** [Remember that **líng** means zero]

Exercise 49

Tell the time in Chinese:

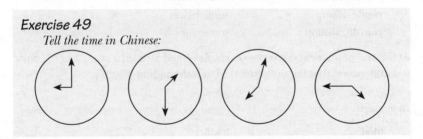

7.11 Hi, ho, hi, ho!

'To go to work' is **shàng bān**. As we saw in **6.17 shàng** means 'to go up to' or 'to ascend', and its opposite word is **xià** 'to go down to', 'to climb down'. It is not illogical, then, that 'to finish work' is **xià bān**. This same pair **shàng/xià** will occur again. **Bān** means 'shift'.

7.12   Open and shut

Kāi mén means 'to open the door'. Its opposite is **guān mén** 'to shut the door'. But when **kāi mén** is used of shops being 'open for business' its opposite is **xiūxi** 'resting', 'closed for lunch', 'closed for the day' rather than **guān mén**. There is nothing wrong with **guān mén**, but it also can mean 'closed down', 'ceased to trade', and some people prefer to avoid mentioning such an unlucky possibility.

7.13   Sentences without verbs

Where there can be no ambiguity about the connection between two nouns, Chinese sometimes is content to do without the verb **shì**:

Jīntiān xīngqījǐ?	What day of the week is it today? [See **7.8**]
Tā Měiguó rén.	He's American.
Běijīng hǎo dìfang.	Beijing is a great place.

(115) 7.14   'Yǒude' *some*

To express an indefinite number of anything you simply need to put **yǒude** in front of the noun:

yǒude rén	some people
yǒude dìfang	some places
yǒu(de) shíhou	sometimes

At the end of the next conversation **yǒude** is used without a noun, but of course it is understood that the noun referred to is **shāngdiàn** 'shops'.

(116) *New words*

biǎo	a watch
cāntīng	restaurant
fànguǎnr	restaurant (not part of hotel or institution)
jiā	(measure for shops and businesses)
shāngdiàn	shop, store
shíjiān	time
xiànzài	now
xiǎoshí	hour

⸨117⸩ CONVERSATION 7C

A tourist asks the hotel receptionist about eating.

T : **Qǐng wèn xiànzài jǐ diǎn le? Wǒde biǎo hái shi Lúndūn shíjiān.**
Excuse me, what's the time? My watch is still on London time.

R : **Shíyī diǎn shí fēn.**
Ten past eleven.

T : **Cāntīng hái kāi ma?**
Is the restaurant still open?

R : **Duìbuqǐ, cāntīng yǐjing xià bān le.**
Sorry, it's closed already.

T : **Fùjìn yǒu fànguǎnr ma?**
Are there any restaurants nearby?

R : **Zhǐ yǒu yì jiā Màidāngláo, èrshisì xiǎoshí dōu kāi.**
There's only a Macdonald's, which is open 24 hours.

T : **Xièxie, Màidāngláo wǒ bù chī. Míngtiān xīngqītiān, shāngdiàn dōu kāi mén ma?**
No thank you, I don't eat Macdonald's. Tomorrow is Sunday. Will all the shops be open?

R : **Kāi. Xīngqītiān shāngdiàn bù xiūxi.**
Yes. They don't close on Sundays.

T : **Jǐ diǎn kāi mén?**
What time do they open?

R : **Yǒude bā diǎn bàn, yǒude jiǔ diǎn.**
Some at half past eight, some at 9 o'clock.

7.15 What's it like?

We saw in **6.1** that **zěnme?** means 'how?' **Zěnme?** also combines with **yàng** ('kind', 'type', 'sort') to make the word **zěnmeyàng?** meaning 'What's it like?', 'What was it like?', 'How was it?', 'How's it going?', 'What do you think?', and so on:

Nèi ge huàjù zěnmeyàng?
How was that play?

Jiǔ zěnmeyàng?
What's the wine like?

⸨118⸩ 7.16 Morning, noon and ...

Morning (after dawn) is 'above noon' **shàngwǔ**
Afternoon (before dark) is 'below noon' **xiàwǔ**
Mid-day is 'mid-noon' **zhōngwǔ**

Note the appearance of **shàng** and **xià** again. Another way of saying 'morning' or 'in the morning' is **zǎoshang**, and 'evening' or 'in the evening' is **wǎnshang**. Here you will also see the reappearance of another pair of words: **zǎo** 'early' and **wǎn** 'late'.

Exercise 50

Answer the questions using the information provided:

1. **Nǐ míngtiān shénme shíhou qù jīchǎng?** (10:00 a.m.)
2. **Wǒmen jǐ diǎn zhōng kāi huì?** (4:15 p.m.)
3. **Huǒchē jǐ diǎn zhōng dào?** (12:48 p.m.)
4. **Tā qǐng nǐ jǐ diǎn zhōng chī fàn?** (7:30 p.m.)

7.17 Exceedingly so

Jíle can be tacked on to adjectives to give great emphasis to them:

hǎo jíle	superb, wonderful, fantastic
rè jíle	extremely hot, sweltering

You may remember that in **4.15** we met this same **le** as part of another 'excessive' pattern, as in **tài hǎo le!** 'Great!'

7.18 To invite

Qǐng has cropped up before, first of all in Chapter One in a number of polite expressions, and then in Chapter Five as part of the expression **Qǐngwèn** 'Please may I ask ...?' As well as 'please' **qǐng** also means 'to invite' or 'to stand treat':

Tā yào qǐng wǒ hē píjiǔ. He's inviting me to have a beer.

7.19 Two-faced constructions

The example sentence in **7.18** is interesting because **wǒ** has two jobs to do. Looked at one way it is the object of the verb **qǐng**, but you can also see that it is the subject of the verb **hē**. The Chinese construction is straightforward, though the English disguises this two-faced role by using the infinitive 'to have'. In the following example English uses 'who is surnamed', but the Chinese remains simple, with **yí ge péngyou** acting as both object and subject at the same time:

Wǒ yǒu yí ge péngyou xìng Wáng.   I've got a friend who is surnamed
Wang.

Exercise 51

Translate into English and note how the structures of the two languages differ:

1. **Wǒ yǒu yí ge péngyou shi Xiānggǎng rén.**
2. **Tā yào qǐng wǒ qù hē jiǔ.**
3. **Tā wèn wǒ yǒu duōshao qián.**
4. **Wǒ rènshi yí ge Huáqiáo yǒu shí ge Zhōngguó fànguǎnr.**

(119) 7.20 See you!

We met the word **jiàn** ('to see') in the expression **zàijiàn** 'goodbye' in Chapter
One. **Jiàn** is often used with other words as well when saying goodbye:

Míngtiān jiàn.	See you tomorrow.
Liù diǎn jiàn.	See you at six o'clock.
Běijīng jiàn.	See you in Beijing.

(120) New words

ānpái	to arrange, arrangements
chī fàn	to eat, to have a meal (Literally: to eat rice)
fàn	cooked rice; meal; cuisine
gāo'ěrfū(qiú)	golf
qiú	a ball
huì	a meeting
kāi huì	to hold/attend a meeting
jiē	to meet, pick up someone
kǎoyā	(Peking) roast duck
máng	busy

(121) CONVERSATION 7D

Old Wang invites Peter to eat Peking duck.

W : **Wéi, shì Peter ma?**   Hello, is that Peter? It's Old
   Wǒ shi Lǎo Wáng a.   Wang here.

P : **Èi, Lǎo Wáng, nǐ hǎo!**   Eh, Old Wang, how are you?

W : **Zhèi liǎng tiān zěnmeyàng?**   How's it been these last couple of
   Máng ma?   days? Busy?

P : **Zuótiān hěn máng, jīntiān bú tài máng.** — Very busy yesterday, not too busy today.

W : **Jīntiān yǒu shénme ānpái?** — What arrangements have you got for today?

P : **Shàngwǔ shí diǎn zhōng yǒu ge huì, zhōngwǔ shí'èr diǎn Huáyuǎn Gōngsī qǐng chī fàn.** — I've got a meeting at 10 o'clock this morning, then at midday the Huayuan Company is giving a lunch.

W : **Xiàwǔ méi shìr le ba?** — But you've got nothing in the afternoon, have you?

P : **Xiàwǔ, wǎnshang dōu méi shìr.** — Nothing this afternoon or evening.

W : **Hǎo jíle. Wǒmen xiàwǔ qù dǎ gāo'ěrfū, wǎnshang qǐng nǐ chī kǎoyā, zěnmeyàng? Liǎng diǎn yí kè wǒ lái fàndiàn jiē nǐ.** — Splendid. How about if we go and play golf in the afternoon, and this evening I'll invite you to have Peking Duck. I'll come to the hotel at 2.15 to pick you up.

P : **Tài hǎo le, xièxie, xièxie. Liǎng diǎn yí kè jiàn.** — Excellent, thank you very much indeed. See you at 2.15.

Exercise 52

Pronunciation practice:

1. **Jǐ yuè jǐ hào jǐ diǎn jǐ fēn lái?**
2. **Sì yuè sì hào sì diǎn sìshisì fēn lái.**
3. **Jǐ yuè jǐ hào jǐ diǎn jǐ fēn qù?**
4. **Qī yuè qī hào qī diǎn qī fēn qù.**

Exercise 53

Translate into Chinese:

1. A: When will you go to Japan?
   B: The fifth of September.

2. A: Is she coming on Saturday?
   B: No, she's coming on Sunday.

3. A: Have you got the time, please?
   B: Ten past ten.

4. A: What time do you get off work on Saturday?
   B: Twelve-thirty.

5. A: Do you know Manager Li of the Huayuan Company?
   B: No, I don't, but I have a good friend who knows him.

6. A: What time does the train get in?
   B: It's already in.

Chapter **8**

DESCRIBING THINGS

Describing things and people is not always easy, and it doesn't help that different cultures sometimes see things in different ways. When westerners speak of a 'big' person, they mean either a 'large' or a 'tall' one, but in Chinese **dàrén** 'big person' means 'a grown-up', 'an adult'.

Colours are not necessarily the same either. What is called a 'brown cow' in English is described as 'yellow' (**huáng**) in Chinese; someone who is jealous is said to be 'green-eyed' in English but 'red-eyed' (**hóng**) in Chinese; and we saw in **4.11** that 'black tea' is 'red tea'.

It all means more work for you, but it is the kind of thing that makes language learning so interesting.

8.1 Adverbs of degree

Adjectives can be modified with other words just as in English. **Hěn** 'very', **zhēn** 'truly', and **tài** 'too' all work as in English, though you will remember from **4.15** that **tài** usually has the particle **le** to help it out:

hěn hǎowánr	very good fun
zhēn piàoliang	really beautiful
tài rè le	too hot

Two other words which can modify adjectives are **zhème** and **nàme**. They both mean 'so', but you will probably have realised that they are variants of our old friends **zhè** and **nà**, so that there is a slight difference. **Zhème** really means 'so much as this', and **nàme** means 'so much as that':

zhème rè	so hot as this
nàme chǎo	so noisy as that

Hěn seldom carries the emphasis that 'very' does in English. The translation of **Tā hěn lǎo** is 'He's old' or 'He's quite old' rather than 'He's terribly ancient':

A: **Tā hěn lǎo ma?**   Is he old?

B: **Tā bù lǎo.** *or*   No.
   Tā hěn lǎo.   Yes.

(123) 8.2 Comparison

To make straightforward comparisons between two things you use the formula

<u>XXX **bǐ** YYY adjective</u>:

Jīntiān bǐ zuótiān lěng.   Today is colder than yesterday.[**lěng** = cold]
Zhè ge bǐ nà ge hǎo.   This one is better than that one.
Xiǎo Wáng bǐ xiǎo Lǐ piàoliang. Wang is prettier than Li.

If you want to say 'even more so than', you simply add **gèng** into the pattern:

<u>XXX **bǐ** YYY **gèng** adjective</u>:

Jīntiān bǐ zuótiān gèng lěng.   Today is even colder than yesterday.
Zhè ge bǐ nà ge gèng guì.   This is even dearer than that.

8.3 The measure word 'dù'

Dù means 'a degree', as in measuring heat or angles:

sānshiwǔ dù   35°C

In China temperature is measured in Centigrade (Celsius).

8.4 Location again

Here are four more place words which use the **shàng** and **xià** pair:

shānshang	on the mountain, up the hill
shānxia	at the foot of the mountain / hill
lóushang	upstairs
lóuxia	downstairs

Exercise 54

Make sentences showing simple comparison, as in the following example:

Běijīng líng dù, Lúndūn wǔ dù. > <u>Běijīng bǐ Lúndūn lěng</u>.

1. **Shǒudū Fàndiàn yǒu jiǔshí ge fángjiān, Huáyuán Fàndiàn yǒu qīshí ge fángjiān. >**

2. **Píjiǔ ¥3.50, kuàngquánshuǐ ¥2.80. >**

3. **Shānshang 5°C, shānxia 15°C. >**

4. **Lóushang de zhōng 10.55, lóuxia de zhōng 10.50. >** *[Tip: The Chinese word for 'fast' came in the expression 'fast train' in 7.6]*

(124) 8.5 It would be better if ...

'You'd better ...' or 'It would be better if ...' is translated by **háishi ... ba.**

Zhèi ge dà, háishi mǎi zhèi ge ba.	This one's bigger, it'd be better to buy this one.
Jīntiān tài wǎn le, nǐ háishi míngtiān qù ba.	It's too late today, you'd better go tomorrow.
Háishi qǐng tā lái ba, wǒ bú rènshi lù.	It'd be better to ask him to come along, I don't know the way.

8.6 To straddle

The verb **qí** 'to straddle' is used for riding horses, and it has been adopted for riding bicycles too:

Tā xǐhuan qí mǎ [horse].	She likes riding horses.
Wǒ qí zìxíngchē [bicycle] **qu.**	I am going by bike.

(125) 8.7 *Duration of time*

Yì nián 'for one year', **yí (ge) xiǎoshí** 'for an hour', **wǔ fēn zhōng** 'for five minutes' are time expressions which show duration, the time over which something goes on. Chinese puts such expressions after the verb;

zuò liǎng tiān (de) huǒchē	travel by train for two days
qí sìshí fēn zhōng (de) chē	ride a bike for 40 minutes
hē yì wǎnshang de jiǔ	to be drinking all evening

The marker **de** is often inserted between the time expression and the object of the verb.

Exercise 55
For how long? Try these:

1. **zhù sān ge xīngqī**
2. **chī liǎng nián de Zhōngguó fàn**
3. **shàng bā (ge) xiǎoshí de bān**
4. **zuò shíwǔ ge xiǎoshí de fēijī**
5. **qí èrshí fēn zhōng de chē**

(126) 8.8 *How come?*

We met **zěnme?** meaning 'how?' in **6.1**. It also means 'how come?' or 'how could it not be?':

Nǐ zěnme bú rènshi wǒ le?	How come you don't recognise me?
Jīntiān zěnme zhème rè?	How come it's so hot today?

(127) *New words*

dǎ dī	to take a taxi [**dǎ** means 'to hit', and **dī** can mean 'the target', but it is probable that this term is a corruption of the Cantonese term for 'to take a taxi', so the literal meaning is not really relevant]
jǐ	crowded, packed
kōngtiáo	air-conditioning
lèi	tired, weary
liàng	(measure for wheeled vehicles)
liángkuai	pleasantly cool
tiānqi	weather
wánr	to play, amuse oneself

(128) *CONVERSATION 8A*

A tourist discusses an outing with a Chinese friend in Beijing.

T : **Jīntiān zhēn rè!**

It's really hot today!

F : **Shì a! Bǐ zuótiān gèng rè le. Wàitou yǐjing sānshiwǔ dù le.**

You're right. It's even hotter than yesterday. It's already 35°C outside.

T : **Tiānqi zhème rè, dào nǎr qù wánr ne?**

The weather's so hot, where can we go to amuse ourselves?

F : **Qù Xiāngshān zěnmeyàng? Shānshang liángkuai.**

How about the Fragrant Hills? It's cool in the mountains.

T : **Hǎo a. Zěnme qù ne?**

Great. How do we get there?

F : **Zuò gōnggòngqìchē ba. Zuò chē bǐ qí chē kuài.**

Let's take a bus. It's quicker than going by bike.

T : **Gōnggòngqìchē tài jǐ le, háishi qí chē qu ba.**

The bus is too crowded. It'd be better to go by bike.

F : **Lù nàme yuǎn, děi qí liǎng ge xiǎoshí; nǐ bú pà lèi a?**

It's such a long way, it'd take two hours by bike; aren't you afraid of getting tired?

T : **Zěnme bú pà? Kěshi wǒ gèng pà jǐ.**

How couldn't I be? But I mind the crowding even more.

F : **Zuò chē pà jǐ, qí chē pà lèi … Nà wǒmen dǎ dī qu ba.**

Too crowded by bus, too tiring by bike… So let's go by taxi.

T : **Hǎo. Zhǎo liàng yǒu kōngtiáo de.**

Good idea. We'll find one that's air-conditioned.

8.9 To go or not to go?

Zǒu and **qù** both can be translated as 'to go', but they are not really the same. **Zǒu** often means 'to leave', while **qù** means 'to go somewhere'. Compare the following two sentences:

Tā míngtiān zǒu.

He's going (leaving) tomorrow.

Tā míngtiān qù.

He's going (there) tomorrow.

(129) *8.10* '*Shàng*' *and* '*xià*' *again*

Used with 'week' and 'month' yet another function of this pair is to indicate 'last' and 'next':

shàng xīngqī	last week
xià xīngqī	next week
shàng (ge) yuè	last month
xià (ge) yuè	next month
shàng xīngqīliù	last Saturday
xià (ge) yuè bā hào	8th of next month

8.11 Really?

Zhēn means 'true' 'real', and **Zhēnde ma?** is the idiomatic way to say 'Really?!', 'Is that true?! '

8.12 More on '*le*'

The sentence particle **le** which we met in **6.5** shows that a new state of affairs has come about. When it is used with a negative (**bù** or **méi**) the translation in English is usually 'no longer' or 'no more':

Xièxie nín, wǒ bù hē le.	Thank you, I won't have any more.
Tā bù lái le.	He's not coming any more (though he said he would.)

Exercise 56
Complete the following, showing change of state:

e.g. ***Zuótiān hěn lěng, jīntiān ...*** (*bù lěng le.*)

1. **Zuótiān tā yǒu qián, jīntiān ...**

2. **Qiántiān tā xiǎng chī kǎoyā, jīntiān ...**

3. **Shàngwǔ hěn máng, xiànzài ...**

4. **Zuótiān chē hěn jǐ, jīntiān ...**

8.13 *It's raining*

The Chinese for 'to rain' is **xià yǔ**, literally 'comes down rain'. Similarly, 'to snow' is **xià xuě** 'comes down snow'. Note that 'It's raining now' is **Xià yǔ le**, the **le** showing that, while it wasn't raining before, things have changed. (There is no equivalent for the 'It' of the English 'It's raining'.)

(130) *New words*

cháng	often
děng	to wait, to wait for
dōngtiān	winter
Guǎngzhōu	Guangzhou (Canton)
nuǎnhuo	warm
shàng wǎng	to go on the internet
tiānqi yùbào	weather forecast
zhàng	account
zhàngdān	the bill
jié zhàng	to settle the bill

(131) ## *CONVERSATION 8B*

A tourist in search of good weather wants to check out of his hotel.

T : **Wǒ míngtiān zǎoshang liù diǎn qù Guǎngzhōu, xiànzài jié zhàng hǎo ma?**

I'm going to Guangzhou at 6 o'clock tomorrow morning; can I settle the bill now?

R : **Nín shì shuākǎ háishi fù xiànjīn?**

Are you paying by card or cash?

T : **Shuākǎ.**

By card.

R : **Hǎo … zhè shi nín de zhàngdān. Nín bú shi xià xīngqīyī zǒu ma?**

Fine, here is your bill. Weren't you leaving next Monday?

T : **Běijīng tài lěng le, wǒ xiǎng zhǎo ge nuǎnhuo de dìfang.**

Beijing is too cold. I want to find somewhere warm.

R : **Guǎngzhōu shì bǐ Běijīng nuǎnhuo, kěshi dōngtiān cháng xià yǔ.**

Guangzhou is indeed warmer than Beijing, but it frequently rains in winter.

T : **Shì ma?**

Is that so?

R : **Nín děng-yi-děng, wǒ xiān shàng wǎng kànkan tiānqi yùbào.**

If you'll just wait a moment, I'll go on the net and have a look at the forecast.

T : **Zěnmeyàng?**	What's it like?
R : **Guǎngzhōu míngtiān yǒu yǔ.**	Guangzhou will have rain tomorrow.
T : **Běijīng ne?**	And what about Beijing?
R : **Běijīng kěnéng xià xuě.**	Beijing may have snow.
T : **Zhēnde ma? Tài hǎo le! Wǒ** **bù zǒu le. Wǒ jiù xǐhuan kàn** **xià xuě.**	Really? Terrific! I won't leave. I just love to watch it snowing.

8.14   Male and female

Although the words **nánren** 'a male person' and **nǚren** 'a female person' do exist, they are best avoided as general words for 'man' and 'woman'. It is more colloquial to say **nán de** and **nǚ de**. A more formal pair is **nánshì** 'gentleman' and **nǚshì** 'lady, woman', and the latter is now the standard translation of the English title 'Ms'.

8.15   The topic of conversation

Quite often Chinese states at the beginning of a sentence or speech the topic under discussion. It is rather like the English 'As for X, …'. To translate it formally each time as 'As for X' would be tedious and unnatural-sounding, but it is helpful to understand that the stating of this topic allows a full sentence to be used as a comment upon it. We could analyse the statement **Tā rén hěn hǎo** 'He is a very nice person' as:

Tā	Topic = 'As for him'
rén	subject = 'as a person'
hěn hǎo	comment = 'is very nice.'

If you now check back to **7.13**, you will see that you have already met some similar sentences there.

Exercise 57
Translate into English:

1. **Nèi ge dìfang, tiānqi bù hǎo, dōngxi yě guì.**
2. **Shānshang, fēngjǐng piàoliang, tiānqi liángkuai.**
3. **Shǒudū Fàndiàn, dìfang hǎo, fángjiān dà.**
4. **Dàhuá Cāntīng, lù yuǎn, kěshi kǎoyā hǎo.**

8.16 Sure to

It is strange that sometimes we use the word 'certainly' when the fact is that we cannot be certain at all. The Chinese word **yídìng** works just like 'certainly':

Míngtiān yídìng xià yǔ.	It will certainly rain tomorrow.
Wǒ yídìng lái kàn nǐ.	I will surely come to see you.

8.17 A little while

Yíhuìr works either as a time word showing when something happens ('in a little while', 'in a moment') or as a duration of time showing how long something goes on for ('for a moment', 'for a while'). In the first case it comes before the verb:

Tā yíhuìr jiù lái.	He will be here in a moment.

But 'duration of time' words come after the verb (See **8.7** above), so:

Tā xiǎng qù wánr yíhuìr.	He wants to go to play for a while.
Wǒmen xiūxi yíhuìr ba.	Let's rest for a bit.

(132) *New words*

ài	to love, to love to
cháng	long
dǎ lánqiú	to play basket-ball
lánqiúduì	basket-ball team
dài	to wear (accessories)
gāo	tall, high
gèzi	build, stature
pàng	fat (of people)
shòu	thin, slim, skinny
tóufa	hair (on the head)
yǎnjìngr	glasses, spectacles

⁽¹³³⁾ *CONVERSATION 8C*

Describing Ms. Wang over the phone.

A :	**Wéi, qǐngwèn Xiǎo Wáng zài ma?**	Hello, is Little Wang there, please?
B :	**Něi ge Xiǎo Wáng? Wǒmen zhèr yǒu liǎng ge Xiǎo Wáng.**	Which Little Wang? We have two Little Wangs here.
A :	**Duìbuqǐ, wǒ bù zhīdao tā de míngzi, shi wèi nǚshì.**	I'm sorry, I don't know the name, but it's a lady.
B :	**Liǎng ge Xiǎo Wáng dōu shi nǚ de.**	Both the Little Wangs are women.
A :	**Tā tóufa hěn cháng, gèzi hěn gāo.**	She has long hair, and she's very tall in build.
B :	**Rén pàng bu pàng?**	Is she on the large side?
A :	**Hěn shòu.**	No, slim.
B :	**Dài yǎnjìngr ma?**	Does she wear glasses?
A :	**Bú dài. Tā hěn ài dǎ lánqiú, shi lánqiúduì de.**	No. She loves playing basket-ball, she's in the team.
B :	**Nà yídìng shi Wáng Huá. Qǐng děng yíhuìr, wǒ qù jiào tā.**	That's bound to be Wang Hua. Please wait a moment, I'll go and call her.

⁽¹³⁴⁾ *8.18 Colours*

Some common colour words are:

hóng	red
huáng	yellow
lǜ	green
lán	blue
bái	white
hēi	black

The word for 'colour' is **yánsè**, and it often combines with the basic colour words to make the colour adjectives. **Hóng yánsè de chē** is 'a red car'. **Hóng sè de** is a shorter version of this, so **hóng sè de chē** also means 'a red car'.

Sometimes a colour word does not need these props but attaches direct to a noun. **Hēi yǎnjìngr** is a word for 'sunglasses', and **hóng tóufa** is 'ginger hair'.

Colours

Colours carry different symbolic meanings. Red is certainly the favourite Chinese colour. It is the colour of happiness and joy and good fortune, and usually when you meet the lucky character **Fú** 福 (see Conversation 8D) it will be written on red paper. White was traditionally the colour for mourning, not for a bride's dress. Yellow was the colour of China and only the imperial family could use yellow tiles on their roofs.

Exercise 58

Add a bit of colour:

1. **Yīngguó rén xǐhuan hē ____ chá.**
2. **Fǎguó rén xǐhuan hē ____ jiǔ.**
3. **Zhōngguó rén de tóufa shi ____ yánsè de.**
4. **Tiānqi hěn hǎo, tiān shi ____ yánsè de.**

[Tip: *tiān* means 'heaven' or 'sky' as well as 'day'.]

8.19 Size

We have met **hào** before in the sense of 'number'. It is also used in the terms for size, usually with the **-er** ending:

xiǎo hàor	small size
zhōng hàor	medium size
dà hàor	large size
tè-dà hàor	extra-large size
liù hàor	size six

(135) 8.20 Enough

Gòu means 'enough'. As an adverb it goes in front of adjectives:

gòu dà	big enough
bú gòu dà	not big enough

but unlike most Chinese adjectives **gòu** cannot occur in front of a noun, it can only follow the noun:

rén gòu	enough people
rén bú gòu	not enough people
Wǒ de qián bú gòu.	I haven't got enough money.

(136) *New words*

chuān	to wear
chuānshang	to put on (clothes)
"Fú" *	"Good Fortune"
fúqì	good fortune
jiàn	(measure for items of clothing)
T-xùshān	T-shirt
yìsi	meaning
zì	a Chinese character

(137) *CONVERSATION 8D*

A tourist is buying a T-shirt.

T : **Xiáojie, kànkan nèi jiàn T-xùshān kěyǐ ma?**

May I have a look at that T-shirt, Miss, please.

S : **Něi jiàn? Shì zhèi jiàn lǜ de ma?**

Which one? Is it this green one?

T : **Bú shì. Shì nèi jiàn huáng de, shàngtou yǒu ge dà hēi zì de.**

No, it's that yellow one, the one with the big black character on it.

S : **Nà shi zhōng hàor de. Nín chuān dà hàor de ba?**

That's a medium. You take a large surely?

T : **Dà hàor de hái shi bú gòu dà.**

Large is still not big enough.

S : **Wǒmen yǒu tè-dà hàor de.**

We have extra-large.

T : **Kànkan kěyǐ ma?**

May I see?

[The sales assistant searches for a long while]

S : **Duìbuqǐ, méi yǒu huáng de le. Hóng de kěyǐ ma?**

Sorry, there are no yellow ones left. Will a red one be OK?

T : **Wǒ bù xǐhuan hóng yánsè. Yǒu lán de ma?**

I don't like red. Have you got it in blue?

S : **Lán de yě méi yǒu tè-dà hàor de le. Bái de zěnmeyàng?**

We've got no more extra-large in blue either. How about white?

T : **Hǎo ba, wǒ mǎi jiàn bái de.**
Qǐng wèn shàngtou zhèi ge zì
shi shénme yìsi?

Alright, I'll buy a white one.
May I ask what this character on
it means?

S : **Zhè shi ge "Fú" zì, chuānshang**
zhèi jiàn yīfu, nín jiù gèng yǒu
fúqì le!

This is the character for "Good
fortune". If you put this shirt on,
you will have even better fortune
than now!

Exercise 59
Pronunciation practice:

1. **Wǒ xǐhuan qí chē; tiān rè qí, tiān bú rè yě qí.**

2. **Tā xǐhuan kàn huàjù; xià yǔ qù, bú xià yǔ yě qù.**

Exercise 60
Translate into Chinese:

1. A: What is winter like in Canada?
   B: It's extremely cold.

2. A: Is it very warm in Hong Kong in March?
   B: Yes, it's warmer than Shanghai.

3. A: Does your friend wear glasses?
   B: No, she doesn't.

4. A: What size do you take?
   B: I don't know. It could be size 42.

5. A: What colour would you prefer?
   B: I like the yellow one.

6. A: How come you don't want to go any more?
   B: I haven't got enough money.

Chapter 9

LIKES AND DISLIKES

English and Chinese word orders are frequently different, and for the most part you will find that the Chinese order is the more logical one. 'To go to China by train' is fine in English, but the Chinese order says 'sitting on a train to go to China', and it is true enough that you must be on the train before you arrive at your destination, so why not say it that way? Whether logical or not, word orders are very important in Chinese, and you will need to pay close attention to them. Of course languages are never 'right' or 'wrong', they just have different ways of going about things — when we point out differences we are not talking about 'better' and 'worse' ways of expressing thought. Comparisons in any case are odious, it is said.

But comparisons are necessary too, and in this chapter we explore them further, and see how they fit into a regular word order pattern. And where there's a comparative there are often superlatives and equivalents, so these are covered too. Once you have mastered them you will be able to express yourself with much greater subtlety.

9.1 *Verb after verb*

Whole series of verbal expressions can succeed each other in Chinese provided they are in a logical sequence:

Tā <u>dào Rìběn</u> <u>qù</u> <u>kāi huì</u>.	He's going to Japan to a conference.
Wǒ <u>qù</u> <u>mǎi dōngxi</u> <u>gěi tā</u> <u>chī</u>.	I'm going to buy something for her to eat.
Wǒ děi <u>jiē tā</u> <u>qù yínháng</u> <u>huàn qián</u>.	I have to meet him to take him to the bank to change money.

And the same idea of a procession of verbs can be seen where the use of prepositions in English rather obscures the pattern:

<u>zuò huǒchē</u> qù Zhōngguó	to go to China <u>by train</u> [sit train go China]
<u>zài Shànghǎi</u> kāi huì	to attend / hold a meeting <u>in Shanghai</u> [be at Shanghai attend / hold meeting]

gěi péngyou mǎi dōngxi	to buy something <u>for a friend</u> [provide for friend buy thing]
tì tā wèn-yi-wèn	to ask a question <u>on his behalf</u> [substitute him ask]
gēn Wáng xiáojie shuō	to speak <u>with Miss Wang</u> [go along with Miss Wang speak]

In these five examples, **zuò**, **zài**, **gěi**, **tì** and **gēn** are translated as prepositions, but they are all verbs in Chinese — we call them 'coverbs'. Coverb phrases always appear before the main verb in a sentence.

Exercise 61
Add the information in brackets to the sentences:

1. **Tā yào qù Zhōngguó.**   (by air)
2. **Qǐng nǐ bié chōu yān.**   (here)
3. **Qǐng nǐ mǎi píng píjiǔ.**   (for me)
4. **Nǐ kěyǐ qǐng Wáng Xiānsheng lái ma?**   (on our behalf)

9.2 'Bǐ' as coverb

You can now see that the comparative pattern which we met in **8.2** (<u>XXX bǐ YYY adjective</u>) is actually another example of the pattern in **9.1**. The coverb **bǐ** is placed in front of adjectival verbs ('to be big', 'to be expensive' etc.):

Nǐ <u>bǐ tā</u> gāo.	You are taller than he is. [you compared to him are tall]
Tā <u>qí chē</u> qù fànguǎnr.	He cycles to the restaurant. [straddling the bike goes to the restaurant]

(140) 9.3 More about comparison

To say something is 'a bit more ...' than something else, the expression **yìdiǎnr** is added to the comparative pattern we met in **8.2**:

<u>XXX **bǐ** YYY adjective **yìdiǎnr**</u>

Kāfēi bǐ chá guì yìdiǎnr.	Coffee is a little more expensive than tea.
Shànghǎi bǐ Xiānggǎng lěng yìdiǎnr.	Shanghai's a bit colder than Hong Kong.

Tā de tóufa bǐ wǒ (de [tóufa])
  cháng yìdiǎnr.
         Her hair's a bit longer than mine.

And to say it is 'a lot more … ', use **duōle** instead of **yìdiǎnr**:

<u>X X X **bǐ** Y Y Y adjective **duōle**</u>

Tā de tóufa bǐ wǒ de cháng duōle.   Her hair's a lot longer than mine.
Zhōngguó bǐ Yīngguó dà duōle.   China is much bigger than Britain.
Tā de qián bǐ wǒ (de) duō duōle.   She's got a lot more money than I.

Exercise 62
Make a comparison between A and B.

  e.g. A. **Kāfēi ¥3.00.**   B. **Píjiǔ ¥3.50.**

    Answer: **Píjiǔ bǐ kāfēi guì yìdiǎnr.**

  1. A. **Běijīng shí dù.**   B. **Shànghǎi shí'èr dù.**
  2. A. **Qù Tiān'ānmén sān zhàn.**   B. **Qù Shǒudū Jùchǎng bā zhàn.**
  3. A. **Lǎo Lǐ de biǎo 7:32.**   B. **Huǒchēzhàn de zhōng 7:30.**
  4. A. **Zuò fēijī qù liǎng xiǎoshí.**   B. **Zuò huǒchē qù èrshiyī xiǎoshí.**

9.4 Although

'Although' is **suīrán**, and it is usually followed in the second half of the sentence by **kěshi** ('but'):

Tā suīrán shi Běijīng rén, kěshi   Although he's from Beijing, he doesn't
  bú ài chī Běijīng kǎoyā.   like Peking Duck.

9.5 No need to

In Chapter Six we met **děi** 'must', 'need to'. **Bù** is never used to make the negative of **děi**: the negative is usually **búbì** 'no need to':

A: **Wǒ děi qù Běijīng.**   I must go to Beijing.
B: **Wáng jīnglǐ bú zài nàr,**   Manager Wang isn't there, so there's no
  nǐ búbì qù le.   need for you to go any more.

Another way of saying 'no need to' is **kěyǐ bù**:

Nǐ kěyǐ bú qù le.   It's alright for you not to go any more.

Note that in all these cases a second verb (**qù** in these examples) follows.

9.6   More doubling up

In Conversation 9A Mr Li uses **tiāntiān** (literally: 'day day') to mean 'every day'. All measure words can be doubled in this way, and so can the noun **rén** (**rénrén** 'everybody').

(141) 9.7   Electronics

Here is a small selection of common electronic terms:

diànzǐ	electronic
diànzǐ yóujiàn	email message
diànzǐ biǎo	a quartz watch
diànzǐ jìsuànjī	computer (literally: electronic calculating machine)
diàn nǎo	computer (literally: electric brain)
hùliánwǎng	the internet (literally: mutual link net)

And some terms betray their foreign origin, like "**yīntè**" **wǎng** 'the internet' and "**yīmèi'ér**" 'an email message'.

9.8   Do a bit of

Yíxiàr added to a verb often gives the idea of 'just doing a bit of', 'having a crack at'. We call it a 'verbal measure'. In the conversation John Smith asks his friend to **chá yíxiàr** his emails for him. **Chá** means 'to examine', 'to check', and the **yíxiàr** gives a sense of little effort being expended on the verb: it makes the request seem less tedious or less difficult than it might be. It is much the same trick that English speakers play when they are asking a favour of someone — 'Would you mind just checking that for me?' 'Could you perhaps run a little check for me?'

Qǐng nǐ wèn yíxiàr.	Please make a little enquiry.
Qǐng nǐ děng yíxiàr.	Please wait a bit.
Tián yíxiàr biǎo.	Just fill in the form.

(142) *New words*

fāngbiàn	convenient
fángzi	house
huánjìng	surroundings, environment
píngcháng	normally, usually
shuō	to speak, to say
shuōdào	to mention
yòng	to use
zhǐyào	provided that, so long as
zìjǐ	self, oneself

(143) CONVERSATION 9A

John Smith is travelling in China. Today he goes to the new home of his old friend Li Ming.

J : **Xiǎo Lǐ, wǒ zhēn xǐhuan nǐ zhè fángzi. Bǐ lǎo dìfang dà duōle ba.**

Xiao Li, I really like this house of yours. It's much bigger than your old place surely?

L : **Shì dà yìdiǎnr, huánjìng yě bǐ nàr hǎo yìdiǎnr.**

Yes, it's a bit bigger, and the surroundings are nicer too.

J : **Shàng-xià bān fāngbiàn ma?**

Is it convenient for getting to and from work?

L : **Suīrán lù yuǎn duōle, kěshi xiànzài wǒ búbì tiāntiān qù gōngsī le.**

Although it's a lot further away, I don't need to go to the office every day any more.

J : **Wèishénme ne?**

Why's that?

L : **Píngcháng wǒ jiù zài jiā li shàng bān. Dàjiā dōu yòng diànnǎo, zhǐyào yǒu hùliánwǎng, rén zài nǎr méi guānxi.**

Normally I work right here at home. Everyone uses computers, and provided there's an internet connection it doesn't matter where the people are.

J : **Shì a. Shuōdào hùliánwǎng, Xiǎo Lǐ, nǐ néng bu néng tì wǒ shàng wǎng chá yíxiàr wǒ de diànzǐ yóujiàn?**

That's right. And talking of the internet, Xiao Li, could you get on it and check my emails for me?

L : **Méi wèntí. Gēn wǒ lái, diànnǎo zài zhèr, nǐ zìjǐ chá ba.**

No problem. Come with me, the computer is here, and you can check them for yourself.

J : **Hǎo. Xièxie, xièxie.** Great. Thank you very much.

(144) *9.9 Vegetarian cuisine*

Sùcài is a 'vegetable dish' or 'vegetarian food', and a **sùcàiguǎnr** is 'a vegetarian restaurant'. A 'vegetarian' is a **chīsùde** (**rén**) 'a person who eats vegetables'.

As well as 'vegetable' **cài** means 'a cuisine', 'a style of cooking'. Here are three well-known cuisines:

Sìchuān cài	The cuisine of Sichuan (Szechuan) province: hot and spicy.
Guǎngdōng cài	Cantonese food, the cuisine of Guangdong (Kwangtung) province: sophisticated, great variety, and particularly strong on fresh seafood.
Fǎguó cài	French food.

(145) *9.10 What's it made of?*

To say what something is made of or from, the formula is:

XXX **shi yòng** YYY **zuò de** (literally: X is using Y made)

Yòng means 'to use', and **zuò** is 'to make':

Zhè shi yòng niúnǎi zuò de.	This is made from milk.
Zhè jiǔ shi yòng shénme zuò de?	What's this wine made of?

(146) *9.11 Similarity*

To show similarity, another coverb pattern is used:

XXX **gēn** YYY **yíyàng** (literally: X with Y the same)

The coverb **gēn** means 'with' and **yíyàng** is 'the same' (literally: 'of one kind'):

Nǐ de biǎo gēn wǒ de (**biǎo**) **yíyàng.** Your watch is the same as mine.

And you can add an adjective to the pattern very easily:

<u>XXX **gēn** YYY **yíyàng** adjective</u>

Tā gēn wǒ yíyàng gāo.   He is as tall as I am.

Lóushang gēn lóuxia yíyàng rè.   Upstairs is just as hot as downstairs.

Exercise 63   All the same
  Use the 'similarity' pattern to make new sentences:

e.g. A. **Jīntiān Lúndūn èr dù.**   B. **Běijīng yě shi èr dù.**
   = **Jīntiān Lúndūn gēn Běijīng yíyàng lěng.**

1. A. **Biyānhú ¥95.**   B. **Diànzǐ biǎo yě shi ¥95.**
2. A. **Qù Tiān'ānmén sì zhàn.**   B. **Qù Bǎihuò Dàlóu yě shi sì zhàn.**
3. A. **Zuò chē qù bàn xiǎoshí.**   B. **Qí chē qù yě shi bàn xiǎoshí.**
4. A. **Xiǎo Wáng chuān sìshisì hàor de.**
   B. **Xiǎo Lǐ yě chuān sìshisì hàor de.**

9.12   Even better than best

We met in **8.2** the pattern <u>XXX **bǐ** YYY **gèng** adjective</u> for 'X is even more so than Y'. Very similar is the pattern:

<u>XXX **bǐ** YYY **hái** adjective</u>

Zhèi jiàn bǐ tè-dà hàor de hái dà. This one is even bigger than extra-large.

You have met **hái** before, and you can probably feel how its original meaning of 'yet' or 'still' works here. This pattern is stronger than the one using **gèng**, and gives the feeling that something is almost 'still better than the best'.

9.13   Ducks

The list of non-vegetarian foods in the conversation ('chicken, duck, fish, meat') is a neat collection of single-syllable nouns in Chinese, but, apart from in such lists, you should remember that 'duck' is usually the two-syllable word **yāzi**. There are quite a lot of words like **yā** which cannot normally be used on their own, and we mark them with an asterisk (**yā***) to warn you.

(147) *New words*

búcuò	not bad (= very good)
cài	vegetables; food; cuisine
càidān	menu
cháng	to taste
dòufu	beancurd, tofu
jī	chicken
Ǹg	Mm
ròu	meat (usually pork)
tǔdòur	potato
wèidao	flavour
yāzi or **yā***	duck
yàngzi	appearance
yú	fish

(148) ## *CONVERSATION 9B*

A vegetarian in a vegetarian restaurant.

V : **Shīfu, nǐmen zhèr bú shi sùcàiguǎnr ma?**

Waiter, isn't this a vegetarian restaurant?

W : **Shì a. Wǒmen zuò de dōu shi sùcài.**

Yes, it is. Everything we cook is vegetarian.

V : **Kěshi càidān shang zěnme jī, yā, yú, ròu dōu yǒu a? Wǒ shi chīsùde.**

But how come there are chicken, duck, fish, and meat all on the menu? I'm a vegetarian.

W : **Nà dōu bú shi zhēn de.**

None of those are the real thing.

V : **Bú shi zhēn de jī, yā, yú, ròu?**

Not real chicken, duck, fish and meat?

W : **Bú shi. Jī, yā shi yòng dòufu zuò de; yú shi yòng tǔdòur zuò de.**

Not real. The chicken and duck are made of beancurd, the fish from potato.

[The food arrives]

V : **Zhè yú de yàngzi gēn zhēn de yíyàng; wèidao yě yíyàng hǎo ma?**

This fish looks exactly like the real thing. Is the flavour as good?

W : **Nín chángchang, wèidao bǐ zhēn de hái hǎo.**

Try it; the flavour is even better than the real thing.

V : **Ǹg, shì búcuò.**

Mm, it's really not bad.

9.14 Coming and going

We have up to now used **lái Lúndūn** for 'to come to London', and **qù Běijīng**
for 'to go to Beijing'. There is an alternative pattern which can be used:

dào Lúndūn lai	to come to London
dào Běijīng qu	to go to Beijing

The two patterns are equally acceptable — you may take your pick — but note
that in final position both **lái** and **qù** normally lose their tone, so that they are
shown as **lai** and **qu**.

(149) 9.15 In the process of happening

To show that something is going on at a particular time Chinese uses **zài** before
the verb, often adding **ne** at the end of the sentence too:

Tāmen zài kāi huì.	They are in a meeting.
Lǎo Wáng zài chī fàn ne.	Old Wang is eating.

The negative ('something is <u>not</u> going on') is formed by putting **méi** (**yǒu**)
before the **zài**:

Tāmen méi zài kāi huì.	They are not in a meeting.

9.16 Measure words again

The measure word **xiē** is very useful for indicating an unspecified plural
number of things. It can be used with any noun, regardless of which measure
word that noun usually takes:

liǎng ge rén	two people
zhèi ge rén	this person
něi xiē rén?	which people?
nèi xiē rén	those people

Xiē also acts as a measure for uncountable things like 'water' which do not have
a 'singular' measure word:

nèi xiē niúnǎi	that milk

Xiē (or **yì xiē**) can also be used to mean 'a few', 'some', 'a certain amount of':

yìxiē rén	some people, a few people

9.17 Seems like

Hǎoxiàng means 'seems like', 'seems as if', 'seems to be':

> **Tā hǎoxiàng shi Rìběn rén.**   She seems to be Japanese.
> **Hǎoxiàng yào xià yǔ.**   It seems like it will rain.

(150) 9.18 Some action verbs

liàn qìgōng	to practise *qigong* [deep breathing exercises]
dǎ tàijíquán	to do *taiji* ['shadow-boxing' exercises]
dǎ yǔmáoqiú	to play badminton [literally: hit feather ball]
tiào wǔ	to dance

Exercise 64
What are they doing now? Say it in Chinese:

1. They are resting.
2. They are dancing.
3. They are drinking downstairs.
4. They are reading the weather forecast.
5. They are not smoking.

(151) New words

duànliàn	to do physical training
gànmá?	doing what? Why on earth?
hǎokàn	attractive, good-looking, pretty
kōngqì	air
lǎoshī	teacher

lǎo tàitai
  tàitai
	old lady, old woman
	  Mrs. (mainly used outside Mainland China)

qīngchu	clear
shǎo	few
xíng	OK, alright, will do
xué	to learn
zǎochen	in the morning

(152) *CONVERSATION 9C*

Jane Jones goes for an early morning walk in the park with a Chinese friend.

J :	**Gōngyuánr li rén zhēn bù shǎo!**	What lots of people in the park!
F :	**Zǎochen kōngqì hǎo, dàjiā dōu ài dào zhèr lai duànliàn.**	In the morning the air is good, so everyone likes to come here to exercise.
J :	**Éi, nèi xiē rén zài gànmá ne?**	Eh, what are those people up to?
F :	**Wǒ yě bù qīngchu, hǎoxiàng shi zài liàn qìgōng.**	I'm not sure either, they seem to be practising *qigong*.
J :	**Nèi biānr hái yǒu rén dǎ yǔmáoqiú.**	There are some other people over there playing badminton.
F :	**Shì a, wǒ yǒu shíhou yě lái dǎ.**	That's right, I sometimes come here to play it as well.
J :	**Zhè jǐ wèi lǎo tàitai tiào de shi shénme wǔ a?**	What dance is it that these old ladies are doing?
F :	**Zhè bú shi tiào wǔ, tāmen zài dǎ tàijíquán ne.**	That isn't dancing, they are doing *taijiquan*.
J :	**Tàijíquán a? Zhēn hǎokàn; wǒ yě xiǎng xuéxue.**	*Taijiquan?* It's really attractive; I'd like to learn it too.
F :	**Hǎo a. Míngtiān bié zǒu le, wǒ gěi nǐ zhǎo wèi lǎoshī.**	Great. Don't leave tomorrow, and I'll find a teacher for you.
J :	**Zhèi cì bù xíng. Míngnián wǒ yídìng lái xué.**	It's no good this time. Next year I'll certainly come here to learn it.

(153) *9.19 All alone*

Yígerén literally means 'one person', but it is used often to mean 'all by oneself', 'all alone', 'alone and unaided':

Tā yígerén qù.	He's going alone.
Nǐ yígerén hē jiǔ bù xíng.	You shouldn't drink alone.
Wǒ xǐhuan yígerén dǎ tàijíquán.	I like doing *taiji* on my own.

(154) 9.20 *The adverbs 'zài' and 'yòu'*

Yòu and **zài** can both be translated as 'again' and both come in front of verbs, just as **dōu**, **yě** and **jiù** do. **Zài** means 'a second time' or 'on another occasion' and usually refers to an event which has yet to happen: remember you met it in **Zàijiàn** 'See you again', 'Goodbye'. **Yòu** means 'furthermore' or 'yet again', usually refers to an event which has already occurred, and is often quite a forceful word, used in moments of exasperation (**Yòu shi nǐ!** 'What, you again!' — the bad penny syndrome). Here are the two words in examples which show the difference:

Tā zuótiān láile, jīntiān yòu lái le, míngtiān hái yào zài lái.	He came yesterday, again today, and he'll be here again tomorrow.
Tā ài hē jiǔ: zuótiān hē le, jīntiān yòu hē le, míngtiān yídìng hái yào zài hē.	He loves drinking wine: he drank yesterday, again today, and he's sure to drink again tomorrow.

9.21 *Is it the case that?*

Shì bu shi can be inserted into a sentence to highlight a question about what follows it:

Tā shì bu shi ài tiào wǔ?	Does she like dancing? (Is it the case that she likes dancing?)
Míngtiān shì bu shi yào xià yǔ?	Will it rain tomorrow?

Exercise 65   Revision
Say it in Chinese:

1. those who smoke
2. those who do not eat meat
3. those who love to drink tea
4. those who want to go to China
5. those who do *taiji* in the morning

(155) ## 9.22   Most

The superlative is simply formed by putting **zuì** 'most' in front of the adjective or verb:

zuì dà de chē	the biggest car
zuì guì de cài	the most expensive dishes
Tā zuì xǐhuan tiào wǔ.	He likes dancing best.
Tā shuō chī sù zuì hǎo.	She says it is best to eat vegetarian food.

9.23   Verbs in need

Many single-syllable Chinese verbs need to have an object, except when one is clearly understood from the context. If there is no specific object to use, then a generalised object has to be supplied. So there is no problem with a sentence like **Tā shuō Zhōngwén** ('She speaks Chinese') where **Zhōngwén** is of course the object of the verb **shuō**. But to translate 'to speak' or 'speaking', where there is no object, the generalised object **huà** 'speech' is supplied. 'She is speaking.' is **Tā zài shuō huà.** Just to be clear, the generalised object is of course never used as well as a specific object, it is one or the other. You have met several of them already:

Verb	Object	Literally	Meaning
chī	**fàn**	eat meal	to eat (a meal)
chī	**dōngxi**	eat thing	to eat (something)
chōu	**yān**	drag smoke	to smoke
hē	**jiǔ**	drink wine	to drink (alcohol)
shuō	**huà**	speak speech	to speak
zǒu	**lù**	walk road	to walk
zuò	**fàn**	make meal	to cook

Exercise 66
How would you put these needy-verb sentences into English?

1. **Gōnggòngqìchē shang bù zhǔn chōu yān.**
2. **Zhèr bù zhǔn chī dōngxi.**
3. **Chī dōngxi de shíhou bié shuō huà.**
4. **Shéi gěi nǐmen zuò fàn?**

(156) *New words*

chūqu	to go out
jiànmiàn	to meet face to face
kǒuyǔ	oral, spoken language
liànxí	to practise
liáotiānr	to chat
shàng kè	to go to class
wǎngyǒu	internet friend
yùndòng	to exercise; exercise, sport

(157) *CONVERSATION 9D*

Two foreign students are in their hostel.

A : **Tiānqi zhème hǎo, wǒmen chūqu yùndòng yùndòng ba.**

It's such nice weather, let's go out for a bit of exercise.

B : **Nǐ yígerén qù ba, wǒ hái yào gēn wǎngyǒu liáotiānr ne.**

You go on your own, I still have to chat to my internet friends.

A : **Yòu yào shàng wǎng! Nǐ tiāntiān bú shàng kè, jiù zài wǎng shang liáotiānr. Shì bu shi bù xiǎng xué Zhōngwén le?**

On the net yet again! You're out of class every day, just chatting on the net. You don't want to learn Chinese any more, is that it?

B : **Bù xiǎng xué Zhōngwén wǒ dào Zhōngguó lái gànmá?**

Why would I have come to China if I didn't want to learn Chinese?

A : **Nà nǐ wèishénme bú shàng kè?**

Well then, why not come to class?

B : **Zài wǎng shang yòng Zhōngwén liáotiānr jiù shi shàng kè.**

Using Chinese to chat on the internet is going to class.

A : **Shénme? Liáotiānr jiù shi shàng kè?**

What? Chatting is attending class?

B : **Duì, nà xiē wǎngyǒu dōu shi wǒ zuì hǎo de lǎoshī.**

Yes, those internet friends are all my best teachers.

A : **Nà nǐ háishi bù néng liànxí kǒuyǔ a.**

But then you still have no chance to practise speaking.

B : **Shéi shuō de? Míngtiān wǒ jiù yào gēn yí wèi wǎngyǒu jiànmiàn. Liǎng ge rén jiànmiàn, néng bù shuō huà ma?**

Who said? Tomorrow I'm going to meet an internet friend. When two people meet, can they fail to speak?

(158)

Exercise 67
Pronunciation practice:

1.

> yā
> kǎoyā
> Běijīng kǎoyā
> chī Běijīng kǎoyā
> xǐhuan chī Běijīng kǎoyā
> dōu xǐhuan chī Běijīng kǎoyā
> shí ge rén dōu xǐhuan chī Běijīng kǎoyā
> Wǒmen shí ge rén dōu xǐhuan chī Běijīng kǎoyā

2.

> yú
> mǎi yú
> tiāntiān mǎi yú
> rén tiāntiān mǎi yú
> sān ge rén tiāntiān mǎi yú
> nèi sān ge rén tiāntiān mǎi yú
> chī yú de nèi sān ge rén tiāntiān mǎi yú
> Ài chī yú de nèi sān ge rén tiāntiān mǎi yú

Exercise 68
Translate into Chinese:

1. A: Will you buy one for me, please?
   B: OK. I think the red one is the best.

2. A: Are you two the same height?
   B: No, he is slightly taller than I am.

3. A: Shall we invite her to have roast duck?
   B: That won't do. She is a vegetarian.

4. A: What is he doing now?
   B: He's just resting.

5. A: I would like to learn *taiji*; can you find me a teacher?
   B: No problem.

6. A: Have you been on the internet today?
   B: My computer has gone wrong and I cannot get onto the net.

Chapter 10

ACTIONS

Although Chinese grammar is not organised in such a way that there are tenses as we know them in English, it would be strange if it were not possible to be clear about the order in which things happen. Of course time words like 'yesterday' and 'next week' help a lot to show tense, but Chinese likes to show what the state of affairs at a particular time is, and that may not have much to do with time sequence or tense. Take the English phrase "having had his lunch". On the face of it it is set in the past, but in fact it could be followed by "he is now having a siesta" or "he will go for a walk" just as well as by "he suffered a bad bout of indigestion". The point is that "having had his lunch" has nothing to do with past, present or future, it is about the aspect of matters at the relevant time. Different 'aspects' are shown in various ways. You have already met **zài ... ne** which is a way of showing 'ongoing aspect', and in this chapter you will meet another use of **le**, this time as a verb-ending showing 'completion of verb action aspect'.

And just in case it should give you a headache (**tóuténg**), Conversation 10D tells you how to consult a doctor.

(159) *10.1 Final particle 'le'*

We saw in **6.5** that **le** at the end of a sentence indicates that a new state of affairs has come about. A further use of this particle is to show that some event has taken place:

Nǐ hē jiǔ le ma?	Did you have a drink / Have you had a drink?
Tā qù Zhōngguó le.	He's gone to China / He went to China.

In the negative **méi** ('not', as in **méi yǒu**) is used, but **le** is not:

Tāmen zuótiān méi kāi huì.   They didn't have a meeting yesterday.

There are various question forms which can be used; all the following mean 'Did he take photos?':

Tā zhào xiàng le ma?
Tā zhào xiàng le méi yǒu?
Tā zhào xiàng le méi zhào?

Exercise 69   Where is he?
Translate into English:

1. **Tā bú zài zhèr, tā qù gōngyuán le.**
2. **Tā bú zài jiā, tā dào gōngsī qu le.**
3. **Tā méi lái shàng bān, tā mǎi dōngxi qu le.**
4. **Tā yě qù hē jiǔ le ma?**

10.2   Returning

'To go abroad' is **chū guó** (literally: 'to exit the country'). 'To return from abroad' is **huí guó** (lit: 'to return to the country'). 'To return home' 'to go home' 'to come home' is **huí jiā**. It would be cumbersome to translate **huí** every time as 'to return to where you belong', but that is really what it means. Mrs Wang would say to someone who has come to call on her husband:

Lǎo Wáng liù diǎn zhōng huílai.   Old Wang will return at 6 o'clock.

and the visitor would reply:

Hǎo, wǒ liù diǎn zài lái.   Fine, I'll return at six.

Both **zài lái** and **huílai** are translated as 'return', but only Mr Wang is returning to where he belongs.

10.3   Along with

Gēn means 'the heel' and it is also a verb which means 'to follow'. From this come the meanings 'along with', 'with' and 'and':

Lǎo Wáng gēn Lǎo Lǐ   Old Wang and Old Li

This is in fact the same **gēn** that we met as a coverb in **9.1** and **9.11**:

Wǒ gēn Wáng lǎoshī xué.   I study with Teacher Wang.

10.4 'Àiren'

Àiren means 'loved person' and is used for either 'husband' or 'wife'.

10.5 To and from

In **9.14** you met **dào X lai** 'come to X' and **dào Y qu** 'go to Y'. You will probably not be surprised to find that the same pattern can be used for 'come from' and 'go from', and the word for 'from' you have already met (**cóng**).

cóng Běijīng lai	to come from Beijing
cóng Lúndūn qu	to go from London

And you can combine 'to' and 'from' if you wish:

cóng Lúndūn dào Běijīng qu	to go to Beijing from London
cóng Běijīng dào Lúndūn lai	to come to London from Beijing

BUT notice that the Chinese order is more logical than the English — it would of course be necessary to leave one city before arriving in the other, and the language follows the same order: always **cóng** before **dào**!

(160) *New words*

bìng	illness, disease
bìng le	to become ill
Fēizhōu	Africa
gāng + verb	to have just …
háizi	a child
shēng háizi	to give birth to a child
Ōuzhōu	Europe
yīyuàn	hospital

(161) *CONVERSATION 10A*

A customer phones a big company.

R : **Nǐ hǎo, Dàhuá Gōngsī.**   Hello, Dahua Company.

C : **Wéi, qǐng wèn Wáng jīnglǐ**   Hello, is Manager Wang there,
zài ma?   please?

R : **Wáng jīnglǐ bú zài, tā chū guó le.** No, he's gone abroad.

C : **Chū guó le? Tā dào nǎr qu le?** Out of the country? Where's he gone?

R : **Dào Ōuzhōu qu le.** He's gone to Europe.

C : **Lǐ jīnglǐ yě qù le ma?** Has Manager Li gone too?

R : **Lǐ jīnglǐ méi qù. Tā gāng cóng Fēizhōu huílai.** No. He's just come back from Africa.

C : **Wǒ kěyǐ gēn Lǐ jīnglǐ shuō huà ma?** May I speak with him?

R : **Duìbuqǐ, Lǐ jīnglǐ jīntiān méi lái. Tā dào yīyuàn qu le.** I'm sorry, Manager Li hasn't come in today. He's gone to the hospital.

C : **Òu, tā bìng le.** Oh, he's ill.

R : **Méiyǒu. Tā àiren zài yīyuàn shēng háizi ne.** No, his wife is having a baby in there.

10.6 Still and yet

Hái means 'still' or 'yet' (as we saw in **6.10**) and very often is accompanied by the final particle **ne**:

> **Tā hái bù zhīdao ne.** She still doesn't know.
>
> **Tā hái méi chī ne.** She has not yet eaten.

Exercise 70   'Already' and 'not yet'.
Give both affirmative and negative answers to the questions.

Example: **Tā qù Rìběn le ma?**   a) **Yǐjing qù le.**   b) **Hái méi qù ne.**

1. **Nǐ chī fàn le ma?**   2. **Wáng jīnglǐ lái le ma?**

3. **Nǐmen jié zhàng le méiyǒu?**   4. **Dōngxi dōu mǎi le ma?**

10.7 Running sounds together

It is quite possible to have more than one particle at the end of a sentence, and sometimes one can fuse with the other. By fusion **le + a** becomes **la**, and **ne + a** becomes **na**:

> **Tā zhēn lái la?!**   She's really arrived?!

Hái méi chī fàn na?!	Still not eaten?!

10.8 It says in the newspaper

Bào is 'a newspaper'. 'It says in the newspaper' is **bào shang shuō**:

Bào shang shuō míngtiān yào xià yǔ.   It says in the newspaper that it
will rain tomorrow.

10.9 Let me ...

You met **gěi** in Chapter Nine meaning 'for'. The basic meaning of **gěi** is 'to give', and **gěi wǒ kànkan** 'give it to me to see' is a neat way of saying 'Let me have a look'.

(163) 10.10 News and news

There are two different words in Chinese for two different meanings of 'news'. **Xīnwén** is news which is in the newspapers or in a broadcast, news in the public domain; **xiāoxi** is 'tidings', information about certain people or events:

Bào shang yǒu shénme xīnwén?	What news is there in the paper?
Nǐ yǒu méi you Lǎo Wáng de xiāoxi?	Have you any news of Lao Wang?

10.11 Active or passive?

Many Chinese verbs work either actively or passively depending on context:

Zuótiān méi zhào xiàng a?	(We) weren't photographed yesterday, surely?//(We) didn't take any photos yesterday, did we?
Tā shi něi nián shēng de?	In which year was she born?//In which year did she give birth?

(164) New words

jìzhě	a reporter
kàn bào	to read the newspaper
shuì jiào	to sleep

| **zǎofàn** | breakfast |
| **zhàopiàn** | a photograph |

🔟 *CONVERSATION 10B*

Delegates chatting at an international conference.

A : **Yóuyǒng qu la?! Chī zǎofàn le ma?**   Oh, you've been swimming?! Have you had breakfast?

B : **Hái méi ne, xiànzài qù chī. Nǐ ne?**   Not yet, I'm going to have it now. What about you?

A : **Wǒ yǐjing chī le. Kàn bào le ma?**   I've already eaten. Have you read the newspaper?

B : **Hái méi ne. Yǒu shénme xīnwén?**   Not yet. What's the news?

A : **Bào shang yǒu wǒmen kāi huì de xiāoxi.**   There's some news about our conference.

B : **Shì ma? Zài nǎr? Gěi wǒ kànkan.**   Is there? Where? Show me.

A : **Jiù zài zhèr. Nǐ kàn, hái yǒu wǒmen de zhàopiàn.**   Just here. Look, there are our photographs as well.

B : **Zuótiān méi zhào xiàng a?**   We weren't photographed yesterday, surely?

A : **Zhào le. Yǒu hěn duō jìzhě zài nàr zhào xiàng.**   Yes we were. There were lots of reporters there taking photos.

B : **Wǒ zěnme bù zhīdao a?**   How come I didn't know?

A : **Nǐ kàn, zhè bú shì nǐ ma? Zài nàr shuì jiào ne!**   Look, isn't this you? You were sleeping!

🔟 *10.12   Verb + '-le'*

The sentence particle **le**, as we have seen in **6.5** and **10.1**, shows that the general state of affairs has changed or that a certain event has taken place. When attention is focused on the *detail* of how that action was carried out, and especially when that detail takes the form of a numbered or quantified object, **-le** is attached to the verb in order to emphasise the completion of the action. So:

'Sentence particle **le**' is used where the completion of the whole process is covered by **le**:

Tā zuótiān qù mǎi dōngxi le ma?   Did she go shopping yesterday?

‘Verb + **-le**’ is used to stress the completion of the action itself:

A: **Tā zuótiān mǎile shénme?**   What did she buy yesterday?

B: **Tā mǎile nǐ zuì ài chī de dōngxi.**   She bought what you most like to eat.

Tā jīnnián láile sān cì Xiānggǎng.   He came to Hong Kong three times this year.

Tā qiántiān kànle liǎng ge péngyou.   He visited two friends the day before yesterday.

Exercise 71
Shift of emphasis:

Sentence particle **‘le’** versus verb + **‘-le’**

Translate into English:

1. A: **Nǐ zuótiān hē jiǔ le ma?**   B: **Hē le.**
   A: **Nǐ hēle jǐ píng (jiǔ)?**

2. A: **Nǐ qù kàn péngyou le ma?**   B: **Qù le.**
   A: **Nǐ kànle jǐ ge (péngyou)?**

3. A: **Nǐ qù Rìběn le ma?**   B: **Qù le.**
   A: **Nǐ zài Rìběn zhùle jǐ tiān?**

4. A: **Nǐ mǎi bíyānhú le ma?**   B: **Mǎi le.**
   A: **Nǐ mǎile jǐ ge (bíyānhú)?**

5. A: **Nǐ dǎ tàijíquán le ma?**   B: **Dǎ le.**
   A: **Nǐ dǎle duōshao fēn zhōng (de tàijíquán)?**

---

(167) 10.13 *Hit the phone, Jack*

The verb **dǎ** means ‘to hit’, so **dǎ rén** means ‘to hit someone’. But **dǎ** has additional uses beyond ‘to hit’:

dǎ diànhuà	to make a phone call
dǎ yú	to catch fish
dǎ zhēn	to have / give an injection (**zhēn** is ‘a needle’)
dǎ quán	to box

dǎ dī	to take a taxi
dǎ zì	to type (**zì** is a Chinese character, remember?)
dǎ qiú	to play ball
dǎ yǔmáoqiú	to play badminton
dǎ lánqiú	to play basketball
dǎ gāo'ěrfū	to play golf

10.14   Verbal measure words

We met in **6.14** the word **cì** ('time'). It is helpful to think of **cì** as a 'verbal measure word' which counts the number of times the verb takes effect:

qù liǎng cì Zhōngguó   to go to China twice

There are a number of other verbal measure words. You have already met **xiàr** in **9.8**, and here are two more of them:

zhēn: dǎ èrshí zhēn	to have / give twenty injections
tàng: qù yí tàng	to go once (**tàng** 'a trip' and **cì** 'a time' are interchangeable here).

(168) 10.15   Finishing off

Wán means 'to end', 'to finish'. It can be attached to other verbs to show that the action has finished:

shuōwán	to finish speaking
chīwán	to finish eating

Hǎo, as we know, means 'good'. It too can be attached to certain verbs to show that the action has been completed:

zuòhǎo	to finish doing
Fàn zuòhǎo le.	The food is cooked (and ready to eat).

Later we shall be meeting quite a few other verb endings like **-wán** and **-hǎo**, all of which show the result of the action initiated by the verb.

Exercise 72   Action sequences

Practise repeating these sequences which show three stages of action:

Planning	→	Carrying out	→	Result
xiǎng chī	→	**zài chī**	→	**chī wánle**
(want to eat)		*(eating)*		*(finished eating)*
xiǎng kàn (bào)		**zài kàn (bào)**		**kàn wánle**
xiǎng zhào (xiàng)		**zài zhào (xiàng)**		**zhào wánle**
xiǎng kāi (huì)		**zài kāi (huì)**		**kāi wánle**

(169) *New words*

bǎi	a hundred
chàbuduō	almost, more or less
Chángchéng	the Great Wall
diànchí	battery
néng	to be able, can
quán (or **wánquán**)	completely
shàng	to go to (literally: to go up to)
shōushi	to pack, to put in order
wàng	to forget
xíngli	luggage
yígòng	altogether
(zhào)xiàngjī	camera
zhǔnbèi	to prepare, to get ready

(170) *CONVERSATION 10C*

Describing what went on before.

A : **Nǐ zuótiān dào nǎr qu le? Wǒ dǎle sān cì diànhuà, nǐ dōu méi kāi jī.**

Where did you go yesterday? I phoned three times but each time you hadn't switched on.

B : **Duìbuqǐ, wǒ shǒujī diànchí méi diàn le. Zuótiān qùle yí tàng Chángchéng.**

I'm sorry, my mobile had nothing left in the battery. I took a trip to the Great Wall yesterday.

A : **Zěnme yòu qù Chángchéng le?**

How come you went there again?

B : **Shàng cì qù, wàngle dài xiàngjī, méi zhào xiàng.**

Last time I went I forgot to take my camera, so I didn't get any photos.

A : **Zuótiān zhàole hěn duō zhāng ba?**

You took lots yesterday, did you?

B : **Liǎng zhāng SD kǎ quán zhàowán le. Yígòng zhàole sānbǎi duō zhāng.**

I filled two SD cards completely; over three hundred shots altogether.

A : **Nǐ zhēn ài zhào xiàng!**

You really like photography!

B : **Nàme hǎo de fēngjǐng, zěnme néng bú zhào?**

It's such wonderful scenery; how could I not take it?

A : **Nǐ jǐ diǎn zhōng zǒu a? Xíngli dōu shōushihǎo le ma?**

What time are you leaving? Is your luggage all packed?

B : **Chàbuduō le. Chīwán fàn jiù zhǔnbèi shàng jīchǎng.**

More or less. When the meal is over I'll get ready to go to the airport.

The Great Wall

The Great Wall is justly famous as one of the wonders of the ancient (and indeed the modern) world. It has not always followed the same line, and in some places there are spurs and unconnected stretches, but in some form it has existed for 2,200 years, a more or less continouous 1300 mile long barrier between Chinese civilization and the nomadic people to the north. It was completed by the First Emperor of China, Qin Shi Huang, but some parts of it pre-date him, where he just joined up existing stretches built by some of the small states which had controlled different areas of north China before succumbing to his Qin armies. It was by no means all the impressive fired-brick and cut stone, battlemented structure which is commonly shown in photographs, and much of it consisted of a mud-brick or tamped earth defensive line. Nor was it always manned or kept in good repair, but it served to warn the Chinese to stay inside, as much as it tried to shield China from outside attack.

10.16 'Bù shūfu'

Shūfu means 'comfortable' and '**bù shūfu**' should therefore mean 'uncomfortable'. And so it does, but **bù shūfu** has another meaning too: 'unwell', 'off colour'.

10.17 Diarrhoea

In the next conversation a tourist suffers from the common ailment of many who travel abroad. He says **Xièle liǎng cì.** 'I have had diarrhoea twice'. **Xiè** means 'to rush down' 'to flood', and like other single-syllable verbs it needs a noun object if there is nothing more specific to be said. In this case the generalised object is **dùzi** 'stomach', so the full expression for 'to have diarrhoea' is **xiè dùzi.** And while we are on the subject, you might like to learn the word for 'a laxative'. It is 'rush down medicine' **xièyào.**

(171) 10.18 Three times a day

Yì tiān sān cì ('one day three times') is the way to say 'three times a day'. Notice that the number of occurrences follows the time during which they happen. When a verb is involved, it splits the number of occurrences from the specified time:

yì tiān chī sān cì	eat three times a day
yí ge xīngqī qù liǎng tàng	go twice a week

Exercise 73
Say it in Chinese:

1. once a week
2. twice a month
3. three trips a year
4. four injections a day

10.19   Insignificant

Yàojǐn means 'important'. The negative **bú yàojǐn** 'unimportant' is often used to mean 'that doesn't matter', both in the sense of 'that's insignificant' and in the polite sense as a response to someone's apology.

Exercise 74
Say it in Chinese:

1. I bought a new mobile phone last week.
2. How many times did you go to Australia last year?
3. Have you packed your luggage yet?
4. I phoned him three times yesterday.

(172) *New words*

dàifu	a doctor
dùzi	stomach, belly
fāshāo	to have a fever
měi	each, every (usually followed by a measure word)
tāng	soup
téng	to ache, hurt
tù	to vomit
wǎn	(measure for 'bowls of'); a bowl
yào	medicine
chī yào	to take medicine
yàopiànr	(medicinal) tablet
piànr	(measure for tablets)
zhī	(measure for most animals)

(173) CONVERSATION 10D

A tourist sees the doctor.

D : **Shénme dìfang bù shūfu?**　　　What's the problem?

T : **Dùzi téng, xiǎng tù, xièle**　　　My stomach aches, I feel sick, and
　　liǎng cì.　　　　　　　　　　I've had diarrhoea twice.

D : **Zhōngwǔ chī shénme le?**

What did you have for lunch?

T : **Péngyou qǐng chī fàn, chīle yì zhī kǎoyā.**

A friend invited me: a whole roast duck.

D : **Shénme?! Nǐ yígerén chīle yì zhī kǎoyā?**

What?! You had a whole roast duck to yourself?

T : **Bú shì, wǒmen sì ge rén.**

No, there were four of us.

D : **Hē jiǔ le ma?**

Did you have any alcohol?

T : **Tāmen sān ge rén hēle liù píng píjiǔ. Wǒ zhǐ hēle yì wǎn tāng.**

The three of them drank six bottles of beer. I only had a bowl of soup.

D : **Nǐ méi fāshāo, bú yàojǐn, dǎ yì zhēn jiù hǎo le.**

You aren't running a temperature, so it isn't serious. One injection and you'll be better.

T : **Ēi, dàifu, wǒ zuì pà dǎ zhēn, chī yào kěyǐ ma?**

Oh, doctor, I hate injections; could I take some medicine (instead)?

D : **Zěnme wàiguó rén dōu pà dǎ zhēn? Hǎo ba, gěi nǐ diǎnr yàopiànr, yì tiān sān cì, měi cì liǎng piànr.**

Why is it that foreigners are all scared of injections? Alright then, I'll give you some tablets; three times a day, two tablets each time.

(174) **Exercise 75**

Pronunciation practice:

1. **Shéi yào qù yīyuàn, gōngyuánr gēn fànguǎnr?**
2. **Tā cháng shuō, méi shìr liáotiānr hěn hǎowánr.**

Exercise 76

Translate into Chinese:

1. A: Hello, can I speak to Mr. Li please?
   B: I'm sorry, he has already gone back to his country.

2. A: How many phone calls did you make yesterday?
   B: One hundred and twenty-three altogether.

3. A: What's the news in the paper?
   B: It says there are a lot of people going abroad this year.

4. A: Have you finished eating?
   B: Not yet, I'll come when I finish my soup.

5. A: Has he got a fever?
   B: 39°. Shall we send for a doctor?

6. A: Do you often have Chinese food?
   B: Yes, about twice a month.

Chapter 11

ARRIVING IN CHINA

This chapter could be called 'Whodunnit?' It focuses on the important matter of getting details and relationships of time, place, and person right. In particular there are several grammar patterns that help you to establish the timing of events relative to each other (before, at the time when, after), so sloppy alibis will be of no use.

And one by one we are introducing some verb-endings (verb suffixes) which show different aspects (initiation, continuation, completion, for example) of the action of the verbs to which they are attached. In this chapter you meet **-guo**, which indicates that the action of the verb has been experienced at some time.

Chinese verbs often pair up, one verb showing an action and the other showing the result of the action. We call these paired verbs 'result verbs' or 'resultative verbs'. Most people will be familiar with the expression 'to have a look-see'. It comes from Chinese originally, via the medium of 'Pidgin English', the half-and-half language which developed on the China coast to facilitate business between Chinese and foreign traders. 'Look' is an action verb of 'trying' and 'see' is a verb showing that the result of the looking has been a success ("Look over there!" "Yes, I can see it.") . Understand this distinction and you are well on your way to coping with a major point of Chinese grammar.

11.1 To know how to

Huì means 'to know how to', 'to be able to (because of knowing how)':

Tā huì zuò kǎoyā.	She can cook [make] roast duck.
Wǒ bú huì chōu yān,	I don't smoke or drink. (This is a polite
yě bú huì hē jiǔ.	formula for declining a cigarette or a drink)

11.2 Languages

In Chapter Ten we met **shuō huà** 'to speak' [to speak speech]. From this root it is easy to form the names of languages: **Rìběn** is 'Japan', so 'to speak Japanese' is **shuō Rìběn huà. Pǔtōnghuà** is 'Universal language' (Mandarin), **Guǎngdōng huà** is 'Guangdong language' (Cantonese), and there are many other dialects in China all of whose names are formed with **huà** in the same way.

Yǔ also means 'language' and it too can be combined with country names, though it is done in an abbreviated form:

Yīngyǔ	English
Déyǔ	German
Fǎyǔ	French
wàiyǔ	foreign language

In this style 'Chinese' is **Hànyǔ**, the language of the **Hànrén**, the majority (Chinese) people of China. **Hànyǔ** therefore does not include the languages of the many minority peoples of China. Note that **Zhōngguó huà** also refers to the language of the **Hànrén**, but it is used when thinking of that language in contrast with the languages of other countries. Yet another word is **Huáyǔ**, which Chinese people in Southeast Asia and other parts of the world often use to mean 'Chinese' as opposed to the other languages of the areas in which they live: **Huá*** means 'China' in a number of idiomatic expressions, but be warned — you will not be understood if you try to use it as an everyday word for China.

11.3   A few

Apart from its function as the question word ('how many'), **jǐ** can be used without stress to mean 'a few', 'several':

> **Tā zhǐyǒu jǐ ge Zhōngguó**   He has only a few Chinese friends.
> **péngyou.**

11.4   Before and after

Yǐqián means 'before' and **yǐhòu** 'after'. Both of them come after the words they refer to (sometimes dropping the **yǐ**):

shuì jiào yǐqián	before going to bed
chī fàn yǐhòu	after eating
sān tiān (yǐ) qián	three days ago / before
sān tiān (yǐ) hòu	three days afterwards / later

Yǐqián and **yǐhòu** can also stand alone as time-words meaning 'formerly' and 'afterwards':

> **Tā yǐqián zài zhèr mài bào.**   He sold newspapers here formerly.

(175) *11.5   The verb-ending '-guo'*

Guò means 'to go through', and as a verb-ending it means 'to have gone through the experience of', 'to have experienced':

Tā qùguo Zhōngguó.	She has been to China.
Wǒ xuéguo Yīngyǔ.	I have learned English.

The negative is formed by adding **méi** before the verb, but note that unlike the verb-ending -**le**, the -**guo** does not drop off in the negative form:

Wǒ méi chīguo Sìchuān cài.   I've never had Szechuanese food.

The question forms are **qùguo ma?** or **qùguo méi you?** 'have you ever been (there)?'.

> ### Exercise 77
> *Answer the questions using Chinese:*
>
> 1. **Yīngguó nǚwáng** (the Queen) **qùguo Zhōngguó ma?**
> 2. **Mǎgē Bōluó** (Marco Polo) **zài Běijīng zhùguo ma?**
> 3. **Dèng Xiǎopíng qùguo Fǎguó ma?**
> 4. **Nǐ gēn Láng Lǎng** (the pianist) **shuōguo huà ma?**

11.6   Ordinal numbers

The ordinal numbers (the first, the second, the third, …) are shown by using the ordinal marker **dì-** before a number:

dì-yī bēi chá	the first cup of tea
dì-qī tiān	on the seventh day

(176) *11.7   Or is it …?*

Just to remind you of an important pattern you met in **6.3**. To ask someone to decide between two alternatives the pattern used is **shi … háishi …?**:

Tā shi Yìdàlì rén háishi Xībānyá rén?	Is he Italian or Spanish?
Nǐ (shi) ài hē chá háishi ài hē kāfēi?	Do you prefer tea or coffee?

11.8 When

Yǐqián and **yǐhòu** show that something happens either before or after something else, but if the event is going on at the same time as something else, 'when' is translated by **de shíhou**.

> **Wǒ zuò fēijī de shíhou bù xǐhuan hē jiǔ.**   I don't like to drink when I'm flying.

Again you will notice that **de shíhou** comes after the words it refers to.

Exercise 78
*Is it -**guo** or -**le**?*

1. **Tā méi chī____ Sìchuān cài.**
2. **Nǐ qù____ Shànghǎi ma? Méi yǒu, zhè shi dì-yī cì.**
3. **Tā yǐqián xué____ tàijíquán, kěshi xiànzài quán wàng le.**
4. **Tā zuótiān mǎi____ yí jiàn gǔdǒng.**

---

(177) *New words*

cānjiā	to take part in
chūjìng	to exit a country
chū	to exit
jiǎnchá	to check, examine
jiāoyìhuì	a trade fair
jù	(measure for speech); a phrase, sentence
rù*	to enter
rùjìngkǎ	immigration card
shōu	to receive, accept
yāoqǐng	to invite
yāoqǐngxìn	invitation letter

(178) ## CONVERSATION 11A

A businessman arrives at the Immigration desk.

B : **Nǐ hǎo! Zhè shi wǒ de hùzhào.**   Hello. This is my passport.

O : **Òu, nín huì shuō Zhōngguó huà a.**   Oh, you can speak Chinese.

B : **Zhǐ huì shuō ji jù.**   Only a few phrases.

O : **Nín de rùjìngkǎ ne? Tiánhǎole ma?**

Your immigration card? Has it been filled in?

B : **Tiánhǎole. Zài zhèr.**

Yes, here it is.

O : **Yǐqián láiguo Zhōngguó ma?**

Have you been to China before?

B : **Shí nián qián láiguo yí cì. Zhè shi dì-èr cì.**

I came once ten years ago. This is my second time.

O : **Zhèi cì shi lái lǚyóu háishi lái ...?**

Have you come as a tourist this time, or...?

B : **Shì lái cānjiā jiāoyìhuì.**

I've come to take part in a trade fair.

O : **Něi ge jiāoyìhuì?**

Which one?

B : **Chóngqìng jiāoyìhuì. Zhè shi yāoqǐngxìn.**

The Chongqing Trade Fair. This is the invitation letter.

O : **Hǎo, xíng le. Qǐng nín shōuhǎo zhèi zhāng kǎ. Chūjìng de shíhou hái yào jiǎnchá.**

OK, that's fine. Please keep the card, it will be checked again when you leave the country.

B : **Zhīdao le. Xièxie, zàijiàn.**

Understood. Thank you. Goodbye.

11.9 Graded Learning

In English we speak of primary, secondary and tertiary education. Chinese has the same progression, but uses a different set of terms: **dà** 'big', **zhōng** 'middle' and **xiǎo** 'small':

xiǎoxué	primary school [small learning]
zhōngxué	secondary school [middle learning]
dàxué	university [great learning]

You will remember from **8.19** that the same set of terms is used for the sizing of clothes — small, medium and large.

11.10 Final particle 'lei'

In Conversation 11B the taxi-driver who picks up the student at the airport says **Hǎo lei** when told the destination. **Hǎo** of course is 'good', 'fine' and the final particle **lei** is used when being pleasant and obliging, so an English equivalent might be 'With pleasure', or 'Right you are' or 'Certainly, Sir' or 'No problem'.

11.11 Verb + result

In **10.15** we met **-wán** and **-hǎo** as verb-endings which show the completion and result of the verb's action. You may perhaps not have noticed that we naughtily slipped in **shōuhǎo** 'receive and thoroughly', 'keep safely', 'hold on to' in Conversation 11A? **Dào** 'to arrive' is another such ending, used to show that as a result of the verb's action some desirable point has been reached. In fact you have already met it in **6.18** in the expression **kāidào** 'to drive and arrive at', 'to reach'. In the next conversation the student says **méi xiǎngdào** (literally: I thought but did not think of) 'I didn't realise', 'I didn't imagine', 'I didn't expect' and the taxi-driver later says **Zhēn méi xiǎngdào** 'I truly would never have guessed'.

Exercise 79
Fill in the blanks with 'results':

1. **Wǒ yǐjing mǎi ___ dōngxi le.** (to have done the shopping)
2. **Hóng de yǐjing mài ___ le.** (to be sold out)
3. **Biǎo yǐjing tián ___ le.** (to have completed)
4. **Zhèi píng jiǔ méi yǒu hē ___.** (to be drunk up)
5. **Méi xiǎng ___ Shànghǎi zhème rè.** (to expect)

Dragon

The Dragon (**lóng**) has a special place in Chinese hearts. It doesn't breath fire or ravish fair maidens, on the contrary it is auspicious, bringing rain to the farmer's fields and symbolising fertility, joy and strength. It is the only mythical creature among the twelve animals which govern the cycle of years, and those who are born during a Dragon year are considered very fortunate. In imperial times the Dragon was closely associated with the Emperor, and his descendants were known as 'the seeds of the dragon'. Only the Emperor was permitted to have representations of dragons with five claws, ordinary people had to content themselves with the less powerful four-clawed variety.

In the next conversation the newly built third terminal at Beijing Airport is said to be like a **jù lóng**. Somehow **jù***, which means 'huge', 'enormous', seems appropriate with 'dragon', but it is not a word which can be freely used in normal speech and you should stick to **dà**, which is easy to use.

11.12 Never before

Cónglái ('always', 'at any time', 'ever') makes the verb-ending **-guo** even more emphatically negative:

Tā cónglái méi chīguo Shànghǎi cài.   She has never ever eaten
                                            Shanghainese food.

Wǒ cónglái méi zhème lèiguo.   I've never been so tired before.

(179) 11.13 The 'shi ... de' construction

This useful construction allows you to pick out one circumstance surrounding an action (the part immediately following **shi**) for special emphasis. In response to the statement:

Tā mǎile yí ge zhàoxiàngjī.   He bought a camera.

the following questions might be asked:

Tā shi zài nǎr mǎi de?   Where was it that he bought it?
Tā shi shénme shíhou mǎi de?   When was it that he bought it?
Tā shi gēn shéi qu mǎi de?   With whom did he go to buy it?

This pattern generally operates for actions which have already taken place.

Exercise 80
Answer using the information provided:

1. **Yīngguó nǚwáng shi shénme shíhou dào Zhōngguó qù de?**
                                            (October 1986)

2. **Zhèi píng jiǔ shi zài nǎr mǎi de?**   (Hong Kong)

3. **Tā shi zěnme lái de?**   (by air)

4. **Tā shi qùnián jǐ yuè zǒu de?**   (July)

5. **Zhèi ge cài shi shéi zuò de?**   (Miss Wang)

11.14 No more

In **8.12** you learned that final particle **le** with a negative gave a meaning of 'not any more.' In the next conversation you will meet **Bié kèqi le**: literally it means 'don't be polite any more' 'stop being polite', but its real sense is the flattering 'You're just being modest' (which is in itself of course a very polite thing to say!)

11.15   That old pal of mine.

When a possessive is used with specifying words like **nèi / zhèi** it goes at the front of the phrase, not behind as in English:

wǒ nèi wèi péngyou	that friend of mine
tā zhèi píng jiǔ	this bottle of wine of his

(180) *New words*

cái	merely
fàng	to put in / on, to place
hángzhànlóu	airport terminal building
jiànzhù	building, structure
màozi	hat, cap
shèjì	to design
tīngshuō	it is said that, I gather, I've heard that
xiàng	like, to resemble

(181) CONVERSATION 11B

A British student arrives in Beijing for the first time.   At the airport he takes a taxi.

S : **Shīfu, wǒ qù Běijīng Dàxué.**
I'm going to Beijing University, driver.

D : **Hǎo lei. Xíngli gěi nín fàng hòutou.**
Fine. I'll put the luggage in the back for you.

[On the way]

S : **Méi xiǎngdào Běijīng Jīchǎng zhème dà. Zhèi ge hángzhànlóu zhēn shi tài piàoliang le.**
I didn't think Beijing Airport was so big. This terminal is too too beautiful!

D : **Cóng fēijī shàng kàn, shì bu shì xiàng yì tiáo jù lóng?**
Seen from the plane, is it like a huge dragon?

S : **Shì a. Wǒ cónglái méi kànjianguo zhème dà de jiànzhù.**
Yes it is. I've never seen such a large structure before.

D : **Xiānsheng, nín de Hànyǔ zhēn bú cuò, shi zài nǎr xué de?**
Sir, your Chinese is really not bad, where did you learn it?

S : **Lúndūn Dàxué. Cái xuéle yì nián; hái bù xíng.**
London University. I've only studied for one year; it's still no good.

D : **Bié kèqi le. Xiānsheng, nín shi Yīngguó rén a, zhè Sān Hào Hángzhànlóu bú jiù shi nǐmen Yīngguó rén shèjì de ma?**

You're just being modest. So, you are from Britain, sir. Wasn't this No.3 Terminal designed by you British?

S : **Shì a, wǒ yě tīngshuō le.**

Yes, I've heard that too.

D : **Wàiguó rén shèjì de dōngxi shì gēn Zhōngguó rén bù yíyàng. Nín kàn, nín zhè màozi jiù hěn tèbié, shi zài Yīngguó mǎi de ba?**

Things designed by foreigners really are different from Chinese ones. Just look at your hat, it's quite special … bought in England presumably?

S : **Shì, kěshi shi zài Zhōngguó zuò de.**

Yes, but it was made in China.

D : **Òu, shì ma? Zhēn méi xiǎngdào.**

Oh, really? I would truly never have guessed.

🎧182 11.16 *Multi-functional words*

Dàibiǎo can be a verb meaning 'to represent', or a noun meaning 'a representative':

> **Tā shi Hélán dàibiǎo.** She is the Dutch representative.
>
> **Tā yào dàibiǎo Hélán dào Rìběn qù kāi huì.** He is going to Japan to represent the Netherlands at a conference.

Many other Chinese words have more than one function like this. You have met **yùndòng** 'to take exercise' or 'a movement' or 'sport'; **dǎsuan** is 'to plan' or 'a plan'; **shèjì** is 'design' or 'to design'; **yāoqǐng** is 'to invite' or 'an invitation'; and later (in Conversation C of this chapter) you will learn **gōngzuò** 'to work' or 'work':

> **Tā hěn xǐhuan gōngzuò.** She loves to work.
>
> **Tā hěn xǐhuan tā de gōngzuò.** She loves her job.

11.17 *Transport delayed*

When a scheduled train / bus / flight is delayed it is said to be **wǎndiǎn** 'behind (scheduled) time'.

11.18   For a long time

Jiǔ means 'a long while', 'for a long while':

> **Tā zài Shànghǎi zhùle hěn jiǔ.**   He lived in Shanghai for a long while.

11.19   This many so far

The sentence **Tā zài Zhōngguó zhùle sān nián** means 'He lived in China for three years'. With another **le** added to the end of the same sentence the meaning changes:

> **Tā zài Zhōngguó zhùle sān nián le.**   He has been living in China for three years.

So the use of verb-ending **-le** and final particle **le** with a numbered object shows that the action of the verb has gone on up to a certain time. That time might be past, present or future, so there are two other possible translations of this double **le** sentence: 'He had been living...' and 'He will have been living...'

> **Wǒ jīntiān yǐjing chōule wǔ**   I have already smoked five cigarettes
> **zhī yān le.**   today. (so far)
>
> **Tā lái yǐqián, yǐjing wènle**   Before he came he had already asked
> **bā ge rén le.**   eight people. (up to then)

Exercise 81   So far
Translate into English:

1. **Tā zài Shànghǎi zhùle sān nián le.**
2. **Wǒmen xuéle liǎng nián Hànyǔ le.**
3. **Tā yǐjing mǎile shí tiáo yú le.**
4. **Tā yǐjing shuōle wǔ ge xiǎoshí le.**
5. **Wǒ yǐjing zhàole liǎng bǎi zhāng le.**

11.20   That's all that matters

Jiù hǎo le tacked on to the end of a remark gives the idea of 'that's all that matters', 'then everything would be OK', or 'I wish …':

> **Nǐ dàole jiù hǎo le.**   Just so long as you've got here.
> **Wǒ huì shuō Zhōngguó huà jiù hǎo le.**   I wish I could speak Chinese.

11.21   Good to eat

Phrases such as 'good to eat' are formed very easily in Chinese:

| **hǎochī** | good to eat, delicious |
| **hǎokàn** | good to look at, good-looking, pretty. |

Tīng means 'to listen to', and **hǎotīng** therefore means 'good to listen to', 'pleasant sounding'. On the same basis **róngyi** 'easy' can be added to **dǒng** 'to understand' to make **róngyi dǒng** 'easy to understand', 'easily understood'.

11.22   Soon

Kuài means 'fast', as we saw in **7.6**. It has a secondary meaning of 'soon':

| **kuài èrshí nián le** | it will soon be twenty years |
| **kuài wǔ diǎn le** | it's nearly 5 o'clock |

The final particle **le** is often used with **kuài** and with other words which convey a sense of immediacy or imminence.

11.23   City wall

In Chapter Five we met **Chénghuáng** the City God. **Chéng** means a defensive wall, and comes to mean 'city' because important cities were walled until very recent times. The expression **jìn chéng** 'to enter the city', 'to go into town' derives from 'to go inside the wall'. **Chéngli** means 'in the city', and **chéngwài** means 'outside the city'.

11.24   Of course

Dāngrán is an adverb meaning 'of course'. As with other adverbs, its usual place is before the verb:

| **Tā dāngrán zhīdao wǒ shi shéi.** | Of course he knows who I am. |
| **Dāngrán yīnggāi wènwen tā.** | Of course we should ask him (about it). |

11.25   This having been done

To show that one action has been completed before another began or begins, -le is attached to the first verb:

Wǒ **chīle fàn** jiù qù.   I am going when I've eaten. [Having eaten I then go]

Wǒ **chīle fàn** jiù qù le.   I went when I'd eaten. [Having eaten I then went]

Exercise 82
Translate into English:

1. Wǒ dàole Shànghǎi yídìng gěi nǐ dǎ diànhuà.
2. Tāmen zhàole xiàng jiù zǒu le.
3. Wǒ huànle qián jiù qù mǎi dōngxi.
4. Nǐ xiàle bān jiù děi huí jiā.
5. Tā shàngle fēijī jiù shuì jiào.

11.26   Action postponed

Děng, as you know, means 'to wait' and in much the same way as **gěi** (see **10.9**) its meaning extends to 'let' ('wait for me to …' = 'let me …'). Very often **děng** introduces the postponement of an action ('*Wait* until …'), and its partner word **zài** tells what the action will be ('…and *then* we'll …'):

Děng tā míngtiān láile *zài* shuō.   Let's talk about it tomorrow when he comes.

Exercise 83   Revision practice on word-orders
*Make a meaningful sentence from each jumbled set below, remembering that the general word-order is **Subject-time-place-action**.*

1. a) qù Zhōngguó   b) míngnián   c) tāmen   d) lǚyóu

2. a) zài fànguǎnr   b) wǒmen   c) zuótiān   d) hēle sān píng píjiǔ

3. a) kāi huì   b) xīngqīliù   c) wǒmen
   d) zài Běijīng Fàndiàn

4. a) dào Měiguó qu   b) tāmen   c) wǔ yuè bā hào
   d) kàn péngyou

5. a) jìn chéng qu   b) míngtiān   c) mǎi dōngxi   d) shéi

(184) *New words*

bīnguǎn	guest-house, hotel
búguò	but, however
gàosu	to tell, inform
qíshí	actually, in fact
sòng	to escort, see someone to
Wénhuàbù	Culture Ministry
wénhuà	culture
yìzhí	(of time) all along
zháojí	anxious, worried, in a rush

(185) ## *CONVERSATION 11C*

Another arrival at the airport. Dr Jones is met by Mr Wang.

W : Excuse me, are you Dr Jones?

J : Yes. **Nín shi ...?**   Yes. You are...?

W : **Wǒ xìng Wáng, dàibiǎo**
Wénhuàbù lái huānyíng nín.

My name is Wang, I've come to
welcome you on behalf of the
Culture Ministry.

J : **Xièxie, xièxie. Fēijī wǎndiǎn**
le. Nín děngle hěn jiǔ le ba?

Thank you very much.
The plane was delayed.
You must have been waiting
for a long while?

W : **Méi shìr. Nín dàole jiù hǎo le.**
Tāmen méi gàosu wǒ nín huì
shuō Zhōngguó huà.

It doesn't matter. The main
thing is that you have arrived.
They didn't tell me you could
speak Chinese.

J : **Zhǐ huì shuō ji jù. Wáng**
xiānsheng de Běijīng huà zhēn
hǎotīng, yě róngyi dǒng.

I can only say a few words.
Your Beijing accent sounds
wonderful, and it's easy to
understand too.

W : **Shì ma? Qíshí wǒ shi Shànghǎi**
rén, búguò zài Běijīng zhùle
kuài èrshi nián le.

Really? Actually I'm from
Shanghai, but I've lived in
Beijing for nearly twenty
years now.

J : **Yìzhí dōu zài Wénhuàbù**
gōngzuò ma?

Have you always worked in the
Culture Ministry?

W : **Shì a. Nín yídìng lèi le ba.**
     Wǒ xiān sòng nín jìn chéng
     dào bīnguǎn xiūxi ba.

Yes. You must be tired.
I'll see you into town to the
guest-house for a rest first of all.

J : **Wǒ bú lèi. Zhèi ge hángzhànlóu**
     zhème dà, zhème piàoliang,
     wǒ xiǎng zhào ji zhāng xiàng,
     kěyǐ ma?

I'm not tired. This terminal is
so big and so beautiful, I'd like
to take some photos, would it
be OK?

W : **Dāngrán kěyǐ, bù zháojí.**
     Děng nín zhàole xiàng,
     wǒmen zài zǒu.

Of course it's OK, there's no
rush. We'll go when you've
taken your photos.

Exercise 84
Translate into Chinese:

1. A: How many years have you been studying English?
   B: About ten years, but I still can't speak it.

2. A: When do you practise *taiji*?
   B: Just before I go to bed.

3. A: Have you ever been to Japan?
   B: Yes, I used to go there once a year.

4. A: Will you do it or will he?
   B: Neither of us knows how to do it.

5. A: Is he coming to the meeting?
   B: No, he phoned and asked me to let you know that he can't come.

6. A: There are no buses today. How did you come?
   B: I came by taxi.

Chapter 12

NEW FRIENDS, OLD FRIENDS

You will probably have realised that starting with Chapter Eleven you are now covering some of the same ground that you trod in the first half of this book. This is quite deliberate. So here we are, going through introductions again, only this time you are trotting steadily where before you could only crawl and stumble. You now have a solid foundation of grammar and vocabulary, and new things that you meet can be seen to fit into patterns which are no longer unfamiliar.

In this chapter you learn not only how to sit down but how to remain seated, how to take something and how to hold on to it. You also find out how to make an adjective work as an adverb, and that allows you to say in what manner an action is performed.

To indicate the time when something happened is already easy for you, and you have also learned how to show duration of time. Now you will learn a third notion, elapsed time. As is almost always the case with Chinese grammar, there is nothing very tricky about this, it is just a matter of internalising a clear word order pattern.

12.1 'Lái'

Lái has the basic meaning 'to come':

Lái, lái, lái; nǐ lái kànkan!   Come over here and have a look!

Sometimes, though, **lái** is used as a substitute verb for other verbs with more specific meanings, rather as English uses 'do':

Tā bú huì zuò, wǒ lái.   He can't do it, let me have a go.
Zài lái yí ge.   Bring another one; 'encore!'

12.2 General before particular

You are now familiar with the order in which dates and times are given — always the larger before the smaller (year before month before day. See **7.2**), and addresses observe the same principle (county before town before street before house number). In the conversation you can see it at work again. Mr Young's company is given before his name and position in the company. Of course his title (Representative) comes after his surname, just as do other titles such as Mr., Miss, or Dr.

12.3 The bureau

Jú* is a word meaning 'a bureau', 'an office'. It usually appears in combinations such as:

Gōng'ānjú	Public Security Bureau (Police)
Lǚyóujú	Tourist Bureau

Zhǎng* means 'the head' (of an organization or department):

júzhǎng	bureau chief; director
Wénhuàbù Bùzhǎng	Minister for Culture

(186) 12.4 The manner of its doing

To comment on the way in which an action is performed Chinese links the comment to the action verb with the marker **de**:

Tā zǒu de hěn kuài.	He walks very quickly. [Literally: He walks in such a way that it is very quick]
Tā xué de hěn bù hǎo.	He learns very badly.

The marker **de** in this pattern must come immediately after the verb, so that if an object has to be mentioned it is necessary to state it first, with or without stating the verb before it:

Tā (chī) fàn chī de hěn kuài. He eats his food very quickly.

You will notice that what is happening here is that the pattern makes an adjective (quick, good, etc) into an adverb (quickly, well, etc).

Exercise 85

Answer the following with the information provided:

Example: **Tā Yīngyǔ shuō de zěnmeyàng?** (beautifully)
 Tā Yīngyǔ shuō de hěn piàoliang.

1. **Tā Hànyǔ xué de zěnmeyàng?** (very fast)

2. **Tā cài zuò de zěnmeyàng?**   (extremely well)
3. **Nǐ zuótiān shuì jiào shuì de zěnmeyàng?**   (not very well)
4. **Tā zhào xiàng zhào de zěnmeyàng?**   (very beautifully)

12.5 *Where did you get that idea?*

We met **nǎr?** 'where?' in Chapter Five. A variant form of **nǎr?** is **nálì?**, and **nálì?** is often used as a polite self-deprecating response to praise or flattery, as much as to say 'Wherever did you get that idea?', 'How could that be the case?':

A: **Nín zhèi ge cài zuò de zhēn hǎo.**   You've cooked this dish beautifully.
B: **Nálì, nálì.**   I wish I had!

It is a mark of changing cultural values that young people increasingly do not pay attention to such niceties, and they are just as likely to accept the compliment with a grateful **Xièxie** as they are to turn it away with a denial of any such possibility.

(187) 12.6 *'Duō' = how?*

Duō cháng? means 'How long?' and **duō** can be used with other adjectives in the same way:

Duō dà?   How big? How old? (of children)
Duō guì?   How expensive?
Duō jiǔ?   How long? (in time)

Exercise 86
Answer the following using the information provided:

1. **Guǎngzhōu jīntiān duō rè?**   (42°C)
2. **Nèi ge fàndiàn duō dà?**   (360 rooms)
3. **Tā yào qù duō jiǔ?**   (3 months)
4. **Zhèi ge háizi duō dà le?**   (5 years old)

12.7 *Over the measure*

Sān nián means 'three years'. To say 'more than three years' **duō** ('more', 'many', 'much') is used:

sān nián duō	three years and a bit (but less than four years)

but note:

sānshí duō nián	over 30 (but less than 40) years

12.8   More result verbs

In **10.15** and **11.11** we met result endings such as -**wán**, -**hǎo** and -**dào**. Here are two more: -**cuò** shows that something results in an error, and -**duì** shows that the result is correct:

shuōcuò	to say something wrong, to mispronounce
zuòduì	to do something right

12.9   Doing nothing but ...

We met **zhǐ** 'only' in Chapter Four. Note the following use as the first part of a negative sentence:

zhǐ shuō bú zuò	just talking, not doing (All you're doing is talking, not getting on with things)
zhǐ kàn bù chī	just looking at it, not eating it

12.10   Toasting

The verb **jìng** means 'to respect', 'to salute', and it is often used when toasting someone:

Wǒ jìng nǐ (yì bēi)!	Here's to you! Your health!

(188) *New words*

chángcháng	often
gāoxìng	happy, delighted
gōngfu	free / available time
jièshào	to introduce
liúlì	fluent
màn	slow

(189) CONVERSATION 12A

Mr Wang introduces Mr Young to Bureau Chief Li at a party.

W: **Lái, lái, lái, wǒ gěi nǐmen jièshào yíxiàr. Zhè wèi shi Léikè Gōngsī de Yáng dàibiǎo, gāng cóng Yīngguó lai. Zhè wèi shi Lǚyóujú de Lǐ júzhǎng.**

Come on, I'll introduce you. This is Mr Young, the Laker Company representative. He's just come from Britain. This is Bureau Chief Li of the Tourist Bureau.

Y : **Nín hǎo. Rènshi nín hěn gāoxìng.**

How do you do. I'm very pleased to know you.

L : **Nín hǎo. Nín Hànyǔ shuō de zhēn liúlì.**

How do you do. Your Chinese is really fluent.

Y : **Náli! Shuō de bù hǎo.**

I'm afraid not, I don't speak it well.

L : **Xuéle duō cháng shíjiān le?**

How long have you been learning?

Y : **Yì nián duō le. Méi gōngfu liànxí, xué de tài màn le.**

Over a year. I have no time to practise, so I learn too slowly.

L : **Bú màn. Wǒ xuéle shí nián Yīngyǔ le, hái chángcháng shuōcuò.**

That's not slow. I've been learning English for ten years and still often get it wrong.

W: **Éi, nǐmen zěnme zhǐ shuō huà, bù hē jiǔ? Lái, zài lái yì bēi. Wǒ jìng nǐmen: gānbēi!**

Hey, how come you're just talking and not drinking? Come on, have another glass. A toast to you both: Cheers!

Y/L : **Gānbēi!**

Cheers!

W: **Lái, chī diǎnr dōngxi. Jīntiān diǎnxin zuò de bú cuò.**

Come on, have something to eat. The titbits are pretty good today.

Y/L : **Hǎo, wǒmen zìjǐ lái.**

Fine, we'll help ourselves.

(190) 12.11 Verb-ending '-zhe'

a) The suffix **-zhe** is attached to activity verbs to indicate that the action is prolonged rather than over in one fell swoop:

Qǐng zuò.   Please sit down.

Qǐng zuòzhe.   Please remain seated.

Qǐng nǐ tì wǒ ná yì bēi jiǔ.	Please take a glass of wine for me. [**ná** 'to take']
Qǐng nǐ tì wǒ názhe zhèi bēi jiǔ.	Please hold this glass of wine for me.

b) Another function of **-zhe** is to attach to a verb in subordinate position, giving the meaning 'When it comes to ...', 'So far as ... is concerned':

Tā kànzhe xiàng Rìběn rén.	When you come to look at him, he's like a Japanese.
Zhèi ge cài chīzhe hǎo chī, kànzhe bù hǎo kàn.	This dish isn't nice to look at but it's good to eat.

Exercise 87
What's going on?

1. **Shéi zài mén wàitou zuòzhe?**
2. **Tā chuānzhe shénme?**
3. **Tā názhe shéi de fēijī piào?**
4. **Tā děngzhe nǐ ne.**
5. **Tā kànzhe hěn shòu.**

12.12   To graduate

Bìyè literally means 'finish the course' and nicely translates 'to graduate', but it is used more widely in Chinese than in English, because it is not confined to universities:

xiǎoxué bìyè	to finish junior school
zhōngxué bìyè	to finish middle school
dàxué bìyè	to graduate from university

12.13   Studying

Shū is 'a book', and from this come the terms **jiāo shū** 'to teach' [literally 'teach books'] and **niàn shū** ['read books out loud'] 'to study'. **Xué**, as you know, means 'to learn', and 'a school' is **xuéxiào**, while 'a student' is a **xuésheng**. 'A fellow student' is a **tóngxué** [someone one 'learns with'].

12.14   I thought so, but ...

The verb **yǐwéi** means 'to think', 'to regard … as …':

Wǒ yǐwéi zhème zuò zuì hǎo, nǐ shuō ne?	I think it would be best to do it this way. What do you say?

But **yǐwéi** is often used in the sense 'I thought so, but now I know I was wrong':

Wǒ yǐwéi tā shi Déguó rén.	I thought he was German (but he's actually ...).
Wǒmen yǐwéi nǐ bù lái le.	We thought you wouldn't come (but here you are).

12.15   Getting married

Jiéhūn [literally: to tie up a marriage] is 'to marry':

Tāmen míngtiān zài Běijīng jiéhūn.	They are getting married in Beijing tomorrow.

'X marries Y' is <u>X gēn Y jiéhūn</u>:

Wáng xiáojie bù xiǎng gēn Lǎo Lǐ jiéhūn le.	Miss Wang no longer wants to get married to Old Li.

Exercise 88
Translate into Chinese:

1. After finishing middle school she went to America.
2. I thought Old Li was also teaching in your school.
3. He's already been dancing for three hours.
4. Who said that Young Zhang is going to marry Miss Wang?

(191) *New words*

érzi	son
jiǔbēi	wine glass
nǚ'ér	daughter
qípáo	cheongsam, high-necked slit-skirted dress
shǒu	hand

🎧 CONVERSATION 12B

That person over there looks interesting. Young Zhang talks to Mr. Brown.

B : **Ēi, Xiǎo Zhāng, nèi wèi chuānzhe qípáo de xiáojie shi shéi?**	Hey, Young Zhang, who's that girl wearing the cheongsam?
Z : **Něi wèi? Shi shǒu shang názhe jiǔbēi de nèi wèi ma?**	Which one? That one with a wine glass in her hand?
B : **Bú shì, shi zài nàr zuòzhe de nèi wèi.**	No, that one seated over there.
Z : **Òu, tā a, wǒ rènshi, xìng Liú, shi wèi lǎoshī.**	Oh, her. I know her, she's called Liu. She's a teacher.
B : **Tā kànzhe xiàng Zhōngguó rén, kěshi Yīngyǔ zěnme shuō de nàme piàoliang a?**	She looks like a Chinese, but how come she speaks English so marvellously?
Z : **Tā shi Yīngguó Huáqiáo. Lúndūn Dàxué bìyè yǐhòu, jiù dào Zhōngguó jiāo shū lai le.**	She's an overseas Chinese from Britain. After graduating from London University she came to China to teach.
B : **Nǐ shi zěnme rènshi tā de?**	How did you get to know her?
Z : **Wǒ érzi gēn tā nǚ'ér zài yí ge xuéxiào niàn shū.**	My son and her daughter are studying in the same school.
B : **Òu, tā yǐjing yǒu nǚ'ér le, wǒ hái yǐwéi ...**	Oh, she's already got a daughter. And I was under the impression that ...
Z : **Yǐwéi tā méi jiéhūn, shì bu shi?**	You thought she wasn't married yet, right?

Marriage

Many of the old customs of China have died out over the past sixty years. Marriage used to be a matter for the family to arrange, and the man and woman concerned often had no say in the choice of their spouse. One of the first acts of the Communist Government after assuming control was to pass a new Marriage Law, which made the consent of the couple a requirement, while at the same time it did away with the taking of concubines (secondary wives), and of course abolished the arrangement of marriages between children and the bizarre practice of arranging marriages of children before they were born or even before they were conceived. In **12.15** you met the sentence 'Miss Wang no longer wants to get married to Old Li' – it might not have appeared in a textbook a century ago.

12.16 Another result verb

The verb **jiàn** 'to see' which we have met before can also be used to show result ('to succeed in seeing', 'to perceive'):

kànjian	to see [literally: look at-perceive]
tīngjian	to hear [literally: listen-perceive]

Exercise 89

Fill in the blanks with result verbs, as in the example:

Action	*Action + result*
Kàn, shānshang yǒu rén.	**Zài nǎr? À, wǒ kàn<u>jian</u> le. Zài nàr!**
1. **Tīng, fēijī lái le.**	**Shì ma? À, wǒ tīng (____) le.** **Zhēnde lái le.**
2. **Shuō, nǐ hái xiǎng shuō shénme?**	**Méi yǒu le. Wǒ yǐjing shuō(____) le.**
3. **Chī le ma?**	**Chīle yìdiǎnr, méi chī(____).**
4. **Qù mǎi le ma?**	**Qù le, kěshi méi mǎi(____).**

(193) 12.17 Long time no see

The English expression 'long time no see' is actually a literal translation from the idiomatic Chinese **hǎo jiǔ bú jiàn** 'very long time not see', 'Haven't seen you for ages'. **Hǎo** is the same word 'good' that you already know, but when it is used to mean 'very' it is stronger and more emphatic than **hěn**, which we have warned you before is a bit of a weakling as far as emphasis goes. Note the word order: when time has elapsed while something has *not* been happening, the period of time is placed *before* the verb:

Hǎo jiǔ méi kànjian nǐ le.	Not seen you for a long time.
Sān nián méi chī Zhōngguó fàn le.	Haven't had Chinese food for three years.
Liǎng ge xīngqī méi kàn bào le.	Haven't read a newspaper for two weeks.

Remember that when something does go on for a length of time, the length of time goes *after* the verb:

Chīle sān nián Zhōngguó fàn.	Ate Chinese food for three years.

Exercise 90
Translate into English:

Time duration	*Time elapsed*
1. **xuéle sān nián**	**sān nián méi xué**
2. **tīngle liǎng tiān**	**liǎng tiān méi tīng**
3. **liànxíle sān ge yuè**	**sān ge yuè méi liànxí**
4. **xiàle wǔ ge xīngqī yǔ**	**wǔ ge xīngqī méi xià yǔ**

12.18 'Shēntǐ'

Shēntǐ literally means 'the body', but it also means 'health'. It would be odd to translate **Tā shēntǐ hěn hǎo** as 'He has a good body': it normally means 'He's very healthy'.

12.19 All things considered

The expression **hái kěyǐ** means 'passable'. In the same way **hái hǎo** and **hái bú cuò** both mean 'not bad'. **Hái** imparts a kind of slightly grudgingly conceded approval.

12.20 Away on business

Chū chāi means 'to be away on official business', 'to be on a business trip':

chūle sān cì chāi   was away three times on business

12.21 To see one another

You met **jiànmiàn** 'to meet' in Chapter Nine, but because it is already a verb + an object [literally: 'see face' (**miàn**)] it cannot take another object directly. As with the example in **12.15**, it needs **gēn** to do that:

gēn Lǎo Lǐ jiànmiàn   to meet (with) Old Li

(194) **12.22   To be in the role of**

Dāng means 'to serve as', 'to be in the position of', 'to be in the role of':

Tā xiǎng dāng lǎoshī.	She wants to be a teacher.
Tā kuài dāng bàba le.	He'll soon be a father.

12.23   Comparison again

We saw in **9.3** that a straightforward comparison can be modified with **yìdiǎnr** 'a little bit' or **duōle** 'a lot'. Further modification can be achieved by using a number and measure:

X **bǐ** Y **guì sān kuài qián.**	X costs three yuan more than Y.

> ### Exercise 91
> *Make sentences expressing degree of comparison, as in the example:*
>
> **Lǎo Wáng 32 suì, Xiǎo Lǐ 28 suì. > <u>Lǎo Wáng bǐ Xiǎo Lǐ dà sì suì.</u>**
> 1. **Lǎo Wáng chuān 40 hàor de, Xiǎo Lǐ chuān 36 hàor de. >**
> 2. **Tā de biǎo 8:15, nǐ de biǎo 8:10. >**
> 3. **Tā yǒu 200 ge, tā érzi yǒu 150 ge. >**
> 4. **Yú mài wǔ kuài qián, jī mài bā kuài qián. >**

12.24   Every (with 'dōu')

You have met two ways of saying 'each', 'every'. **Měi tiān** and **tiāntiān** both mean 'every day'. It is common for the adverb **dōu** to be used with these forms, and **dōu**, as always, comes *after* what it refers to and *before* the verb:

Wǒmen měi nián dōu qù yí cì Lúndūn.	We go to London once every year.
Tā niánnián dōu lái.	He comes every year.
Gègè dōu piàoliang.	Every one of them is beautiful.

12.25　Simply must

To convey the idea 'simply must', Chinese often uses a double negative construction:

bú qù bù xíng　　　　　　　　simply must go [If don't go, won't do]

bù gěi bù xíng　　　　　　　　just have to give

12.26　Even (with dōu)

The adverb **dōu** has many uses. We have met it meaning 'all', 'both', and it commonly reinforces expressions of completeness and plurality, as we saw in note **12.24** above. Another use is to give the meaning 'even':

Zhème dà de xīnwén, tā dōu　　He doesn't even know such an
bù zhīdao.　　　　　　　　　important piece of news as this.

Again **dōu** must come *after* not *before* the words it refers to (**Zhème dà de xīnwén**).

(195) *New words*

fù*	assistant-, deputy-, vice-
fùjúzhǎng	Deputy Bureau Chief
fùdàibiǎo	Deputy Representative
gōngjīn	kilogram
pèngjian	to bump into, to meet
zhìshǎo	at least
zuìjìn	recently

(196) **CONVERSATION 12C**

Meeting an old friend.

L : **Èi, Lǎo Zhāng, hǎo jiǔ bú jiàn!**　　Eh, Old Zhang, long time no see.

Z : **Shì nǐ a, Xiǎo Lǐ. Méi xiǎngdào**　　Oh, it's you, Young Li. I didn't
　　zài zhèr pèngjian le.　　　　　　expect to bump into you here.

L : **Zuìjìn shēntǐ zěnmeyàng?**　　　　How's your health been recently?

Z : **Hái kěyǐ. Hěn jiǔ méi kànjian**　　　It's OK. Haven't seen you for ages.
　　nǐ le. Chū chāi le ma?　　　　　Have you been away on business?

L : **Dào Shēnzhèn qùle bàn nián.** Went to Shenzhen for six months.

Z : **Nà hǎo a. Zài Shēnzhèn pèngjian Wáng Jiànhuá le ba?** That's great. You must have met Wang Jianhua in Shenzhen, I suppose?

L : **Wǒmen měi ge xīngqī dōu jiànmiàn. Tā dāngle fùjúzhǎng le.** We met every week. He's become a Deputy Bureau Chief.

Z : **Shì ma? Rén háishi lǎo yàngzi ma?** Really? Is he still the same?

L : **Bǐ yǐqián pàng duōle; zhìshǎo pàngle èrshi gōngjīn.** Much fatter than before; at least 20 kilos heavier.

Z : **Hái nàme ài hē jiǔ ma?** Is he still as fond of drinking?

L : **Dāngle fùjúzhǎng, tiāntiān yǒu rén qǐng chī fàn. Tā xiǎng bù hē dōu bù xíng!** Since becoming Deputy Bureau Chief, he gets invited out to dinner every day. He has no choice but to drink!

Exercise 92

Translate into Chinese:

1. A: He looks very tired this morning.
   B: Yes, he didn't sleep very well last night.

2. A: Does she cook fish well?
   B: She doesn't often cook fish. I'll do it.

3. A: Your spoken Chinese is excellent.
   B: Far from it, I often make mistakes.

4. A: What is he holding in his hand?
   B: It must be his passport.

5. A: We haven't had chicken for three months.
   B: Alright, I'll go and buy one straight away.

6. A: Which T-shirt is more expensive: the yellow one or the blue one?
   B: The blue one is $2 more than the yellow one.

Chapter 13

ASKING FOR IT

Electronic communications have taken China by storm, with huge numbers of people using personal computers, the internet, and the latest in mobile telephones. We can only introduce some very basic terms here, but of course if you want more there is always the internet — you can find up-to-date English-Chinese dictionaries there.

Credit cards are becoming more common in the big cities of China, but it is largely a cash economy still, and you may need to change money from time to time. In Conversation C you find how to do it, but you should take to heart the message about trying to change defaced or damaged banknotes. You will see some pretty scruffy Chinese notes, but when it comes to foreign currency, banks and hotels will only accept nice clean ones. You have been warned!

13.1 Dialling up

Bō is the verb used for 'to dial' a telephone:

zhí bō	to dial direct
bō (diànhuà) hàomǎ	to dial a (phone) number

13.2 'Xiān ... zài ...'

Xiān 'first' and **zài** 'next' are used to show the sequence of events. Both these words are adverbs which must be placed before verbs:

Wǒmen xiān qù Shànghǎi,	We'll go to Shanghai first, and then to
zài qù Guǎngzhōu.	Guangzhou.

Exercise 93   Revision: How do you ... ?
Translate into English:

1. **Qù huǒchēzhàn zěnme zǒu?**
2. **Zhèi ge cài zěnme zuò?**
3. **Zhèi ge dōngxi zěnme yòng?**
4. **Wèishēngjiān de mén zěnme kāi?**
5. **'Cheers!' Zhōngguó huà zěnme shuō?**
6. **Běijīng zěnme zhí bō?**

13.3   To tell a fact

Gàosu, as you learned in Chapter Eleven, means 'to tell a fact' 'to tell something'. In English the same word 'tell' is also used 'to tell someone to do something', but Chinese does not then use **gàosu**. Note carefully the difference between the following:

Tā gàosu wǒ tā xìng Wáng.	He told me he is called Wang.
Tā jiào wǒ lái kàn nǐ.	He told me to come to see you.

13.4   'Āiyā!'

This is the most commonly heard exclamation. It is generally, but not always, used when something unpleasant happens, like 'My goodness!', 'Oh dear!', 'Oh!' in English:

Āiyā, wǒ wàngle dài hùzhào!   Oh dear, I've forgotten to bring my passport!

13.5   To hit or not to hit

As you know, 'to make a telephone call' is **dǎ diànhuà** (literally: to hit the electric speech). The newer expressions **chuánzhēn** ('facsimile, fax') and (**diànzǐ**) **yóujiàn** do not use **dǎ** but instead take **fā** 'to send out', 'to emit'. So 'to send a fax' is **fā chuánzhēn** and 'to send an email' is **fā yóujiàn**.

13.6 There's something else

In Chapter Six you met **hái** meaning 'still', 'yet', and in Chapter Nine you learned that it could mean 'even more so' in comparative sentences. It also can mean 'in addition', 'there's something else':

Tā mǎile liǎng jiàn T-xùshān,　　She's bought two T-shirts, and
　hái yào mǎi yí jiàn qípáo.　　wants to buy a cheongsam as well.

And **hái** combines with **yǒu** ('there is/are') as a kind of interjection, 'By the way', 'And another thing', 'And there's something else':

Òu, hái yǒu, qǐng nǐ gàosu　　Oh, by the way, will you please
　Lǎo Lǐ …　　tell Old Li that …

13.7 To return

In Conversation 10A we introduced **huílai** 'to come back' without explanation, but it is time now to look at this more carefully. **Huí** means 'to return'. The addition of **lái** 'come' or **qù** 'go' shows whether 'return' means 'come back' or 'go back':

Tā yǐjing huí Rìběn qu le.　　She's already gone back to Japan.

Chūqu de rén duō, huílai de　　Many people go out, but few come
　rén shǎo.　　back.

So **lái** and **qù** give a sense of 'in this direction' and 'in that direction' respectively. In Conversation 13A you will see that **huí** can also indicate direction ('back to where it belongs'). The hotel guest says he wants to send (he uses **chuán** 'to transmit') a document 'back' to London — **chuánhuí Lúndūn (qu)**.

(197) 13.8 Machines and gadgets

Chuánzhēn [literally 'transmit truly'] is a fax, and 'a fax machine' is **chuánzhēnjī**. **Jī** 'machine' is added to many other words to indicate the physical machine/gadget/set. Thus:

diànhuà 'the telephone'	>	**diànhuàjī** 'the telephone set'
fēi 'flying'	>	**fēijī** 'an aircraft'
jìsuàn 'to calculate'	>	**jìsuànjī** 'computer'
shǒu 'hand'	>	**shǒujī** 'cellphone', 'mobile phone'

zhào xiàng 'to photograph'	>	**zhàoxiàngjī** 'a camera'
zǒng* 'general'	>	**zǒngjī** 'switchboard', 'operator'

(198) *13.9 Trouble*

The word **máfan** means 'trouble' or 'troublesome':

Nǐ shì bu shi yào zhǎo máfan?	Are you looking for trouble?
Zuò Zhōngguó cài hěn máfan.	Cooking Chinese food is a lot of trouble.

Máfan is also a verb meaning 'to trouble' 'to bother' 'to inconvenience'. It is often used as a polite request, rather like the English 'Could I trouble you to ...?':

Máfan nǐ tì wǒ mǎi zhāng piào, hǎo ma?	Could I bother you to buy a ticket for me?

(199) *New words*

chángtú	long-distance
fèn	(measure for documents, newspapers)
guójì	international
guójì chángtú (diànhuà)	international long-distance call
shāngwù	commercial, business
wénjiàn	a document
zhōngxīn	a centre

(200) *CONVERSATION 13A*

A hotel guest asks about international phone calls.

S :	**Wéi, nín hǎo!**	Hello!
G :	**Wéi, zǒngjī, qǐng wèn guójì chángtú zěnme dǎ?**	Hello, operator, could you tell me how to make an international long distance call?
S :	**Hěn fāngbiàn. Nín kěyǐ zài fángjiān zhí bō.**	It's very convenient. You can dial direct from your room.
G :	**Shì ma?**	Really?
S :	**Nín xiān bō líng-líng, zài bō nín yào de hàomǎ, jiù xíng le.**	You first dial zero-zero, then dial the number you want, and that's it.

G : **Hǎo. Nǐ néng gàosu wǒ xiànzài Lúndūn jǐ diǎn zhōng ma?**

Fine. Can you tell me what the time is in London now?

S : **Lúndūn bǐ Shànghǎi wǎn bā xiǎoshí, xiànzài tāmen shi zǎochen wǔ diǎn.**

London is eight hours behind Shanghai: it's 5 a.m. for them now.

G : **Āiyā, tài zǎo le. Gōngsī hái méi shàng bān ne. Nà ... wǒ zhǐ néng fā yóujiàn le.**

Oh dear, it's too early. The office won't be open yet. In that case... I'll just have to send an email.

S : **Nín zài fángjiān jiù néng shàng wǎng.**

You can go on the internet in your room.

G : **Wǒ zhīdao. Òu, duì le, wǒ hái yǒu yí fèn wénjiàn, děi chuánhuí Lúndūn. Nǐmen zhèr yǒu chuánzhēnjī ma?**

I know. Oh, that's right, I also have a document that I must fax back to London. Do you have a fax machine here?

S : **Yǒu, zài èr lóu shāngwù zhōngxīn, èrshisì xiǎoshí dōu kāi.**

Yes, it's in the business centre on the first floor: that's open 24 hours.

G : **Hǎo, máfan nǐ le.**

Fine, sorry to have troubled you.

S : **Bú kèqi.**

You're welcome.

13.10   Formal group names

We saw in **12.3** that **jú*** meant 'a bureau' (as in **lǚyóujú** 'travel bureau'). Another similar word is **chù*** 'office', as in the term **wàishìchù** 'foreign affairs office'. A **chù*** is a lesser unit than a **jú***. Yet another formal unit is a **tuán*** 'group', as in **lǚyóutuán** 'a tour group' and **dàibiǎotuán** 'a delegation'.

13.11   Leadership

Lǐngdǎo is another multi-functional word. It is a verb meaning 'to lead', but it is also a noun meaning 'leadership', 'the leaders', 'the head'.

13.12   Polite address

Nín is a polite way of saying 'you', as we saw in **2.1**. When addressing more than one person politely it is common to use the expression **Nín jǐ wèi** (literally: you several ladies/gentlemen), or **Nín sān wèi** (you three gentlemen/ladies), etc.

13.13 'Yìsi'

Yìsi means 'meaning', 'idea', as you learned in Chapter Eight:

> **Wǒ bù dǒng zhèi jù huà de yìsi.** I don't understand the meaning of this sentence.

Yìsi also means 'a token of affection', 'a mark of appreciation', 'a symbol of gratitude'. When giving someone a gift it is polite to make light of it by saying:

> **Zhèi shi wǒ de yìdiǎnr xiǎo yìsi.** This is (just) a small mark of my appreciation.

13.14 Just in the act of

To show that some action is happening or going on right now Chinese uses **zhèngzài** 'just -ing', often adding **ne** at the end of the sentence:

> **Tā zhèngzài dǎ diànhuà ne.** She is telephoning.
> **Wǒmen zhèngzài chī fàn ne.** We're having dinner.

Exercise 94 **Tā zhèngzài gànmá ne**? *What's he doing at this moment?*
Finish the following sentences:

1. **Tā zhèngzài** (drinking)
2. **Tā zhèngzài** (sleeping)
3. **Tā zhèngzài gǔdǒng shìchǎng** (shopping)
4. **Tā zhèngzài** (learning Chinese)

13.15 That's settled!

Shuō 'to say' plus the result ending **dìng** 'fix' means 'to settle', 'to agree on':

> **Shíjiān shuōdìng le,** The time is settled, but the place
> **dìfang hái méi shuōdìng.** hasn't been agreed yet.

13.16 To dispatch

Pài means 'to send out', 'to dispatch', 'to deploy' people or perhaps transport:

Qǐng nǐmen pài rén lai kànkan.   Please send someone to have a look.
Wǒ pài chē qu jiē nǐ.   I'll send a car to meet you.

 New words

biǎoshì	to express/show (feelings)
dùn	measure word for 'a meal'
qǐngtiě	invitation card
sòng	to send, deliver
xīcāntīng	restaurant serving Western food
xīcān	Western food
Zhōngcān	Chinese food
Zhōngcāntīng	(hotel) restaurant serving Chinese food

CONVERSATION 13B

A Danish delegation phones to invite the heads of their Chinese host unit to dinner.

H : **Wéi, Wàishìchù Lǐ chùzhǎng ma? Wǒ shi Dānmài dàibiǎotuán de Hán Sēn.**

Hello, is that Mr Li, the Head of the Foreign Affairs Office? This is Hansen of the Danish delegation.

L : **À, Hán Sēn xiānsheng, nǐ hǎo!**

Ah, Mr Hansen, how are you?

H : **Nǐ hǎo! Lǐ chùzhǎng, wǒmen tuánzhǎng xiǎng qǐng nín gēn júli de lǐngdǎomen chī dùn fàn. Bù zhīdao nín ji wèi shénme shíhou yǒu gōngfu?**

Hello. Mr Li, the head of our delegation would like to invite you and the heads of your bureau to a meal. I wonder when you would all be free?

L : **Nǐmen bú yào kèqi le.**

No need to be so polite!

H : **Bú shi kèqi. Wǒmen yídìng yào biǎoshì yìdiǎnr yìsi. Hòutiān wǎnshang fāngbiàn ma?**

This isn't out of politeness. We certainly must show how grateful we are. Would the evening of the day after tomorrow be convenient?

L : **Tāmen ji wèi lǐngdǎo zhèngzài kāi huì. Wǒ qù wèn yíxiàr. Qǐng nín děng-yi-děng... Wéi, Hán Sēn xiānsheng, hòutiān wǎnshang kěyǐ.**

The leaders are in a meeting. I'll go and ask them. Please hang on ... Hello, Mr Han Sen, that evening is OK.

H : **Hǎo jíle. Nà wǒmen jiù shuōdìng: hòutiān wǎnshang liù diǎn bàn zài Guójì Fàndiàn liù lóu xīcāntīng.**

Super. So we'll settle on the day after tomorrow, 6.30 pm in the Western restaurant on the 6th floor of the International Hotel.

L : **Hǎo, xiān xièxie nǐmen.**   Good. Let me thank you in
                                    advance.

H : **Bú xiè. Wǒ mǎshang pài rén sòng**   Not at all. I'll send someone over
    qǐngtiě lai.   with the invitation cards
                                            straight away.

13.17 Banknotes

The common word for a banknote is **chāopiào** (**piào**, you will remember, means 'a ticket'). **Xiànchāo** means 'ready cash', 'money in hand', and **jiǎchāo** is 'a counterfeit note', 'a forgery'.

13.18 Ratios

When changing money the rate can be expressed using **bǐ** 'compared to':

yī bǐ sì diǎn wǔ   1:4.5

The same device is used for giving football and other sports results:

sān bǐ yī   3 – 1

(204) 13.19 In this direction or that

In **13.7** we used **lái** and **qù** with **huí** to show whether 'return' meant 'come back' or 'go back'. **Lái** and **qù** can be used with any verb indicating physical movement:

nálai	to bring here
náqu	to take away
shànglai	to come up
shàngqu	to go up
xiàlai	to come down
xiàqu	to go down
zǒulai	to walk over here
zǒuqu	to walk away

And sometimes other verbs make use of them too:

xiǎnglai xiǎngqu	racking one's brains ['thinking coming and thinking going']

In the next conversation you will meet **qǔlai** 'to withdraw'. The tourist who is talking about withdrawing (**qǔ**) money from the bank is of course seeing the action from his own viewpoint, so the money is coming towards him, and hence the use of **lái**.

Exercise 95
*Fill in the blanks with **lai** or **qu**:*

1. Wǒ bú yòng le, nǐ kěyǐ ná____ gěi Lǎo Lǐ le.
2. Qǐng nǐ sòng____ gěi wǒmen kànkan.
3. Tā gāng cóng yínháng qǔ____ le bù shǎo xiànchāo.
4. Júzhǎng lái diànhuà yào kàn zhèi fèn wénjiàn, kuài gěi tā sòng____.

13.20 One that ...

In **5.14** you met **de** used to link an adjective or descriptive phrase to a noun. In **7.9** we said that if it is clear what that noun is, there is no need to mention it and **de** can stand alone in its place, making a kind of non-specific noun like 'the one that...', 'that which...', 'what...' in English:

Zhè shì wǒ bù xǐhuan de.	This is the one that I don't like *or* This is what I don't like.
Wǒ shi chīsùde.	I am a vegetarian.
Dà de guì, xiǎo de piányi.	The big one's expensive, the small one's cheap.

Exercise 96
Translate into English:

1. Zhèi tiáo yú bú shì zhēn de, shì yòng tǔdòu zuò de.
2. Tā shuō zhèi zhāng yìbǎi yuán de Rénmínbì shi jiǎ de.
3. Zuótiān wǎnshang de cài dōu shi zuì guì de.
4. Tā mǎi de nèi liàng qìchē shi hóng de.

13.21 To do a good turn

Bāng or **bāngmáng** means 'to do a good turn', 'to do a favour', 'to help':

Qǐng nǐ bāng ge máng.   Please lend a hand.

Shéi néng bāng wǒ mǎi piào?   Who can help me out by buying a ticket?

Qǐng nǐ bāng wǒ zhǎo yí wèi   Please could you help me to find a
Zhōngwén lǎoshī hǎo ma?   Chinese teacher?

Exercise 97   Could you help …?
Translate into English:

1. Qǐng nǐ bāng ge máng, gěi wǒmen jiào liàng chūzūchē, hǎo ma?
2. Nǐ néng bāng wǒ zhǎo yí wèi jiāo tàijíquán de lǎoshī ma?
3. Qǐng nǐ bāng wǒmen zhào zhāng xiàng, kěyǐ ma?
4. Máfan nǐ bāng wǒ wèn yíxiàr Lǎo Wáng zài bu zai.

13.22   No way

Fázi means 'way', 'method'. **Méi fázi** is equivalent to the English 'There's nothing to be done about it'. It is often followed in Chinese by a verb:

Méi fázi yòng.   There's no way to use it.

Jīntiān méi huǒchē, méi   There's no train today, so there's no
fázi qù.   way to get there.

Exercise 98   Lodging a complaint
Translate into English:

1. Fángjiān tài chǎo, wǒ méi fázi shuì jiào.
2. Cài dōu lěng le, wǒmen méi fázi chī.
3. Cèsuǒ méi shuǐ, wǒmen méi fázi yòng.
4. Chōu yān de (rén) tài duō, wǒmen méi fázi chī fàn.

13.23   What's to be done?

Bàn means 'to see to things', 'to manage', and **zěnme bàn?** (literally 'How to do it?') means 'What's to be done?', 'How can we cope?'

A: **Qìchē, huǒchē, fēijī dōu méi yǒu,**   There are no buses, trains or
nǐ shuō zěnme bàn?   aircraft, what do you think we
                                 can do?

B: **Wǒ yě méi fázi.**   I have no way out of this either.

13.24 If

Yàoshi means 'if' and is commonly followed in the second part of the sentence by **jiù** 'then':

A: **Yàoshi xià yǔ, nǐ qù bu qu?**　　Will you go if it rains?
B: **Yàoshi xià yǔ, wǒ jiù bú qù le.**　　If it does I won't go after all.

Yàoshi tāmen yǒu chuánzhēn　　It would be great if they
　　jiù hǎo le.　　　had a fax.

If 'yàoshi'

Although there are a number of words for 'if' in addition to **yàoshi,** Chinese often does not feel the need to make use of any of them. **Nǐ bú qù, wǒ bú qù** can easily be understood to mean 'If you don't go, I won't go', and **Chīle fàn qù, jiù tài wǎn le** can hardly mean anythung but 'If (we) go after the meal it will be too late'. And note also that in Conversation 13C there is no **yàoshi** in the Chinese version of 'I don't know if they're forgeries or not' because **yàoshi** does not translate 'if' in the sense of 'whether'.

---

(206) *New words*

guīdìng	to prescribe, to stipulate, to make a rule that
jiù	old (of inanimate things)
páijià	quoted price
pò	damaged, broken, torn
shǔ	to count
wàibì	foreign currency
xūyào	need; to need, to need to
zāng	dirty
zhíjiē	directly, immediately
zìdòng	automatic
zìdòng tíkuǎnjī	automatic telling machine (ATM)

(207) ## CONVERSATION 13C

A tourist finds that changing money is not always straightforward.

T : **Nǐ hǎo. Wǒ xiǎng huàn qián.**　　Hello. I'd like to change money.

C : **Shì wàibì huàn Rénmínbì ma?**   Is it foreign currency to RMB?

T : **Shì, Yīngbàng xiànchāo huàn**   Yes, Sterling notes to RMB.
Rénmínbì. Jīntiān páijià   What is the quoted price today?
duōshao?

C : **Yī bǐ shí diǎn wǔ.**   10.5 to one.

T : **Hǎo. Wǒ huàn liǎng bǎi**   Fine. I'll change £200. Please
Yīngbàng, nǐ shǔshu.   count it.

C : **Duìbuqǐ, zhèi sān zhāng èrshi**   I'm sorry, these three twenties can't
bàng de bù néng huàn.   be changed.

T : **Wèishénme? Shì jiǎchāo ma?**   Why's that? Are they forgeries?

C : **Bù zhīdao shì bu shi jiǎchāo,**   I don't know if they're forgeries or
kěshi yì zhāng tài zāng, yì   not, but one is too dirty, one is too
zhāng tài jiù, hái yǒu yì zhāng   old, and one is damaged. We can't
shi pò de. Wǒmen bù néng shōu.   take them.

T : **Wǒ zhè qián dōu shi zhíjiē**   This money was drawn straight from
cóng yínháng qǔlai de. Nǐ   the bank. Can you help me out and
néng bù néng bāng ge máng,   just change it for me?
gěi wǒ huàn yíxiàr?

C : **Duìbuqǐ, yínháng guīdìng:**   I'm sorry, the bank has ruled that
jiù de, zāng de, pò de dōu bù   old, dirty and damaged notes may
néng shōu, wǒ yě méi fázi.   not be accepted, and there's
     nothing I can do.

T : **Nà wǒ xūyào de Rénmínbì**   Then I won't have enough RMB for
bú gòu, zěnme bàn?   my needs. What shall I do?

C : **Nín yàoshi yǒu yínhángkǎ,**   If you have a bank card, you can use
kěyǐ yòng wàitou de zìdòng   the automatic telling machine
tíkuǎnjī qǔ Rénmínbì.   outside to withdraw RMB.

T : **Òu, shì ma? Nà hǎo ba.**   Oh, really? That's OK then.

Exercise 99

Translate into Chinese:

1. A: Can I dial direct to England?   B: Yes, of course.

2. A: May I trouble you to take me to   B: No problem, get in.
   the station?

3. A: Must we really invite them for a meal?   B: It's OK not to.

4. A: When shall we go to Japan?   B: We can go next month
     if there's no problem
     with visas.

5. A: Where is Miss Wang?   B: She's sending a fax.

6. A: Thank you for your help.   B: Don't mention it.

Chapter 14

WHERE? OH WHERE?

Chinese tends to give the verb a lot of the work in a sentence, while English seems to prefer to work its nouns harder. So in English we might say 'She's a good cook', but Chinese would prefer **Tā zuò fàn zuò de hǎo** ('She cooks well'), where the main information is conveyed by the verb **zuò fàn.** Now you will meet another example of difference, the piling up of verbs such as **zǒuguolai** 'walk cross come', where English would normally say 'walk over here' with only one verb. Perhaps all this seems rather woolly and therefore not very helpful for you the learner, but if nothing else it might guard against the temptation to translate too literally from English into Chinese. In fact the difference is little more than a preference for another way of ordering thoughts in sequence, it is hardly frightening.

Earlier we concentrated quite hard on ways to pinpoint time sequences clearly. There is still plenty to be said about time, indeed you will meet here the very useful pair 'as soon as' and 'not until', but we are looking more closely at place and distance. At first you might find it odd that Chinese says 'A is separated from B closely' when it means 'A is close to B', but you probably don't find 'A is separated from B distantly' strange, and if you think about it they are actually a logical pair of opposites. It's all so interesting, isn't it?

14.1 Correspondence

'A letter' is **xìn**, and the measure word for it is **fēng**, so **liǎng fēng xìn** is 'two letters'. **Duǎn** means 'short', as opposed to **cháng** 'long' (beware that **duǎn** is not the opposite of **gāo** 'tall'), and **duǎnxìn** is 'a brief note' or nowadays 'a text message'. 'To write a letter' is **xiě xìn** and 'to text a message' is **fā duǎnxìn**.

(208) *14.2 Question words as indefinites*

In **11.3** we saw that **jǐ?** 'how many?' can be used as an indefinite number ('several') rather than as a question. In Conversation 14A there is another example, where **shénme?** 'what?' is used to mean 'something', 'anything':

Nǐ zhǎo wǒ yǒu shénme shì ma?　　Was there something you wanted
　　　　　　　　　　　　　　　　　　　from me?

It may help to understand what is happening here if you compare it with the same sentence without the final **ma:**

Nǐ zhǎo wǒ yǒu shénme shì?　　　'What do you want with me?'

And note the following contrasted sentences:

Tā yǒu duōshao qián?　　　How much money has he got?
Tā méi duōshao qián.　　　He hasn't got much money.

Other question words can also be used indefinitely, often translating neatly as '-ever' words:

Tā yào duōshao, wǒmen jiù　　We'll give him however much
　gěi duōshao.　　　　　　　　he wants. (Literally: He wants how
　　　　　　　　　　　　　　　　　much, we'll then give how much)

Nǐ shuō něi ge hǎo, wǒ jiù mǎi　　I'll buy whichever one you think
　něi ge.　　　　　　　　　　　is good.

14.3　Opposite

Duìmiàn means 'opposite', 'facing':

Bīnguǎn zài huǒchēzhàn (de)　　The hotel is opposite the
　duìmiàn.　　　　　　　　　　railway station.

Tā jiā duìmiàn yǒu ge xiǎo　　　There is a little park across
　gōngyuán.　　　　　　　　　from his house.

Exercise 100　Revision: Where is it?
Translate into English:

1. **Yínháng zài fàndiàn de dōngbianr.**
2. **Shāngwù zhōngxīn jiù zài kāfēitīng duìmiàn.**
3. **Nán cèsuǒ zài xīcāntīng hòutou.**
4. **Wǒ de hùzhào zài nǐ yòubianr de lǚyóutú shàngtou.**
5. **Nèi zhāng zhàopiàn jiù zài tā shǒu shang názhe de hùzhào lǐtou.**

(209) *14.4 From A to B*

The pattern used for showing distance from one place to another makes use of **lí** 'separated from':

A **lí** B (**hěn**) **jìn/yuǎn.**   A is very close to/far from B.
Wǒ jiā lí gōngyuán hěn jìn.   My house is very near the park.

To show the actual measured distance the verb **yǒu** is usually added to make the pattern <u>A **lí** B **yǒu** [distance]</u>:

Guǎngzhōu lí Běijīng (yǒu) duō   How far is it from Guangzhou to
yuǎn?   Beijing?

Guǎngzhōu lí Běijīng yǒu duōshao   How many kilometres is it
gōnglǐ?   from Guangzhou to Beijing?
                                                                (**gōnglǐ** = kilometre)

Tā jiā lí jīchǎng zhǐ yǒu wǔ gōnglǐ.   His home is only 5 km from
                                                                the airport.

Exercise 101
True or false?

1. **Lúndūn lí Luómǎ (Rome) chàbuduō yǒu wǔbǎi gōnglǐ.**
2. **Běijīng lí Tiānjīn yǒu yìbǎi sānshi duō gōnglǐ.**
3. **Běijīng lí Shànghǎi bǐ Běijīng lí Guǎngzhōu yuǎn.**
4. **Yīngguó lí Zhōngguó bǐ Měiguó lí Zhōngguó yuǎn duōle.**

14.5 I'm afraid

Kǒngpà means 'I'm afraid' but has nothing to do with real fear: in fact it mirrors the English non-fearful usage. It will also translate quite often as 'perhaps':

Míngtiān kǒngpà bù xíng ba.   I'm afraid tomorrow won't do.

Zhèi ge dōngxi kǒngpà hěn guì ba.   This thing will perhaps be rather
                                                                costly.

14.6 For short

Chinese sometimes neatly shortens ideas which can be quite cumbersome to express in English. **Shàng-xià**, for instance, can stand for 'coming up and going down' or for 'going up and coming down' or for 'ascending and descending' (we met it in Conversation 9A). **Jìn-chū** similarly makes short work of 'entering and exiting':

Guójì Fàndiàn yǒu hěn duō diàntī,
    shàng-xià hěn fāngbiàn.

There are lots of lifts in the International Hotel: it's easy to get up and down.

Nèige dìfang yào jiǎnchá hùzhào,
    jìn-chū hěn máfan.

You have to have your passport checked at that place: it's quite tedious to get in and out.

14.7 'Céng' v 'lóu'

We met in **4.13** the use of **lóu** to mean a storey or floor of a building. But **lóu** also can mean 'a building' or 'a block'. To avoid confusion the word **céng** (literally: a layer, a tier) is now more often used for 'floor':

Tāmen gōngsī zài wǔ lóu
    (or wǔ céng).

Their company is on the 5th floor.

And when both buildings and floors are mentioned then **céng** is more likely to be used:

Tā jiā zài shíbā (hào) lóu sì céng.

His home is on the 4th floor of Block 18.

(210) 14.8 Oh, yes, but ...

Reluctant concession can be shown by using the pattern X **shi** X, **kěshi ...**

1. A: **Nǐ de fángjiān méi diànhuà ma?**   Isn't there a phone in your room?
   B: **Yǒu shi yǒu, kěshi bù néng zhí bō.**   There is, but I can't dial direct.

2. A: **Nèi ge fàndiàn bù hǎo ma?**   Isn't that hotel any good?
   B: **Hǎo shi hǎo, kěshi tài guì le.**   Yes, it's O.K., but it's too expensive.

14.9 'Chū máobìng'

Chū means 'out' or 'to exit'. (Remember that in Chapter Seven we met **chū wèntí** 'to develop a problem'.) **Chū** tends to be associated with unwanted or unpleasant circumstances, and in the conversation we meet another example,

chū máobìng 'to develop a fault', 'to go wrong'. **Máobìng** means 'a defect' or 'a malfunction', and **yǒu máobìng** is often used for 'has broken down, 'is faulty'. Later, in Conversation 14C, you will meet yet another example: **chū shì** means 'to have an accident' (literally 'to develop into a matter/an incident').

14.10 Just about to.

Zhèng xiǎng and **zhèng yào** both mean 'just about to', 'just thinking of':

Wǒ zhèng xiǎng qù kàn tā,	Just as I was about to go and
tā jiù lái le.	see him he arrived.

14.11 Greater before lesser

Another reminder that larger normally comes before smaller (see **7.2** and **12.2**). When giving addresses in Chinese the order is:

Zhōnghuá Rénmín	People's Republic of China, [<u>Country</u>]
Gònghéguó,	
Guǎngdōng <u>Shěng</u>,	Guangdong <u>Province</u>,
Guǎngzhōu <u>Shì</u>,	Guangzhou <u>City</u>,
Zhōngshān <u>Lù</u>,	Zhongshan <u>Road</u>,
145 <u>Hào</u>,	<u>No.</u> 145,
Sān <u>Lóu</u>.	3rd <u>Floor</u>.

14.12 When the time comes

Dào shíhou literally means 'arrived at the time', and it doesn't take much of a stretch of the imagination to understand that it will translate 'when the time comes' very neatly.

New words

bān	to move
bān jiā	to move house
bǐ	a pen
biànfàn	a simple meal, 'pot-luck'

dìzhǐ	address
diànyóu dìzhǐ	email address
wǎngzhǐ	website
qū	district
tiáojiàn	condition, conditions
xīn	new
xīwàng	hope, to hope
zhǎnlǎn	to exhibit

(213) *CONVERSATION 14A*

Wu Qiang (John Woods) is invited by his Chinese friend Young Li to a housewarming.

W : **Wéi, Xiǎo Lǐ ma? Wǒ shi Wú Qiáng.**
Hello, is that Young Li? This is Wu Qiang.

L : **Ēi, Wú Qiáng. Shōudào wǒ de duǎnxìn le ma?**
Oh, Wu Qiang. Did you get my text message?

W : **Gāng shōudào. Nǐ zhǎo wǒ yǒu shénme shì ma?**
Just got it. Was there something you wanted from me?

L : **Wǒmen bān jiā le.**
We've moved house.

W : **Shénme shíhou bān de? Bāndào nǎr le?**
When was this? Where have you moved to?

L : **Shàng yuè bā hào bān de, bāndào Jìng'ānlǐ le, jiù zài Guójì Zhǎnlǎn Zhōngxīn duìmiàn.**
We moved on the 8th of last month, to Jinganli, right opposite the International Exhibition Centre.

W : **Nàme yuǎn a! Lí nǐmen gōngsī kǒngpà yǒu shí gōnglǐ ba. Fángzi zěnmeyàng?**
So far! That's… what? … all of 10 km from your office, isn't it? What's the house like?

L : **Tiáojiàn hái kěyǐ, jiù shi shàng-xià bù fāngbiàn. Wǒmen zài shí céng.**
The (living) conditions aren't bad. It's just that it's not convenient for getting up and down. We're on the 10th floor.

W : **Méi diàntī ma?**
Isn't there a lift?

L : **Yǒu shi yǒu, kěshi cháng chū máobìng. Ēi, Wú Qiáng, zhèi ge xīngqītiān zhōngwǔ yǒu gōngfu ma? Wǒmen xiǎng qǐng nǐ lái chī ge biànfàn.**
Well, there is, but it often breaks down. Eh, Wu Qiang, are you free this Sunday at midday? We'd like to invite you round to have a meal.

W : **Hǎo a, wǒ zhèng xiǎng
kànkan nǐmen de xīn jiā.**

Oh good, I was just thinking
that I'd like to see your new home.

L : **Nǐ nàr yǒu bǐ ma? Wǒ gàosu
nǐ dìzhǐ: Cháoyáng Qū,
Jìng'ānlǐ Lù, Sìshiwǔ Hào Lóu,
Shí Céng, Yāo-líng-èr-liù.
Xīngqītiān zhōngwǔ shí'èr
diǎn zěnmeyàng?**

Have you got a pen I'll tell you
the address: it's 1026, 10th floor,
Block No.45 Jinganli Road,
Chaoyang District. How about
12 noon on Sunday?

W : **Hǎo, xiān xièxie le, xīwàng dào
shíhou diàntī bié chū máobìng.**

Fine. Thank you in advance. I hope
that the lift won't go wrong when
the time comes.

14.13 Busy doing what?

You have met **máng** 'busy' or 'to be busy with', and **máng shénme?** is a
common way of asking 'Busy doing what?':

**Tā zhèng zài máng chū guó
de shì.**

He's busy with the business of
going abroad.

14.14 Long since

Zǎojiù literally means 'early as soon as that', and it very conveniently translates
'long since':

**Wǒ zǎojiù zhǔnbèihǎo le. Nǐ shuō
shénme shíhou zǒu jiù shénme
shíhou zǒu.**

I was ready long ago. We can go at
any time you say.

Tā zǎojiù wàngle wǒ shi shéi le.

She's long since forgotten who I am.

14.15 Opinion

Yìjiàn means 'an opinion', 'an idea', and 'to give an opinion' is **tí yìjiàn**. In the
next conversation the verb **tí** is doubled, and rather as with **kànkan** 'to have a
glance at', the effect is to make the effort seem less strenuous. **Títi yìjiàn** feels
more like 'to pass a few comments on' than 'to express a weighty opinion on'.

14.16 'Gěi' = to

In Chapter Nine you met **gěi** meaning 'for', 'on behalf of'. The basic meaning of **gěi** is 'to give', 'to give to'. In a coincidental similarity to the English expression 'to give him a phone call' Chinese uses **dǎ diànhuà gěi tā**, 'make a phone call to him'. There are a number of other expressions where **gěi** means 'to':

jìgěi tā	'to mail to him' (see Conversation 14B)
nágěi tā	'to take to her'
zuògěi tā chī	'to cook for him to taste'

14.17 'Hǎo ji ge'

Hǎo ji ge is a useful colloquial idiom meaning 'loads of', 'lots of', 'quite a few'. Since **ge** is a measure word, it can of course be followed by a noun like **rén**. If the noun is one that does not take **ge**, then substitute the correct measure for **ge**:

hǎo ji fèn wénjiàn	lots of documents
hǎo ji tiān	quite a few days

14.18 'Wǒ zhèr'

Wǒ zhèr means literally 'I here'. In English 'me' is a place as well as a person, so we can happily say 'Come to me', but **wǒ** does not seem like a place in Chinese, and **zhèr** is added to make it clear. **Nǐ nàr** and **tā nàr** are of course the equivalents for 'over there where you are/she is':

Jīntiān de bào zài nǐ nàr ma?	Have you got today's paper?

Note that the question form **Nǐ nǎr?** has been hijacked for use over the telephone to mean 'Who's calling?'

(214) 14.19 Compound verb endings

In Chapter Thirteen you have already met **lái** 'come', **qù** 'go', and **huí** 'back' indicating the direction of the action of the verb. Other verb endings which give additional sense are **shàng** 'up', **xià** 'down', **chū** 'out', and **jìn** 'in'. **Lái** and **qù** can be used with all of these as well. It sounds complicated, but the following examples show clearly how it works:

Tā cóng lóushang zǒuxialai le.	She walked down from upstairs [towards me]
Shān suīrán hěn gāo, kěshi qìchē háishi kāishangqu le.	Although the mountain was high, the car still went up it.
Tā cóng wàiguó dàihuilai bù shǎo dōngxi.	She brought back lots of things from abroad.
Tāmen de diànhuà yǒu wèntí: zhǐ néng dǎjìnqù, bù néng dǎchūlái.	Their phone is defective: you can only phone in, they can't dial out.

Exercise 102
Fill in the blanks with verb endings:

1. **Tā míngtiān zǎochen qù, hòutiān wǎnshang huí ____.**
2. **Lóushang yào zhèi fèn bào, qǐng nǐ ná ____ ____.**
3. **Yàoshi nǐ pà wàngle, qǐng nǐ xiě ____ ____ ba.**
4. **Zhè shi nǐ de xíngli ma? Nǐ yīnggāi xiě ____ nǐ de míngzi.**

14.20 Inland and abroad

The opposite to **guówài** (literally: outside the country) 'abroad' is **guónèi** (literally: inside the country) 'inland':

Guónèi dǎ tàijíquán de rén dāngrán bǐ guówài duō.	Of course there are more practitioners of *taiji* inside China than abroad.
Zhèi xiē bíyānhú xiān zài guónèi zhǎnlǎn, míngnián zài sòngdào guówài qu.	These snuff bottles will first be exhibited in China, and then next year they'll be sent abroad.

14.21 More on 'huì'

Another use of the verb **huì** (which we met in **11.1**) is to indicate future probability:

Jīntiān xiàwǔ bú huì xià yǔ ba.	It won't rain this afternoon, will it?
Wǒmen shi lǎo péngyou, tā yídìng huì bāngmáng.	We're old friends, he's sure to lend a hand.

(215) *New words*

jiàoshòu   professor

jīngjì	economics
Jīngjì Tèqū	Special Economic Zone (SEZ)
lùnwén	academic paper, essay
piān	(measure for writings)
tuì	to return, withdraw, retreat
tuìhuilai	to return to sender, to send back
yánjiū	research, to do research
yóujú	The Post Office
yóu(zhèng) biān(mǎ)	postcode, zip code

🔊 CONVERSATION 14B

On campus, Peter, a foreign research student, meets Xiao Fang, a fellow student.

F : **Zuìjìn máng shénme?**
What have you been busy at recently?

P : **Hái zài yánjiū Jīngjì Tèqū de wèntí. Éi, Fùdàn Dàxué de Táng jiàoshòu huí Shànghǎi le ma?**
I'm still doing research into problems of the Special Economic Zones. Oh, has Professor Tang of Fudan University gone back to Shanghai?

F : **Zǎojiù huíqu le. Nǐ wèn tā gànmá?**
Some time ago. Why do you ask about him?

P : **Wǒ xiěle liǎng piān lùnwén, xiǎng qǐng Táng jiàoshòu títi yìjiàn.**
I've written a couple of papers, and I'd like to ask him to comment on them.

F : **Nǐ kěyǐ jìgei tā a.**
You could post them to him, you know.

P : **Kěshi wǒ méi yǒu tā de dìzhǐ. Wènle hǎo jǐ ge rén dōu bù zhīdao.**
But I haven't got his address. I've asked lots of people but none of them know it.

F : **Wèishénme bú wèn wǒ? Wǒ zhèr jiù yǒu.**
Why didn't you ask me? I've got it right here.

P : **Tài hǎo le. Kuài gàosu wǒ.**
Marvellous! Tell me it quick.

F : **Hǎo, nǐ xiěxialai ba: Shànghǎi Shì, Huáihǎi Běilù, 268 Hào, Sān lóu. Yóubiān shi 200435.**
OK, write it down: 3rd Floor, No.268 Huaihai Road North, Shanghai Municipality. The zipcode is 200435.

P : **Duìbuqǐ, yóubiān shi shénme yìsi?**
I'm sorry, what does **yóubiān** mean?

F : **Yóubiān jiù shi yóuzhèng biānmǎ. Guónèi de xìn yàoshi bù xiěshang, yóujú jiù huì gěi nǐ tuìhuilai.**

It is the postal administration's coding. If you don't write it on inland letters, the post office will return them to you.

P : **Shì ma? Nà wǒ yídìng děi xiěshang. Jīntiān pèngjian nǐ, yùnqi zhēn hǎo. Zǒu, wǒ qǐng nǐ qù Xīngbākè hē kāfēi.**

Really? In that case I certainly must write it on. It's been really lucky that I ran into you today. Let's go, I'll treat you to a coffee at Starbucks.

14.22 *That's right*

Shìde 'That's right', 'Yes, sir' is the standard respectful reply to someone in authority.

(217) 14.23 *Coming to rest*

Normally phrases describing the location where something happens are introduced by **zài** and come before the verb (See **5.2**). But when the location is where the verb's action comes to rest, the **zài** phrase, quite logically, comes after the verb:

Míngzi yīnggāi xiězai nǎr?	Where should I write my name?
Xíngli fàngzai wàitou kěyǐ ma?	Is it alright to put my luggage outside?
Tā shēngzai Zhōngguó, kěshi liǎng suì jiù dàole Yīngguó.	She was born in China, but she moved to Britain when she was two years old.

Zhù 'to live', 'to dwell' is an accommodating (as it were!) verb, and it is happy to have the **zài** phrase either before or after it:

Zhùzai zhèr de rén (or **Zài zhèr zhù de rén**) **méi yǒu bú rènshi tā de.**	Everyone who lives here knows him. [there is no-one who doesn't know him]

Exercise 103 *Place where/place whither?*
Translate into English:

1. **Nǐ kěyǐ zài nǐ fángjiān xiě. / Nǐ de dìzhǐ kěyǐ xiězai xíngli shang.**

2. **Tā zài Zhōngguó shēngle yí ge nǚ'ér. / Tā nǚ'ér shēngzai Zhōngguó.**

3. **Tā cháng zài gōngyuánr dǎ tàijíquán. / Yǔ dǎzai tā shēn(tǐ) shang, hěn bù shūfu.**

4. **Wǒmen zài nǎr tián biǎo? / Wǒ de míngzi tiánzai nǎr?**

14.24   Expecting a plural answer

When the answer to a question is likely to be in the plural, the questioner often puts in the adverb **dōu**:

Nǐ dōu xiǎng kàn shénme?	What things do you want to look at?
Tā dōu rènshi něi xiē rén?	Which people does she know?

14.25   Not dead but 'gone before'

Like people from many other cultures Chinese are shy of mentioning death too directly, and there are lots of euphemisms which help to avoid the dread word **sǐ le** 'dead'. One very common one is **bú zài le** 'not present any more'.

14.26   Together

Yìqǐ means 'together':

Wǒmen wǔ ge rén zhùzai yìqǐ.	The five of us live together.
Tāmen wǔ ge rén yìqǐ chū guó lǚyóu qu le.	The five of them have gone abroad travelling together.

(218) 14.27   As soon as

The pattern **yī ... jiù** is used to convey the idea 'as soon as this, then that', 'whenever this, then that'. Both words come immediately before the verbs in the two halves of the sentence:

Tāmen yì lái, wǒmen jiù zǒu.	As soon as they come, we'll leave.
Tā yí kànjian jiǔbēi jiù xiǎng hē jiǔ.	Whenever he sees a glass he wants to have a drink.

(219) 14.28   Only then

Cái 'only then' is another very useful fixed adverb:

Zhèi jiàn shì tāmen zuótiān jiù zhīdao le. Wǒ jīntiān cái zhīdao.	They knew about this matter as early as yesterday. I only knew of it today. (literally: I today only then knew.)

Nǐ jiǎole fèi cái néng zǒu.   You can't leave until you've paid up.
                                    (literally: You've paid only then can
                                    leave.)

Go very careful! **Cái** will often be most easily translated by 'not until' in English, but there is no negative in the Chinese version. It helps if you remember that its meaning is 'only then'.

Cái forms a nice contrast with **jiù** ('as late as that' and 'as soon as that' respectively), as Exercise 104 illustrates:

Exercise 104   *Jiù v Cái*
Fill in the blanks with either **jiù** *or* **cái**:

1. **Yóujú jiǔ diǎn kāi mén. Tā bā diǎn bàn ____ dào le: tài zǎo le.**

2. **Wǒmen jiǔ diǎn kāi huì. Tā shí diǎn ____ dào: tài wǎn le.**

3. **Tā jiā lí huǒchēzhàn hěn yuǎn. Zǒu lù qù, yì xiǎoshí ____ gòu.**

4. **Tā jiā lí huǒchēzhàn hěn jìn. Zǒu lù qù, wǔ fēn zhōng ____ gòu le.**

5. **Lái Zhōngguó yǐhòu tā ____ zhīdao Běijīng yǒu zhème yí ge dà zhǎnlǎn zhōngxīn.**

New words

gēge	elder brother
jiéguǒ	result; as a result
kǒuyīn	accent
liúxia	to leave behind (note, address etc)
sǎosao	elder brother's wife
shēng	to be born; to give birth
tōngzhī	to inform, to let know

CONVERSATION 14C

An expatriate interviews for a driver.

E : **Nǐ jiào Zhāng Jūn, shì ba?**   You're called Zhang Jun, right?

D : **Shìde.**   Yes.

E : **Jīnnián duōshao suì le?**   How old are you this year?

D : **Èrshiwǔ.**   25.

E : **Shénme dìfang rén?**   Where are you from?

D : **Sìchuān rén.**	Sichuan.
E : **Nǐ shuō huà zěnme méi yǒu Sìchuān kǒuyīn a?**	How come you don't have a Sichuan accent?
D : **Wǒ shēngzai Sìchuān, kěshi liǎng suì jiā jiù bāndào Běijīng lai le.**	I was born in Sichuan, but my family moved to Beijing when I was two.
E : **Jiā li dōu yǒu shénme rén?**	Who are there in your family?
D : **Fùqin bú zài le. Xiànzài zhǐ yǒu mǔqin, gēge, gēn sǎosao.**	My father has passed away. Now there are only my mother, my elder brother and his wife.
E : **Dōu zhùzai yìqǐ ma?**	Do you all live together?
D : **Shìde.**	Yes.
E : **Yǐqián dōu zài nǎr gōngzuòguo?**	Where else have you worked?
D : **Zhōngxué yí bìyè jiù xué kāi chē, yìzhí kāi chūzū, qùnián cái huàndào Měiguó yínháng.**	As soon as I finished secondary school I learned how to drive, and drove a taxi right up until last year when I went to work for an American bank.
E : **Nǐ kāile zhème duō nián de chē, chūguo shì ma?**	You've driven for so many years, have you ever had an accident?
D : **Méi yǒu, cónglái méi chūguo shì.**	No, I've never had one.
E : **Hǎo, nǐ liúxia dìzhǐ, diànhuà, jiéguǒ wǒmen huì tōngzhī nǐ.**	Fine, leave us your address and phone number, and we'll let you know the result.

Exercise 105
Translate into Chinese:

1. A: Where is the International Exhibition Centre?
   B: It's just opposite the **Xīnhuá** Hotel.

2. A: How far is your house from the railway station?
   B: I think it's about five kilometres.

3. A: Do you have his address in Beijing?
   B: Yes, here it is: 29 **Yǒngdìng** Road, 3rd floor, Beijing 100826.

4. A: When was it that he went back to Shanghai?
   B: He went back as soon as he received your email.

5. A: Mr Wang said that there's nothing to be done about it.
   B: Tell him you're a friend of mine, I am sure he would help.

6. A: Can I sit next to you, Miss Li?
   B: Yes, of course, but I have to leave in a minute.

Chapter 15

GETTING THERE

Beijing is like many other large cities in the world — stop people and ask the way and you will be told that they don't know either, they're just visitors or have only recently moved to the capital. When in doubt, ask a policeman. By the time you have mastered this chapter you should be well able to ask ... and to understand his answer.

But you will first have to find your policeman, and you will discover that there is an intriguing difference between "the policeman appears" and "a policeman appears." So often in Chinese it is word order that shows subtle differences, and that is the case here. And what goes for appearance also goes for disappearance. Puzzled? Read on.

Watch out also for **huí** 'to return' and **zài** 'again'. You met this pair in Chapter Ten. They can both be translated as 'come back', but remember that **huí** means 'to return to where you came from or belong', while **zài** means 'to come back on another occasion'. There are examples of both in this chapter.

15.1 Procedures

'A procedure' is **shǒuxù**, and 'to carry out a procedure' is **bàn shǒuxù** (**bàn**, you will remember from Chapter Thirteen, means 'to do', 'to manage', 'to handle'):

Mǎi fángzi de shǒuxù hěn máfan.	The procedures for buying a house are really troublesome.
Tā yào chū guó, zhèngzài bàn shǒuxù.	She wants to go abroad, and is going through the procedures right now.

15.2 Edition, version

Bǎn means 'a printing block', and has come to mean 'an edition', 'a version'. In the conversation below it combines with **dào*** 'a thief', 'a robber' to make **dàobǎn** 'a pirated copy', 'a pirate version'. And you can no doubt easily enough understand and remember the following:

xīnbǎn	a new version
Yīngwénbǎn	an English language version
chūbǎn	to publish

15.3 Forms

Dān or **dānzi** is 'a bill', 'a form'. It crops up in quite a number of everyday words. In the first conversation you will meet **bāoguǒdān** 'a form to be filled in when sending a parcel', and you will frequently meet **càidān** 'bill of fare', 'menu', and **míngdān** 'a name list'. And there is a recent addition to the list: in restaurants you can call for the bill by saying **Mǎi dān!** 'The buy bill!' This is actually a corruption of a Cantonese expression, and it has come in on the wave of popularity of Hong Kong culture, especially with regard to eating, pop songs, and kungfu movies.

(222) 15.4 More on 'This having been done'

In **11.25** we met sentences of the 'Having eaten I will go' type where the main action is contained in 'I will go'. The dependent (less vital) clause 'Having eaten' would be translated in Chinese by <u>verb-**le** (object)</u>:

Wǒ chīle zǎofàn jiù chūqu le.   Having had breakfast I went out.

There is another example in the conversation: **Tiánhǎole zài lái.** 'Having filled in the form, come here again.' Such dependent clauses can be used regardless of whether the main action is in the past, the present, or the future:

Tā fāle chuánzhēn jiù chūqu le.	He went out after sending the fax.
Tā měi tiān xiàle bān dōu qù mǎi dōngxi.	She goes shopping every day after work.
Wǒ xiàle fēijī jiù xiān qù kàn Chángchéng.	Having got off the plane I will first go to see the Great Wall.

Exercise 106
Using the suggestions in brackets, answer the following questions in Chinese:

1. **Tā shi shénme shíhou qù de?** (After we gave her the money)
2. **Tā shénme shíhou zǒu?** (After watching the news)
3. **Nǐ shénme shíhou qu kàn tā?** (After I post these letters)
4. **Tā měi tiān shénme shíhou chī zǎofàn?** (After doing his *taichi*)

223 15.5 Mail

It is enlightening from time to time to collect together words which have
common elements; it helps to increase your understanding of the basic
meaning of the element, as with **bǎn** and **dān** above. **Yóu** 'mail' appears in
plenty of terms:

yóubiān	postcode, zip code
yóujú	Post Office
yóufèi	postage
yóupiào	postage stamp
píngyóu	surface mail

15.6 A reminder on question words as indefinites

We craftily slipped into **14.2** two examples of 'whatever', 'whoever', 'whenever'
type sentences using question words to translate these indefinite ideas. In the
first conversation you will find another. And just to remind you how it works,
here are a couple more:

Shéi huì shuō Zhōngguó huà, wǒmen jiù qǐng shéi.	We'll invite anyone who can speak Chinese.
Tā érzi yào shénme, tā jiù gěi shénme.	She gives her son anything he wants.

Exercise 107
Fill in the blanks with question words, as in the example:

Example: **Nǐ yào mǎi (duōshao), wǒmen jiù mài (duōshao).**

1. **Nǐ xiǎng qǐng ____, wǒmen jiù qǐng ____.**
2. **Tā xiǎng chī ____, wǒ jiù zuò ____.**
3. **Nǐ shuō yīnggāi ____ zuò, wǒ jiù ____ zuò.**
4. **Nǐ shuō ____ hào qù, wǒmen jiù ____ hào qù.**

224 15.7 The Continents

Àodàlìyà or **Àozhōu**	Australia
Fēizhōu	Africa
Měizhōu	America

Ōuzhōu	Europe
Yàzhōu	Asia
Dōngyà	East Asia
Dōngnányà	Southeast Asia

(225) *New words*

bāoguǒ	a parcel
běn	(measure for books)
chēng	to weigh
guāngpán	CD, DVD, CD ROM
hángkōng	aviation; air mail
hé	and (links nouns only)
jì'niànpǐn	souvenir, memento (literally: 'memory item')
míngxìnpiàn	postcard
piányi	cheap
shūdiàn	bookstore
tiē	to stick, to paste
zhǒng	(measure for 'kind of, type of, sort of')

(226) *CONVERSATION 15A*

A tourist sends a parcel at the post office.

T : **Wǒ yào jì ge bāoguǒ dào Jiānádà.
Děi bàn shénme shǒuxù?**

I want to send a parcel to Canada. What procedures are needed?

C : **Nǐ dōu yào jì shénme dōngxi? Xiān nálai jiǎnchá yíxiàr.**

What things are you sending? Bring them here first for examination.

T : *[opens a cardboard box]* **Jiù shi zhè xiē jì'niànpǐn, guāngpán hé ji běn Zhōngwén shū.**

There are just these souvenirs, DVDs and a few Chinese books.

C : *[inspects the box]* **Guāngpán lǐtou yǒu méi you dàobǎn de?**

Are there any pirated ones among the DVDs?

T : **Dàobǎn de? Méi you, méi you, dōu shi zài dà shūdiàn mǎi de.**

Pirated ones? No, no, they were all bought in major bookstores.

C : **Hǎo, méi wèntí. Nǐ děi xiān qù tián bāoguǒdān. Tiánhǎole zài lái.**

Fine, no problem. You need to go and fill in a parcel form first though. Come back when it's done.

T : *[reads the form]* **Zhè shàngtou yǒu Yīngwén, wǒ kěyǐ yòng Yīngwén tián ma?**   There's some English on this: can I fill it in in English?

C : **Kěyǐ.**   Yes, you can.

T : **Tiánhǎole, yóufèi duōshao?**   It's filled in. What's the postage?

C : **Wǒ chēngcheng kàn. Shi jì hángkōng, háishi jì píngyóu?**   I'll weigh it and see. Is it to go by airmail or surface mail?

T : **Něi zhǒng piányi jì něi zhǒng.**   Send it by whichever is cheaper.

C : **Dāngrán píngyóu piányi: sān bǎi líng wǔ kuài.**   Surface mail is of course cheaper: 305 yuan.

T : **Hǎo. Wǒ hái yào jì míngxìnpiàn, sì zhāng dào Ōuzhōu, liǎng zhāng dào Měiguó. Děi tiē duōshao qián de yóupiào?**   OK. I also want to send some post-cards, four to Europe and two to the States. What value stamps should I stick on?

C : **Guójì hángkōng dōu shi sì kuài wǔ. Liù zhāng èrshiqī kuài … yígòng sān bǎi sānshi'èr kuài.**   All international airmail is ¥ 4.50. Six stamps will be ¥ 27 … ¥ 332 altogether.

15.8   Ambassadors and embassies

The word for an ambassador is **dàshǐ** and an embassy building is called a **dàshǐguǎn**:

Zhōngguó [zhù Àodàlìyà] Dàshǐ   The Chinese Ambassador [to Australia]

Éluósī [zhù Měi(guó)] Dàshǐguǎn   The Russian Embassy [in America] (**zhù** 'to be stationed in')

15.9   Native or not

One's native place is **běndì** (literally: 'this place'), and 'a native', 'a local' is a **běndì rén**. The opposite is **wàidì** ('outside place') and someone who comes from elsewhere in the same country is called a **wàidì rén**.

⁽²²⁷⁾ 15.10   Appearance and disappearance

Rather dramatically, when Chinese mentions something or someone appearing or going away, it changes the normal word order of a sentence and puts the subject after the verb. In Conversation 15B there is an example where the woman says "there's a policemen coming over". Here are some others:

Tāmen jiā láile hěn duō kèrén.	Lots of guests came to their house.
Wǒmen gōngsī zǒule bù shǎo rén.	Many people have left our firm.
Nèi tiáo lù shang duōle yí ge fànguǎnr.	An extra restaurant has appeared on that road.

This change of word order for appearance and disappearance reflects a more general principle. Usually a noun which has a definite article in English ('**the** book', '**the** policeman', '**the** ones we were talking about yesterday') goes before the verb in Chinese, but a noun with an indefinite article in English ('**a** book', '**an** apple', '**some** policemen') goes after the verb in Chinese. In other words Chinese is using word orders to do the job which is done by 'the' and 'a' in English. Compare these two questions:

Bǐ zài nǎr?	Where is **the** pen? (i.e. the specific one already identified)
Nǎr yǒu bǐ?	Where is there **a** pen? (i.e. any old pen will do)

15.11 Good to eat ... again.

In **11.21** we met the adjectives **hǎo** and **róngyi** used as adverbs before verbs to make phrases like 'good to eat' and 'easy to understand'. Sometimes **hǎo** and **róngyi** are used interchangeably. For example, **hǎo zhǎo** and **róngyi zhǎo** both mean 'easy to find'. Another adjective/adverb that can be used like **hǎo** and **róngyi** is **gòu** 'enough':

Wǒ de qián bú gòu yòng.	I haven't got enough money to spend.

And you should note that this type of phrase can be in a negative form as well:

Nèi tiáo lù chē duō, bù hǎo zǒu.	That road has a lot of traffic, it's not easy to travel on.

Exercise 108
Translate into Chinese:

1. Chinese food is good to eat but difficult to prepare.
2. His house is in the mountains and very hard to find.
3. Is one Peking Duck enough for ten people?
4. This phrase is easy to learn.

15.12 More on ordinal numbers

As we saw in **11.6**, ordinal numbers (the first, the second, the third, etc) are easily formed by prefixing **dì-** to a number:

wǔ ge rén	five people
dì-wǔ ge rén	the fifth person

There are a few cases where Chinese does not use **dì-** even though the English seems to call for it. So:

'The second floor' is **èr lóu**
'The No.44 (bus)' is **sìshisì lù**
'No.28 Xinhua Road' is **Xīnhuá Lù èrshibā hào**

15.13 Follow the road

Shùnzhe means 'following':

Shùnzhe zhèi tiáo dà lù wǎng dōng zǒu, yídìng néng dào Zhōngguó.	Go east along this highway and you will certainly be able to get to China.

15.14 Even the most ...

We met **zuì** 'most' in **9.22**. Used with the adverb **yě** it means 'even the most ...':

Chī dùn fàn zuì kuài yě děi bàn xiǎoshí.	To eat even the fastest meal [to eat a meal even at the fastest rate] takes half an hour.
Dǎ guójì diànhuà zuì shǎo yě děi yìbǎi kuài qián.	To make an international phone call even at its cheapest costs ¥100.

It is worth remembering **zuì shǎo** as the standard way of translating 'at least'.

Exercise 109
Translate into English:

1. **Tā zuì zǎo yě děi míngtiān dào.**
2. **Tā jiā lí gōnggòngqìchēzhàn zuì shǎo yě děi zǒu èrshi fēn zhōng.**
3. **Běijīng bā yuè zuì rè yě bú huì dào sìshi dù.**
4. **Cóng Zhōngguó lái de xìn, zuì kuài yě yào yí ge xīngqī.**

(228) *15.15   Rough estimates*

Where English indicates approximate numbers by saying 'one or two', 'five or six', Chinese achieves the same effect by putting two numbers together:

Zuótiān zhǐ yǒu yì-liǎng ge rén méi lái.	There were only one or two people who didn't come yesterday.
Tā dǎsuan zài Xiānggǎng wánr wǔ-liù tiān.	She intends to enjoy herself in Hong Kong for five or six days.

In the same way,   **shísì-wǔ** is 14 or 15

èr-sānshí is 20 or 30

qī-bābǎi is 700 or 800

But note that there is one exception: it is not possible to use the same device for '9 or 10', because **jiǔ-shí** sounds like **jiǔshí** and can be confused with '90'.

15.16   Go careful!

The word **xiǎoxīn** (literally 'little heart') means 'careful', 'go careful', 'beware of':

Zài guówài lǚxíng, chī dōngxi děi tèbié xiǎoxīn.	When travelling abroad one should be especially careful about what one eats.
Xiǎoxīn! Qiántou yǒu rén.	Careful, there's somebody ahead.

(229) *15.17   It would be better if: a reminder*

The pattern **háishi ... ba** translates 'it would be better if', 'had better':

Tāmen dōu bú rènshi lù, háishi nǐ qù ba.	None of them know the way, it'd be better if you went.
Zuò huǒchē tài màn, wǒmen háishi zuò fēijī ba.	It's too slow by train, we'd better go by air.

Exercise 110
Give your advice in Chinese:

1. (**Dàjiā dōu shuō chōu yān bù hǎo**), you'd better give it up.
2. (**Jīntiān tài wǎn le**), we had better do it tomorrow.
3. (**Fēijīpiào bù róngyi mǎi**), you'd better go by train.
4. (**Xìn tài màn**), we had better send them a fax.

(230) *New words*

guò	to cross over
hónglǜdēng	traffic lights
hóngdēng	red light
lǜdēng	green light
huángdēng	amber light
jǐngchá	policeman
lùkǒur	road junction, intersection
mǎlù	major road (**mǎ** means 'horse')
rénxíng héngdào	pedestrian crossing

(231) *CONVERSATION 15B*

A foreign tourist wants to go to the British Embassy. She doesn't know the way and asks a man in the street.

T : **Qǐng wèn nín zhīdao Yīngguó Dàshǐguǎn zài nǎr ma?**

Excuse me, do you know where the British Embassy is?

B : **Duìbuqǐ, bù zhīdao. Wǒ shi wàidì lái de. Ēi, nèibiān zǒuguolai yí ge jǐngchá, nǐ wèn tā ba.**

Sorry, I don't. I'm from elsewhere. Look, there's a policeman coming over. You can ask him.

[Asks the policeman]

T : **Tóngzhì, qǐng wèn Yīngguó Dàshǐguǎn shì bu shì zài zhè fùjìn?**

Comrade, could I ask you if the British embassy is near here?

P : **Shì lí zhèr bù yuǎn, jiù zài Guānghuá Lù.**

Yes it's not far from here, it's on Guanghua Road.

T : **Nín néng gàosu wǒ zěnme zǒu ma?**

Can you tell me how to get there?

P : **Hěn hǎo zhǎo. Dào qiántou hónglǜdēng zuǒ guǎi, yìzhí zǒu, dì-sān ge lùkǒur yòu guǎi, jiù shi Guānghuá Lù. Shùnzhe gōngyuán wǎng qián zǒu, jiù kànjian dàshǐguǎn le.**

It's very easy to find. Turn left at the traffic lights ahead, go straight on, turn right at the third intersection, and that's Guanghua Road. Go ahead alongside the park and you'll see the embassy.

T : **Zǒu lù qù wǔ fēn zhōng gòu ma?**

Is five minutes enough on foot?

P : **Wǔ fēn zhōng bú gòu, zuìshǎo yě děi shíyī-èr fēn zhōng.**

Five minutes isn't enough, it'll take at least 11 or 12 minutes.

T : **Hǎo, duō xiè!**

Fine, many thanks.

P : **Bú kèqi. Ēi, xiǎoxīn qìchē!**
Bié zài zhèr guò mǎlù. Nǐ háishi
zǒu rénxíng héngdào ba.

Not at all. Hey, mind the traffic!
Don't cross here. You'd better use
the pedestrian crossing.

T : **Hǎo, hǎo, hǎo.**

Right, OK, fine.

(232) 15.18 'Huài' and 'huài le'

Huài means 'bad', 'evil', 'rotten', 'broken down':

Hǎo rén zuò hǎo shì, huài rén
zuò huài shì.

Good people do good things,
bad people do bad ones.

Huài le means 'become bad', 'gone rotten', 'gone wrong':

Āiyā! Yú gēn ròu dōu huài le,
bù néng chī le.

Curses! The fish and meat
have both gone bad, and have
become uneatable.

Duìbuqǐ, wǒ lái wǎn le.
Wǒ de chē huài le.

I'm sorry I'm late. My bike
broke down.

15.19 The missing person

As we saw in **9.1**, **gěi** introduces a prepositional phrase before the verb and
means 'for'. Sometimes the object of **gěi** is well enough understood that it can
be left out:

Máfan nǐ gěi (wǒ) xiě yíxiàr.

May I trouble you to write it
(for me).

Nǐ bù shūfu, yīnggāi qǐng dàifu
gěi kànkan.

If you aren't well, you should ask
the doctor to have a look (for you).

15.20 What's the matter?

Zěnme le? means 'What's the matter?', 'What's wrong?':

Tā zěnme le?

What's the matter with him?

Chē zěnme le? Zěnme bù zǒu le?

What's wrong with the bus?
Why won't it go any more?

(You will remember from **8.12** that **bù** plus **le** means 'not any more'.)

Exercise 111   New situation 'le'
  Translate into English:
  1. **Tā de shǒu zěnme le?**
  2. **Tā bìng le, bù néng lái le.**
  3. **Nǐ zěnme méi mǎi piào? Duìbuqǐ, wǒ wàng le.**
  4. **Diàntī huài le, wǒmen zǒushangqu ba.**

15.21   Wheeled vehicles

Chē means any kind of wheeled vehicle, and the measure for all of them is **liàng**. 'A wheel' is **lúnzi**, and **qiánlúnr** and **hòulúnr** are 'front wheel(s)' and 'rear wheel(s)' respectively.

15.22   To rent

In Chapter Six you learned **chūzūchē** 'a taxi'. **Zū** means 'to rent', 'to hire' and **chūzū** means 'out for hire', 'to let'.

15.23   'Dà' for emphasis

Dà means 'big', 'great', and it is used with certain expressions to give them emphasis. So, since **rè tiānr** means 'hot weather', **dà rè tiānr** means 'sizzling hot weather'; and, since **báitiān** means 'in daylight', **dà báitiān** means 'in broad daylight':

Dà rè tiānr bié chūqu le.	Don't go out in this boiling hot weather.
Nǐ zěnme dà báitiān zài jiā li shuì jiào a?	How come you're asleep at home in broad daylight?

15.24   'Zhè shi'

Zhè shi is a colloquial way of adding emphasis to a question. You will see that it can be omitted without affecting the basic sense of the sentence. In the next conversation the bicycle mender says **nǐmen zhè shi shàng nǎr qu a?** 'Where can it be that you are off to?' Here are a couple more examples:

Nǐmen zhè shi zài máng shénme?   What can it be that you are so busy at?

Nǐ zhè shi yào gànmá? Shí'èr   What can you be doing? 12 o'clock
diǎn le hái bú shuì jiào?   and still not in bed?

(233) *15.25 Turn back*

Wǎng, as we saw in **6.4**, means 'towards':

wǎng qián zǒu	go forwards
wǎng dōng zǒu	go east
wǎng xī guǎi	turn west

Huí, of course, means 'to return', and **wǎng huí zǒu** means 'to turn back':

Qiántou lù huài le,   The road ahead is
  wǒmen zhǐ néng   damaged, there's
  wǎng huí zǒu.   nothing for it but
               to turn back.

(234) *15.26 'Shàng' again*

We have met **shàng** many times, most commonly matched by its opposite word **xià**. **Shàng** has an additional function as a verb-ending which indicates that an action or state of affairs is being initiated:

chuān qípáo	to wear a cheongsam
chuānshang qípáo	to put on a cheongsam
dài yǎnjìngr	to wear glasses
dàishang yǎnjìngr	to put on glasses
xiě míngzi	to write one's name
xiěshang míngzi	to write one's name in/on
qí zìxíngchē	to ride a bicycle
qíshang zìxíngchē	to get on a bicycle

> ### The cross
>
> The shape of a cross had no religious significance in traditional Chinese culture, instead it was considered to resemble the Chinese character for **shí** 'ten' (十). Hence the word **shízì lùkǒur**, 'character ten road mouth' for 'crossroads'. And 'The Red Cross' is known in Chinese as **Hóng Shízì Huì**, 'red character ten society'.

(235) *New words*

fāngxiàng	direction
hūrán	suddenly
shìshi	to try, to have a try

xiū or **xiūlǐ**	to mend, repair, fix
yǒu-yìsi	interesting
méi-yìsi	uninteresting
zhuàn	to revolve, turn

Marco Polo Bridge

The Marco Polo Bridge, **Lúgōu Qiáo**, to the south-west of Beijing, is so-called because it was described in *The Travels of Marco Polo*. There is some doubt as to whether he actually went to China at all, because many of the most remarkable features of Chinese culture, such as footbinding, chopsticks, the Great Wall, and the Chinese writing system, are not mentioned in the book, but he certainly had some sound knowledge of the country, so most people continue to believe that he did go there. In 1937 the bridge acquired infamy as the place where the first shots of the Sino-Japanese War were fired. It is a popular scenic spot for tourists now.

(236) *CONVERSATION 15C*

One of a party of cycling tourists chats with an old bicycle repairer.

T : **Lǎo shīfu, wǒ de chē huài le. Máfan nín gěi xiūlǐ yíxiàr.**	My bike's broken down, chief. Could I ask you to mend it for me.
R : **Zěnme le?**	What's wrong?
T : **Bù zhīdao wèishénme, hòulúnr hūrán bú zhuàn le.**	I don't know why, but the back wheel suddenly stopped going round.
R : **Wǒ kànkan ... wèntí bú dà.**	Let me see ... No great problem.
T : **Mǎshang néng xiūhǎo ma?**	Can you fix it straightaway?
R : **Shí fēn zhōng ba. Nǐmen zhè ji liàng chē zěnme dōu yíyàng a? Shi zūlai de ba?**	It'll take about 10 minutes. How come your bikes are all the same? Rented, are they?
T : **Shì a. Wǒmen juéde qí chē lǚyóu cái yǒu-yìsi.**	That's right. We feel that cycling is the only interesting way to do sightseeing.
R : **Dà rè tiānr, nǐmen zhè shi shàng nǎr qù a?**	Where is it that you are off to in such heat?
T : **Lúgōu Qiáo.**	To the Marco Polo Bridge.

R : **Shàng Lúgōu Qiáo zěnme zǒu zhèi tiáo lù a?**

How come you're on this road if you're going to that bridge?

T : **Wǒmen zǒucuò la?! Āiyā! Nà zěnme bàn na?**

Have we gone wrong then? Oh dear! So, what do we do about it?

R : **Bú yàojǐn. Nǐmen xiān wǎng huí zǒu, dào dì-èr ge shízìlùkǒur zài wǎng zuǒ guǎi, shùnzhe dà lù yìzhí xiàqu jiù dào le.**

Nothing to worry about. First go back the way you came, then turn left at the second crossroads, keep on down the main road and you'll be there.

T : **Lúgōu Qiáo zài něi ge fāngxiàng a?**

Which direction is the bridge in?

R : **Zài xībianr.** [points] **Nǐmen wǎng zuǒ guǎi jiù shi wǎng xī guǎi. Hǎo le, xiūhǎo le. Qíshang shìshi.**

West ... Turn left and that's turning west. OK, it's mended. Get on and try it.

T : **Duōxiè nín la, lǎo shīfu!**

Many thanks, chief!

Exercise 112

Translate into Chinese:

1. A: Excuse me, is there a post office near here?
   B: Yes, there's one just in Xinhua Road.

2. A: How much does it cost to send an air mail postcard to Europe?
   B: International air mail postcards all cost ¥4.50.

3. A: Excuse me, where is the nearest bank?
   B: Turn right at the traffic lights. It's at the second crossroads.

4. A: What's wrong with your telephone?
   B: I don't know why but now you can only phone in, we can't dial out.

5. A: Is the fax machine out of order?
   B: Yes, it's been out of order for two days.

6. A: Which road shall we take?
   B: Better take the main road, the minor roads are difficult at night.

Chapter 16

TIME IS MONEY

Way back in Chapter Ten you first met the idea of a 'result verb', a two-parter where the first half initiates an action and the second shows the result. Probably the clearest example to bear in mind is **tīngjian**, because it so neatly breaks down in the same way as English — **tīng** 'to listen' (= to attempt to hear) and **jiàn** 'to perceive' — so **tīngjian** is 'to listen and perceive', and means 'to succeed in hearing', 'to hear'. In this chapter you will learn how to manipulate these result verbs in a simple way to show 'can' and 'cannot' meanings. All of them operate in the same way, so once you learn the pattern you can apply it to all, and that's real value for effort.

And after this chapter you will be able to translate "Can you walk a little faster? said the whiting to the snail" — well, you could if you knew the words for 'whiting' and 'snail'…. How's that for progress?

(237) 16.1 *More on 'dōu'*

a) In answer to the question **Tā yǒu shénme?** 'What has he got?' you might well hear the emphatic **Tā shénme dōu yǒu.** 'He's got everything.' (lit: 'He whatever all has got'). The negative answer in the same vein would be **Tā shénme dōu méi yǒu.** 'He hasn't got anything'. Similarly:

A: **Shéi xǐhuan chī Sìchuān cài?**	Who likes Sichuan food?
B: **Shéi dōu xǐhuan.** *or*	Everyone likes it.
Shéi dōu bù xǐhuan.	No-one likes it.

Any of the question words you have learned can be used in this 'all-inclusive' way. In the negative form you have the choice of using either **dōu** or **yě**.

b) In colloquial usage **dōu** can mean 'already':

Dōu shí'èr diǎn le,	Already midnight and
tā hái méi shuì jiào.	he's not asleep yet.

See if you can spot another example in Conversation 16A.

Exercise 113

Answer the following questions in the way indicated:

1. **Nǐ xiǎng mǎi něi ge?**	(all of them)
2. **Nǎr yǒu Zhōngguó fànguǎnr?**	(everywhere)
3. **Nǐ shénme shíhou yǒu gōngfu?**	(anytime)
4. **Zuótiān wǎnshang nǐ qu kàn shéi le?**	(no one)

(238) 16.2 *Per unit*

There are two ways in which you can ask 'How much for each one?':

Duōshao qián yí ge? or **Yí ge duōshao qián?**   How much for one?

The first of these is probably more commonly used:

Píjiǔ duōshao qián yì píng?   How much is beer a bottle?

16.3 *Going metric*

China has adopted the metric (**gōng**) system, but long before she did so she had met with metric measures and had devised a way of translating them. Wherever possible old Chinese 'market' terms were retained with the word **gōng** prefixed:

jīn a catty (0.5 kg)	>>	**gōngjīn** a kilogram
lǐ a Chinese mile (0.5 km)	>>	**gōnglǐ** a kilometre

16.4 *Import-export*

Jìnkǒu (literally: enter mouth) means 'import', and **chūkǒu** (literally: exit mouth) means 'export':

Tā zài jìn-chūkǒu gōngsī gōngzuò.   She works for an import-export company.

16.5 *Stressing a statement*

The little word **kě** is used to give emphasis, just as in English we use 'really', 'certainly', 'in no way':

Jīntiān kě zhēn lěng.	It's really cold today.
Wǒ kě méi yǒu qián.	There's no way I've got any money.

(239) *16.6 'Duìbuqǐ'*

We met **duìbuqǐ** right at the beginning of the book. It means 'sorry', 'pardon me', 'excuse me', and it is formed of three parts:

duì	to face, to match up with
bù	not
qǐ	to rise up

Literally, then, **duìbuqǐ** means 'face not rise up', and it does not stretch the imagination too far to see that that means 'face you but cannot rise up', that is (to put it dramatically) 'I am prostrate before you (with shame)'. The positive form of this negative phrase is **duìdeqǐ** ('face you can rise up') and it means 'to not let someone down', 'to treat someone fairly', 'to be worthy'. There are many other examples where two verbs have **de** or **bu** sandwiched between them, and sometimes they have meanings which are not readily self-apparent, but all of them have the 'can/cannot' idea in common:

mǎideqǐ	to be able to afford (to buy)
mǎibuqǐ	to be unable to afford (to buy)
chīdeqǐ	to be able to afford to eat
chībuqǐ	to be unable to afford to eat

Exercise 114
Fill in the blanks:

1. **Tā méi yǒu qián, mǎi ___ qǐ zhème guì de dōngxi.**
2. **Tā de qián bǐ shéi dōu duō, dāngrán zhù ___ qǐ dà fángzi.**
3. **Zhèi ge dìfang tài chǎo le, wǒ shénme dōu tīng ___ jiàn.**
4. **Nǐ hē ___ qǐ yì bǎi kuài yì bēi de kāfēi ma?**

(240) *16.7 The four seasons*

chūntiān	spring
xiàtiān	summer
qiūtiān	autumn
dōngtiān	winter

16.8   Guaranteed

Bāo has the meaning 'guaranteed' 'assured' 'absolutely certain to':

> **Chīle wǒ de yào, sān tiān bāo hǎo.**   When you've taken my medicine
> you're guaranteed to be well in
> three days.

16.9   Twice, thrice, fourfold

The word **bèi** is used to indicate multiples:

> **Tā bǐ nǐ kuài sān bèi.**   He's three times faster than you are.
> **Zhōngguó bǐ Rìběn dà èrshiwǔ bèi.**   China is 25 times bigger than Japan.

Note that by a quirk of language **yí bèi** and **liǎng bèi** usually mean the same thing:

> **duō yí bèi** = **duō liǎng bèi** = 'twice as many'

16.10   Another particle 'Ma!'

Ma! is used at the end of a statement to point out rather patronisingly that something is very obvious. It doesn't sound quite like the regular toneless question particle **ma**: the voice is pitched a little higher for the whole of the part ending with **ma!**, and the **ma!** itself tends to be rather drawn out and stressed. Listen carefully to the recording of the conversation and you will hear this.

> **Tā shi Yīngguó Huáqiáo ma**!   She's a British Overseas Chinese: of course
> **Yīngyǔ dāngrán hǎo le.**   her English is good: (surely you know that?)

 New words

bù tóng	not the same, different
jìjié	season
píngguǒ	apple
shuǐguǒ	fruit
tiāo	to choose, pick
xiāngjiāo	banana
xīguā	water melon
Xīnjiāng	Xinjiang (Autonomous Region)
zhǎng	to rise (of prices or rivers)

(242) *CONVERSATION 16A*

A local customer buys fruit in the market.

S : **Xiānsheng, mǎi diǎnr shuǐguǒ ba; wǒmen zhèr shénme dōu yǒu.**

Buy some fruit, sir; we've got all kinds here.

C : **Píngguǒ zěnme mài?**

How much are the apples?

S : **Hóng de sì kuài wǔ yì jīn, huáng de sān kuài liù.**

The red ones are ¥4.50 a catty, and the yellow ones ¥3.60.

C : **Xiāngjiāo ne?**

And the bananas?

S : **Zhèi zhǒng dà de sān kuài èr, shi jìnkǒu de. Nín yào duōshao?**

This big kind are ¥3.20, they're imported. How many do you want?

C : **Wǒ kě chībuqǐ jìnkǒu shuǐguǒ. Nèi zhǒng xiǎo de ne?**

There's no way I can afford to eat imported fruit. How much are the small kind?

S : **Xiǎo de piányi, yì jīn liǎng kuài liù, liǎng jīn wǔ kuài.**

The small ones are cheap, ¥2.60 a catty, and ¥5 for two catties.

C : **Gěi wǒ lái liǎng jīn ba.**

Let me have two catties.

S : **Hǎo lei. Nín zài tiāo ge xīgua ba.**

Certainly. And how about choosing a melon as well?

C : **Qiūtiān dōu kuài guòqu le, zěnme hái yǒu xīgua a?**

Autumn is nearly over, how come there are still water melons?

S : **Zhè shi Xīnjiāng lái de, bāo tián, bù tián bú yào qián!**

These are from Xinjiang, guaranteed sweet, and if they aren't I won't want your money.

C : **Duōshao qián yì jīn a?**

How much a catty?

S : **Piányi, liǎng kuài wǔ.**

Very cheap, ¥2.50.

C : **Shénme? Liǎng kuài wǔ? Xiàtiān cái mài jiǔ máo, zěnme sān ge yuè zhǎngle sān bèi?**

What? ¥2.50? In summer they only cost 90 cents, how can they have gone up threefold in three months?

S : **Jìjié bù tóng le ma! Dàole chūntiān jiù gèng guì le. Nín tiāo něi ge?**

But it's a different season, don't you see? Come the spring they'll be even more expensive. Which one do you choose?

C : **Jīntiān bú yào le, wǒ háishi děngdào míngnián xiàtiān zài chī ba.**

I don't want one today now, I'd better wait till next summer and have some then.

(243) 16.11 Discounts

Dǎ zhékòu means 'to give a discount', but it operates the other way round from English. So **jiǔ-zhé** ('nine **zhé**') is a 10% discount, i.e. you pay 9/10ths, and **qī-wǔ-zhé** is a 25% discount:

> **Dōngtiān lǚxíng de rén shǎo le, zuò fēijī, zhù fàndiàn dōu kěyǐ dǎ zhékòu.**
>
> Fewer people travel in winter, you can get discounts on flights and hotels.

> **Yí jiàn qípáo jiǔ bǎi bā, tài guì le! Dǎ ge bā-zhé ba?**
>
> ¥980 for a cheongsam is much too expensive. How about 20% discount?

Sale

Bargaining died out in China after the 1949 Communist Revolution, and the rather quaint sign **bú èr jià** 'only one price' [literally: not two prices] appeared. Now it is possible to bargain again in some markets and small shops, and even large stores will advertise a 'Sale' **dà jiǎn jià** [literally: great reductions in price] from time to time.

16.12 Scheduled services

In **7.11** you met **bān** 'a shift', 'work period'. The same word is used for other kinds of scheduled service, so **hángbān** is 'an airline flight', and **zhèi bān chē** is 'this train' or 'this bus'. Note that when **bān** is used you don't think of the *physical* bus, aircraft or train, you mean the service provided by it. English distinguishes these two concepts too: consider the difference between 'this aircraft' and 'this flight'. **Xià bān fēijī** is 'the next flight', not the next airliner in a row parked on the apron.

16.13 Difficult

Nán or **kùnnan** mean 'difficult'. **Kùnnan** can also be used as a noun 'difficulty':

> **Qǐng rén bāngmáng hěn (kùn)nán.** — It's very hard to get someone to help.

> **Wǒmen zuì dà de kùnnan jiù shi rén tài duō.** — Our greatest difficulty is that there are too many people.

Note that only **nán** (not **kùnnan**) can be used as an adverb:

> **Hànyǔ bù nán xué.** — Chinese isn't hard to learn.

Exercise 115   Revision
  Give the opposites of the following:

1. **hǎo**	2. **duō**	3. **hēi**
4. **dà**	5. **lěng**	6. **pàng**
7. **zǎo**	8. **kuài**	9. **duì**
10. **yuǎn**	11. **piányi**	12. **róngyi**
13. **nuǎnhuo**	14. **qiántou**	15. **zuǒbian**

16.14   Can-cannot verbs

Result verbs can be split by **bu** or **de** just like **duìbuqǐ/duìdeqǐ** in **16.6**, and again they result in 'unable to/able to' meanings. So **mǎidào** 'to succeed in buying' can be split into **mǎidedào** 'can be bought' and **mǎibudào** 'cannot be bought'. Similarly:

kàndejiàn/kànbujiàn	able to/unable to see
zuòdewán/zuòbuwán	able to/unable to finish doing
bàndechéng/bànbuchéng	able to/unable to succeed in doing (**chéng** = to succeed, to complete)
Zài Lúndūn mǎidedào Zhōngguó píjiǔ ma?	Can Chinese beer be bought in London?
Zhèi jiàn shì sān tiān zuòbuwán.	This thing could not be finished in three days.
Fēijī zài nǎr? Tài yuǎn le, wǒ kànbujiàn.	Where's the plane? It's too far away, I can't see it.

Here are paired sentences which show up some interesting nuances of meaning:

'You can buy it in China.'

(1) **Nǐ kěyǐ zài Zhōngguó mǎi.**

This might be used in a context such as 'You can buy it in China and save yourself the trouble of buying it elsewhere.'

(2) **Nǐ zài Zhōngguó mǎidedào.**

This means 'You can buy it in China, it is available there.'

'He says that I can't see it.'

(1) **Tā shuō wǒ bù néng kàn.**

This means that I am not allowed to see it.

(2) **Tā shuō wǒ kànbujiàn.**

This means that I am unable to see it or incapable of seeing it.

16.15   In time or not in time

Another common can-cannot verb with **de/bu** is **láidejí/láibují**. **Láidejí** means 'to make it in time' 'to be able to catch it':

Tāmen wǔ diǎn bàn xià bān,
  nǐ xiànzài qù hái láidejí.

They come off duty at 5.30,
  if you go now you will catch them.

Huǒchē yǐjing kāi le, láibují le.

The train has already started,
  you won't catch it.

Exercise 116

Fill in the blanks with result verbs:

1. **Zhème duō shì, wǒ jīntiān zuò ____ ____.**
2. **Wǒmen zhǐ yǒu èrshi kuài qián, chī ____ ____ zhème guì de yú.**
3. **Tā bú dài yǎnjìngr, shénme dōu kàn ____ ____.**
4. **Zhǐ yǒu shíwǔ fēn zhōng le, wǒmen zuò chē qù ba, zǒu lù lái ____ ____ le.**
5. **Qù Xīnjiāng de rén bù duō, fēijīpiào yídìng mǎi ____ ____.**

16.16   Abbreviated names

In **14.6** we saw how ideas could be expressed in a shorter form to save time and breath, and when it comes to proper names Chinese has lots of abbreviations that are widely used, much as in English we might say 'the UN' instead of 'the United Nations', or 'the pub' instead of 'the public house'. You don't need to be either from Beijing or an academic to know that **Běi Dà** stands for **Běijīng Dàxué** 'Peking University', it is so well known. In Conversation 16B the clerk in the ticket office refers casually to **Nán Háng**, the abbreviation for **Nánfāng Hángkōng Gōngsī** ('Southern Aviation Company', Southern Airlines), and probably most people would understand it perfectly well, just as in a travel context 'BA' would be understood to mean 'British Airways'. No prizes for guessing which airline is meant by **Yīng Háng**, incidentally, but in general you should not try to make abbreviations up for yourself — the rules of the game are tricky.

16.17 Don't worry

Fàngxīn literally means 'let your heart relax'. It will translate as 'Don't worry' 'rest assured' 'be at ease' and so on:

Tā yígerén chū guó lǚxíng, tā mǔqin hěn bú fàngxīn.	She went travelling abroad on her own; her mother was very worried.
Nǐ fàngxīn ba, wǒmen yídìng láidejí.	Don't worry, we'll make it in time.

16.18 'Hǎo le': then it'll be alright

Jīntiān nǐ zhème máng, wǒ qù hǎo le.	You're so busy today, I'll go (and that'll do it).
Yàoshi nǐ bú fàngxīn, gěi tā dǎ ge diànhuà hǎo le.	If you're worried, phone him up and that'll sort it out.

(246) *New words*

hétong	contract
mǎn	full
míxìn	superstition
qiān	to sign
qǐfēi	to take off (of aircraft)
suǒyǒu de	all that there are, all
wèizi	seat, place
yùnqi	luck, fate

(247) *CONVERSATION 16B*

A Western tourist buys an air ticket.

T :	**Xiáojie, wǒ xiǎng mǎi fēijīpiào.**	Miss, I'd like to buy an air ticket.
C :	**Nín yào qù nǎr? Něi tiān zǒu a?**	Where would you like to go? Which day are you travelling?
T :	**Hā'ěrbīn, shí'èr hào, xià xīngqīsì.**	Harbin, the 12th, next Thursday.
C :	**Nín xiǎng zuò něi jiā gōngsī de fēijī?**	Which company's aircraft do you want to go by?

T : **Něi jiā dōu xíng, zuì hǎo néng dǎ zhékòu.**

Any one will do, but best if there is a discount.

C : **Hā'ěrbīn yǒu jiāoyìhuì, kǒngpà hěn kùnnan.** *[She checks]* **Bù xíng, shí'èr hào suǒyǒu de hángbān quán mǎn le.**

There's a trade fair on in Harbin, I'm afraid it'll be difficult... It's no good, all flights are full on the 12th.

T : **Āiyā, zhè zěnme bàn a? Piào mǎibudào, wǒ de hétong jiù qiānbuchéng le.**

Oh dear, what's to be done? If I can't get a ticket, my contract can't be signed.

C : **Nín shénme shíhou qiān hétong a?**

When are you to sign the contract?

T : **Shísān hào xiàwǔ.**

On the afternoon of the 13th.

C : **Nà nín shísān hào shàngwǔ zǒu yě láidejí a. Wǒ kànkan... éi, nín yùnqi zhēn hǎo, shísān hào Nán Háng de 6202 hángbān hái yǒu wèizi.**

Well then, if you travel on the morning of the 13th you'll still be in time. Let me see... heh, your luck's good, there are still seats on Southern Airlines flight 6202 on the 13th.

T : **Shì ma? Jǐ diǎn néng dào Hā'ěrbīn?**

Really? What time can I get to Harbin?

C : **Shàngwǔ shí diǎn wǔshí qǐfēi, zhōngwǔ shí'èr diǎn bàn dào.**

Take-off at 10.50 a.m., arrival 12.30 midday.

T : **Kěshi... shísān hào shi ge xīngqīwǔ a! Wǒ pà ...**

But... the 13th is a Friday. I'm afraid...

C : **Zhōngguó méi zhèi zhǒng míxìn, nín fàngxīn hǎo le.**

There's no such superstition in China, you shouldn't worry about it.

(248) *16.19   A bit more ...*

'Do it a bit quicker', 'Hit it a bit harder' and so on are expressed in Chinese using the pattern <u>Verb-adjective-(**yì**)**diǎnr**</u>:

Wǒ de Hànyǔ bù xíng, qǐng nín shuōmàn (yì)diǎnr.

My Chinese is no good, please speak a bit slower.

Xià yǔ le, wǒmen zǒukuài (yì)diǎnr ba!

It's raining, let's walk a bit faster!

Tài xiǎo le, qǐng nǐ zuòdà (yì)diǎnr kěyǐ ma?

It's too small, can you make it a bit bigger?

Exercise 117

Use the <u>*verb-adj-*(**yì**) **diǎnr**</u> *pattern:*

What would you say to someone if:

1. he is speaking too fast?
2. she is selling too expensively?
3. he is always late?
4. she doesn't do her work well?

(249) *16.20   From now to then*

The same word **lí** ('separated from') which we met in **14.4** in connection with distances can also be used for time:

Xiànzài lí qǐfēi shíjiān hái yǒu bàn xiǎoshí.	There is still half an hour to take-off time.
Lí kāi huì zhǐ yǒu yí ge xīngqī le.	There's only one week until the meeting takes place.

16.21   Bound to be

Kěndìng can mean 'bound to be', 'sure to', but it is also a verb meaning 'be certain about it', 'to affirm':

Tā shì bu shi zài dàshǐguǎn gōngzuò, wǒ bù néng kěndìng.	I can't be positive whether she works at the embassy or not.
Tā zhèi jiàn xíngli kěndìng méi yǒu èrshi gōngjīn.	I'm sure that this piece of luggage of his is less than 20 kilos.

(250) *16.22   Two more can-cannots*

Kāi, as you know, basically means 'to open', but as a 'success word' it conveys the idea of 'detachment' or 'separation':

Zhèi píng píjiǔ kāibukāi.	This bottle of beer can't be opened.
Wǒ zhèngzài kāi huì zǒubukāi, wǎnshang qù kàn nǐ, xíng ma?	I'm in a meeting and can't leave, is it alright if I go to see you this evening?
Yìbǎi kuài yì zhāng de Rénmínbì, wǒ zhǎobukāi.	A ¥100 note … I can't give change for that.

Another success word is **liǎo***, generally meaning 'to finish', 'to exhaust', 'to complete'. In the next conversation the taxi-driver uses **kāibuliǎo** for 'to really drive', 'to drive properly'. And if you like a good dose of sentimentality you might like to listen to a famous pop-song of the 1960s which has achieved classical status:

> **Wàngbuliǎo!**   Unforgettable!

Exercise 118
Translate into English:

1. **Lóushang shuō huà, lóuxia tīngdejiàn ma?**
2. **Zài Měiguó mǎidedào Zhōngwén shū ma?**
3. **Tā yígerén chībuliǎo yí ge dà xīgua.**
4. **Nǐ fàngxīn, zhèi jiàn shì wǒ yídìng wàngbuliǎo.**

16.23 Forget it!

Suàn means 'to calculate', but the colloquial expression **suànle** or **suànle ba** has the special meanings of 'let it be!' 'let it pass!' 'that'll do!' 'forget it!':

Tiānqi zhème huài, suàn le, bié qù Chángchéng le.	The weather's so bad, let's forget it, we won't go to the Great Wall after all.
Suàn le ba, bié gēn tā shuō le, shuōle yě méi yòng.	Give up, don't talk to her any more; it wouldn't be any good if you did.

 New words

dòng	to move
zǒubudòng	unable to get moving
duàn	(measure) section
gǎn	to catch, catch up with
gǎnbushàng	unable to catch up
gāofēng	high peak, apex
gāofēng shíjiān	peak time
shú or **shóu**	familiar with, well acquainted
tǎoyàn	annoying, tiresome, irritating
wēixiǎn	danger, dangerous
zhuàngshang	to knock into, crash into

(252) *CONVERSATION 16C*

A taxi passenger rushing for the train.

P : **Shīfu, wǒ yào gǎn qī diǎn sìshiwǔ de huǒchē, néng bu néng kāikuài diǎnr?**

Driver, I want to catch the 7.45 train, can you drive a bit faster?

D : **Nín kànkan, chē zhème duō, zǒubudòng a!**

Just look, there's so much traffic, we can't move!

P : **Lí kāi chē zhǐ yǒu èrshi fēn zhōng le, yàoshi gǎnbushàng zhèi bān chē...**

It's only 20 minutes to departure, and if I don't catch this one...

D : **Nín bié zháojí, dà lù zǒubudòng, wǒmen huàn xiǎo lù.**

Don't worry, since the main road is clogged we'll change onto the minor roads.

P : **Gāofēng shíjiān xiǎo lù yě zhème jǐ ... Xiǎoxīn! Bié zhuàngshang rén!**

At peak hour the minor roads are just as crowded ... Watch out! Don't run into anyone!

D : **Méi shìr. Zhè xiē zìxíngchē zhēn tǎoyàn!**

No problem. These bicycles are a real nuisance!

P : **Shīfu, tài wēixiǎn le, háishi qǐng nǐ kāimàn diǎnr ba!**

It's too dangerous, driver, you'd better go slower!

D : **Méi wèntí, guòle zhèi duàn jiù hǎo zǒu le.**

No problem, after this section the going will be easy.

P : **Nǐ lù zhēn shú a.**

You really know your roads!

D : **Lù bù shú kāibuliǎo chūzū. Hǎo le, chēzhàn dào le, nín hái yǒu bā fēn zhōng, kěndìng láidejí.**

If you don't know the roads you can't drive a cab properly. We're alright, we've got to the station and you've still got eight minutes. You're sure to be in time.

P : **Xièxie nǐ a, shīfu.** *[Pays fare]* **zhè shi yìbǎi.**

Thank you, driver ... Here's a hundred.

D : **Āiyā, yìbǎi? Wǒ zhǎobukāi a ....**

Oh dear, a hundred. I can't change it ....

P : *[Looks at watch]* **Suàn le, búbì zhǎo le. Zàijiàn.**

Forget it, no need to give change. Goodbye.

Exercise 119

Translate into Chinese:

1. A: How are the bananas sold?
   B: ¥2.60 a catty, two catties for ¥5.

2. A: Are all fruit getting more expensive?
   B: Yes, apples now cost ¥3.20 a catty: three times more than they were last year.

3. A: I'm afraid that you won't get there in time if you take the train.
   B: It can't be helped: I can't afford an air ticket.

4. A: What can we do if we miss the 6.45 train?
   B: Don't worry, there is another one at 6.55.

5. A: The plane is about to take off; please hurry up.
   B: What did you say? Could you speak more slowly?

6. A: Where are you going this summer?
   B: I shall go wherever is cheap.

Chapter 17

WHAT'S IT LIKE?

Adjectives can be quite tricky — remember how in French some go before and some go behind their nouns? Chinese adjectives (**hǎo, dà, piàoliang**) and even Chinese adjectival phrases and clauses ('with the shiny nose', 'whom I love', 'that I bought yesterday') all come before the noun, so there can be no confusion there. But (there's usually a 'but', isn't there?) when it comes to qualifying the adjectives themselves, the situation is slightly more complicated. You are now very used to **hěn** 'very' and **zhēn** 'truly' popping up before the adjective, just where you'd expect them, and it must have been a little surprising to find in Chapter Seven that **jíle** 'exceedingly' comes after and not before the adjective it qualifies. Here you are going to meet another way of qualifying adjectives sneakily from behind, and it involves that little marker **de** again. Little it may be, but it packs a powerful punch, and you'll find this new usage gives you lots of freedom of expression. And it is worth remembering that an adjective cannot be qualified from front and back at the same time, that would be unfair and against the rules.

Not be outdone, another little word **bǎ** 'to grasp' puts in an appearance. Amongst other things, it lets you change word orders in a sentence in order to stress what it is that is being done to the object, and that's quite useful too.

And in case these are too painful, we take you through another consultation with the doctor.

17.1 *Colour shades*

Chinese uses the words **shēn** (deep) and **qiǎn** (shallow) for 'dark' and 'light' of certain colours:

shēn lán	dark blue
qiǎn lǜ	light green

17.2 *Brands and trademarks*

Páir [or **páizi**] means 'a label', 'a tag', 'a plate', but is also commonly used for a brand or trademark:

xíngli páir   luggage tag/label
Nín yào shénme páir de   What mobile phone brand do
  shǒujī?   you want?

17.3   The 'bǎ' construction

In making sentences we have mostly used the <u>Subject + Verb + Object (S-V-O)</u>
pattern or the <u>Topic + Comment</u> pattern (**8.15**), because these are the basic
ones for Chinese. But sometimes it is necessary to put the Object in front of the
Verb rather than after it, in order to stress what it is that is done to the Object.
To do this, **bǎ**, a word which means 'to grasp' 'to take', is used. Here are some
examples:

Qǐng nǐ bǎ zhèi zhāng piào gěi   Please give this ticket to Mr Wang.
  <u>Wáng xiānsheng</u>.

Tā bǎ dōngxi bān<u>zǒu le</u>.   He moved the things elsewhere.

Qǐng nǐ bǎ chē kāi<u>dào wǒ jiā lai</u>.   Please drive the car over here to my
     house.

Bié bǎ xíngli fàng<u>zài nàr</u>.   Don't put the luggage there.

All these examples show three things which **bǎ** sentences have in common:

1. If the Object had not been moved it would have competed with other things
    (<u>the underlined phrases</u>) for the position after the Verb, and the desired
    stress would have been lost in the clutter.

2. The Object is always a definite one ('the' rather than 'a').

3. The Verb is never left hanging at the end of the sentence; there is always a
    lai, a **qu**, a **le**, a result word like -**wán** or -**hǎo**, or whatever to follow it.

Exercise 120
Translate into English:

1. **Tā yǐjing bǎ qián gěi wǒ le.**
2. **Wǒ kěyǐ bǎ xíngli fàngzài zhèr ma?**
3. **Shéi bǎ wǒ de zhàoxiàngjī názǒu le?**
4. **Qǐng nǐ bǎ zhèi ge nádào lóushang qu.**

(254) ## 17.4 *Have a go*

In Conversation 15A we slipped in **chēngcheng kàn**, hoping that you would feel comfortable with the translation 'I'll weigh it and see.' Now in 17A you meet **cháchá kàn** 'I'll check it out and see', and there are others too:

Wènwen kàn.	Let's ask and see.
Bǐbi kàn.	We'll compare them and see.

Similarly, **shì** 'to try' gives rise to **shìshi kàn** 'try it and see'.

> ### Exercise 121
> *Translate into English:*
>
> 1. **Nǐ shìshi kàn: dà hàor zěnmeyàng?**
> 2. **Dàjiā xiǎngxiang kàn: něi ge fázi hǎo?**
> 3. **Wǒ wàngle fàngzài nǎr le. Wǒ qù zhǎozhao kàn.**
> 4. **Huǒchē shénme shíhou dào, nǐ qù wènwen kàn.**

(255) *New words*

Guó Háng	Air China. It is an abbreviation of **Zhōngguó Guójì Hángkōng Gōngsī** [literally: 'China International Airways Company']
hòu	thick (in dimension)
huī	grey
jiàngluò	to land (of an aircraft)
jìde	to remember
jìxù	to continue, go on
xiāngzi	suitcase, box, trunk
yīfu	clothes

(256) ## CONVERSATION 17A

An airline passenger asks a ground stewardess about his missing luggage.

P :	**Xiáojie, máfan nǐ tì wǒ chá yíxiàr xíngli hǎo ma?**	Could I trouble you to check for my luggage for me, Miss?
S :	**Nín zuò de shi něi ge hángbān?**	Which flight were you on?
P :	**CA108, cóng Xiānggǎng lái de.**	CA108 from Hong Kong.

S :	**Guó Háng 108 yǐjing jiàngluò yí ge bàn xiǎoshí le, xíngli zǎojiù chūlai le.**	It's already an hour and a half since Air China flight 108 landed, and the luggage came out ages ago.
P :	**Kěshi méi yǒu wǒ de xiāngzi.**	But my case wasn't there.
S :	**Nín de xiāngzi shi shénme yánsè de?**	What colour is your case?
P :	**Shēn huīsè de, yǒu lúnzi.**	It's dark grey, with wheels.
S :	**Duō dà?**	How big is it?
P :	**Gēn nèi biānr nèi ge hóng xiāngzi yíyàng dà.**	The same size as that red case over there.
S :	**Shénme páir de?**	What make?
P :	**Wǒ bú jìde le, hǎoxiàng shi Fǎguó zuò de.**	I don't remember, but I've an idea that it was French made.
S :	**Nín bǎ xíngli páir gěi wǒ, wǒ qù gěi nín cháchá kàn.** *[Five minutes later]* **Duìbuqǐ, méi yǒu.**	Give me your luggage ticket and I'll go and check for you … I'm sorry, it's not there.
P :	**Āiyā, nà zěnme bàn? Tiānqi zhème lěng, wǒ de hòu yīfu dōu zài xiāngzi li ne.**	Oh dear, what can I do? It's so cold, and my thick clothes are all in the case.
S :	**Bié zháojí, nín xiān tián zhāng biǎo, liúxia dìzhǐ, diànhuà, wǒmen zài jìxù gěi nín zhǎo. Zhǎodàole, mǎshang gěi nín sòngqu.**	Don't worry. First fill in a form and leave your address and telephone number, then we'll go on looking for it for you. When we've found it, we'll send it to you at once.

17.5 'yòu … yòu…'

You met 'bad penny **yòu**' in **9.20**, meaning 'furthermore' 'yet again'. It is also used like 'both …and…' to tie together two features which something has in common:

Tā de xīn qìchē yòu piàoliang yòu shūfu.	His new car is both handsome and comfortable.

17.6 Service failure

The verb **tíng** means 'to stop'. It appears in two common expressions **tíng diàn** 'power cut' and **tíng shuǐ** 'water shut-off':

> **Sān ge yuè méi xià yǔ le. Zuìjìn**
> **cháng tíng shuǐ, yě cháng tíng**
> **diàn.**

> It hasn't rained for three months.
> Recently there have been frequent
> water stoppages, and power cuts too.

(258) 17.7 *To such an extent that*

We have met several ways of qualifying adjectives:

> **Xīgua <u>hěn</u> guì.**   Water melons are very expensive.
>
> **Xīgua <u>zhēn</u> guì.**   Water melons are really expensive.
>
> **Xīgua guì <u>jíle</u>.**   Water melons are extremely expensive.

More complicated qualifying phrases can be easily dealt with by using the
marker **de**, which gives the sense of 'in such a way that' or 'to such an extent
that'. (You met it used in the same way with action verbs in **12.4**):

> **Xīgua guì de méi rén**
> **mǎideqǐ.**

> Water melons are so expensive that no one
> can afford to buy them. [Water melons
> are expensive to such an extent that no
> one can afford to buy them]

> **Tiānqi lěng de shéi dōu**
> **bù xiǎng chūqu.**

> The weather is so cold that no one wants to
> go out.

Exercise 122

Fuse two together, as in the example:

A **Tiānqi tài rè le.** + B **Wǒ bù xiǎng chī fàn.**

Tiānqi rè de wǒ bù xiǎng chī fàn.

1. A **Tā tài lèi le.**   B **Tā zǒubudòng le.**

2. A **Yǔ tài dà le.**   B **Wǒmen chūbuqù le.**

3. A **Zhōngguó cài tài hǎo chī le.**   B **Shéi dōu xiǎng chī.**

4. A **Tā de xiāngzi tài dà le.**   B **Shí ge rén dōu bānbudòng.**

---

(259) 17.8 *Don't bring that up again!*

Tí means 'to lift up', and **Bié tí le**! is just like the English 'Don't bring that up
again!' 'Don't even mention it!':

> **Zuótiān chī de hǎo ba?**   You ate well yesterday, I suppose?

Bié tí le, nàr de cài yòu guì yòu nán chī.	Don't talk about it, the food there was both expensive and not good.
A: **Nǐ de Hànyǔ hěn liúlì le ba?**	Your Chinese must have become very fluent surely?
B: **Bié tí le, wǒ sān ge yuè méi liànxí le.**	Don't even mention it, it's been three months since I practised it.

17.9 *It would be better if I didn't ...*

The pattern **bu** + verb + **hái hǎo, yi** + verb is used to give the meaning 'It would be better if I didn't ..., because no sooner do I than ...':

Zhèi ge wèntí bù xiǎng hái hǎo, yì xiǎng wǒ jiù zháojí.	It would be better not to think about this problem, because as soon as I do I get anxious.
Dàifu gěi wǒ de yào bù chī hái hǎo, yì chī dùzi gèng téng le.	It would have been better if I hadn't taken the medicine the doctor gave me, because no sooner had I taken it than my stomach ached even worse.

17.10 *'Nòng'*

The basic meaning of **nòng** is 'to play around with', but it has an all purpose use something like the verbs 'to make', 'to get', and 'to do' have in English:

Shéi bǎ wǒ de zìxíngchē nònghuài le?	Who's damaged my bike?
Tā méi bǎ zhèi jiàn shì nòng qīngchu.	He didn't get this clear.

17.11 *Free of charge*

Miǎnfèi means 'gratis' 'free of charge':

A: **Zài zhèr kàn yí cì dàifu duōshao qián?**	How much does it cost here for a consultation with the doctor?
B: **Wánquán miǎnfèi.**	It's absolutely free.

(260) 17.12 *Washing*

The verb to wash is **xǐ**, that's how what is **zāng** 'dirty' is made **gānjing** 'clean':

xǐ yī(fu)   to wash clothes

xǐyījī	washing machine
gānxǐ	dry cleaning
shuǐxǐ	laundry [water wash]

Xǐshǒu is 'to wash your hands' and is also used just as in English as a polite way of saying 'to go to the toilet'. In restaurants and public buildings the sign for the toilet usually calls it the **xǐshǒujiān** 'washing hands room'. **Xǐtóu** means 'to wash your hair' [literally: wash head], and 'to have a bath' is **xǐzǎo**.

Exercise 123
Fill in the blanks with verbs:

1. **Qù Zhōngguó lǚxíng děi ___ shénme shǒuxù?**
2. **Dǎ diànhuà bǐjiào guì, gěi tā ___ ge duǎnxìn ba.**
3. **Zhè bú shi miǎnfèi cèsuǒ, qǐng nǐ xiān ___ fèi.**
4. **Zài dà gōngsī mǎi dōngxi dōu kěyǐ ___ kǎ.**
5. **Duìbuqǐ, láiwǎn le, wǒ de chē ___ máobìng le.**

17.13 Hospitality

The word for 'a reception' is **zhāodàihuì**. **Zhāodài** means 'to serve', 'to entertain':

Chī, zhù búbì gěi qián, jiāoyìhuì miǎnfèi zhāodài.	There is no need to pay for food or accommodation, the Trade Fair provides it all free of charge.

17.14 To set out from home

Chūmén literally means 'to go out of the door', and it is not hard to see that it has an extended meaning of 'to set out from home':

Tā měi tiān zǎochen qī diǎn bàn chūmén.	He leaves home at 7.30 every morning.

17.15 More can-cannot with 'liǎo'

Liǎo*, as we saw in **16.22**, means 'to finish', 'to dispose of'. Here are a couple more verbs which have can-cannot partnerships with it:

<u>chūdeliǎo/chūbuliǎo</u>:

> **Hěn duō shì hái méi zuòwán,**   There's a lot of things I haven't
> **qī diǎn zhōng chūbuliǎo mén.**   finished doing, I cannot leave at
>   7 o'clock.

<u>zuòdeliǎo / zuòbuliǎo</u>:

> **Zhèi jiàn shì yí ge rén**   This thing can't be done by one
> **zuòbuliǎo.**   person.

(261) *17.16 What?!*

Shénme?! of course means 'what?' or 'what kind of?', and it can be used to express disbelief, sarcasm, surprise or disagreement, just as 'what' can be in English ("What £100,000 tax rebate?! Pigs might fly!") :

> **Shénme**?! **Nǐ xiǎng qí zìxíngchē**   What? You intend to cycle to China?!
> **qù Zhōngguó?**
>
> **Zhème hǎo de chá nǐ bù hē,**   Such lovely tea and you don't drink it!
> **hē shénme kāfēi**?!   What do you mean you'll have
>   coffee?
>
> **Yínháng yǐjing xià bān le,**   The bank is shut already, what do you
> **nǐ hái qù huàn shénme qián**?!   mean you're going to change money?

17.17 Another 'dǎ' oddity

We can add another item to the list of versatile things to do with **dǎ** which we gave you in **10.13**. The word for 'a necktie' is **lǐngdài**, and 'to wear a tie' or 'to put on a tie' is **dǎ lǐngdài**.

(262) *New words*

ānjìng	quiet
chuānghu	window
chuī	to blow
dāying	to respond, agree to
fēng	wind, breeze
gōngchǎng	factory
kāishǐ	to begin

tào   (measure for clothes: 'a suit of')

xīzhuāng   a (Western-style) suit

⁽²⁶³⁾ *CONVERSATION 17B*

A hotel guest talks with his Chinese friend.

C : **À, zhè fángjiān zhēn bú cuò, yòu ānjìng yòu liángkuai.**	Ah, this room is not bad at all, it's quiet and cool.
G : **Nǐ zuótiān lái jiù hǎo le.**	You should have seen it yesterday!
C : **Wèishénme?**	Why is that?
G : **Zuótiān zhèi qū tíng diàn, méi yǒu kōngtiáo, rè de wǒ yí yè méi shuìhǎo.**	This district had a power cut yesterday, there was no air-conditioning, and it was so hot that I didn't sleep well all night.
C : **Nǐ kěyǐ bǎ chuānghu dǎkāi ya, lóu zhème gāo, yídìng yǒu fēng.**	You could open the window, this building is so high there'd certainly be a breeze.
G : **Bié tí le, bù kāi chuānghu hái hǎo, yì kāi chuānghu duìmiàn gōngchǎng de hēiyān quán chuījinlai le, bǎ wǒ nèi tào bái xīzhuāng dōu nòngzāng le.**	Don't talk about that, it would have been better not to have opened it, because as soon as I did, all the smoke from the factory opposite blew in and made my white suit filthy.
C : **Nǐ méi zhǎo jīnglǐ ma?**	Didn't you send for the manager?
G : **Zhǎo le, tā dāying miǎnfèi tì wǒ xǐ gānjing.**	I did, and he agreed to have it washed for me free of charge.
C : **Nà hái bú cuò. Ēi, nǐ kuài huàn yīfu ba, dàshǐguǎn de zhāodàihuì qī diǎn kāishǐ.**	That's not so bad. Hey, hurry up and change, the embassy reception starts at 7 o'clock.
G : **Nǐ yígerén qù ba, wǒ de xīzhuāng hái méi xǐhǎo ne, chūbuliǎo mén.**	You go on your own, my suit is still not ready, so I can't go out.
C : **Tiānqi zhème rè, chuān shénme xīzhuāng, dǎ tiáo lǐngdài jiù xíng le. Zǒu, zǒu, zǒu!**	It's so hot, what do you mean a suit? Just put on a tie will do! Come on, let's go!

(264) *17.18   Ailments*

Téng, as you will remember from Chapter Ten, means 'pain', 'to be painful':

tóuténg	headache
yáténg	toothache
dùziténg	stomach ache
hóulóngténg	sore throat
késou	cough

(265) *17.19   Parts of the face*

yǎnjing eyes (not to be confused with **yǎnjìngr** 'glasses')

bízi	nose
ěrduo	ears
zuǐ	mouth

17.20   Getting through

Tōng means 'to get through', 'to communicate', 'to penetrate':

lù bù tōng le	the road is impassable
bízi bù tōng	blocked up nose
diànhuà dǎbutōng	to be unable to get through on the phone

(266) *17.21   To be a bit ...*

Yǒu yìdiǎnr or **yǒu diǎnr** 'to be a little bit', 'to have a little bit' can be used in front of an adjective or auxiliary verb:

Wǒ jīntiān yǒu yìdiǎnr bù shūfu.	I'm a little unwell today.
Mǎibudào piào, tā xīn li yǒu diǎnr zháojí.	She can't get a ticket and she's feeling a bit anxious.
Zhèi zhǒng píngguǒ yǒu (yì) diǎnr guì.	This kind of apple is rather costly. (cf. **Zhèi zhǒng píngguǒ [bǐ nèi zhǒng] guì yìdiǎnr.** This kind of apple is a bit more costly than that kind.)

Tā hǎoxiàng yǒu diǎnr bù gāoxìng.

He seems a bit unhappy. (cf. **Tā hǎoxiàng hěn gāoxìng.** He seems very happy.)

(Note that **yǒu yìdiǎnr** *is only used for things which are undesirable.)*

Exercise 124   Not quite opposite

Make a contrasting statement using **yǒu (yì)diǎnr**, *as in the example:*

Zhèi jiàn shì hěn róngyi. >> <u>**Nèi jiàn shì yǒu diǎnr kùnnan.**</u>

1. **Jīntiān hěn nuǎnhuo.** >> **Zuótiān** _____
2. **Zhèr de dōngxi hěn piányi.** >> **Nàr de dōngxi** _____
3. **Gōngyuánr lǐtou hěn ānjìng.** >> **Gōngyuánr wàitou** _____
4. **Tā de yīfu hěn gānjing.** >> **Tā àiren de yīfu** _____
5. **Zài guónèi lǚxíng hěn róngyi.** >> **Zài guówài lǚxíng** _____

(267) *17.22   More on 'bǎ'*

Quite often the use of **bǎ** stresses the result of an action or gives a sense of deliberateness to it, sometimes even a sense as strong as the English 'He went and ...':

Qǐng nǐ bǎ xínglǐ dǎkai.   Please open your luggage.

Qǐng nǐ bǎ zuǐ zhāngkai.   Please open your mouth.

[**zhāng** 'to stretch open']

Kuài bǎ yīfu chuānshang.   Hurry up and put your clothes on.

Tā yǐjing bǎ chē xiūhǎo le.   She has already mended the car.

Tā bǎ wǒ de xīn chē zhuànghuài le.   He went and smashed my new car.

Exercise 125

Fill in the blanks along the lines suggested:

1. **Shéi bǎ zhèi píng jiǔ hē ____ le?**   (finish drinking)
2. **Wǒ yǐjing bǎ yīfu xǐ ____ ____ le.**   (wash clean)
3. **Qǐng nǐ bǎ dìzhǐ liú ____.**   (leave)
4. **Tā yǐjing bǎ fàn zuò ____ le.**   (make ready)

17.23 The verb 'ràng'

Ràng means 'to let' 'to allow' 'to cause':

Tā zěnme le? Ràng wǒ kànkan.	What's happened to him? Let me see.
Dàifu bú ràng tā zuò fēijī.	The doctor wouldn't let her fly.
Wǒmen xiān gàosu tā ba, bié ràng tā zháojí.	Let's tell her first, we shouldn't let her be worried.

17.24 Another step in time

In **7.1** we saw that 'the day before yesterday' is **qiántiān**. Chinese can go one further step backward by using **dàqiántiān**, but English only has the clumsy term 'the day before the day before yesterday'. Logically enough, **dàhòutiān** means 'the day after the day after tomorrow'.

17.25 Not much good

We have seen in **11.3** and **14.2** that question words can be used as indefinites. Here are more examples of indefinites used in negative sentences:

Zhèi zhǒng yào méi shénme yòng.	This medicine isn't much use.
Jīntiān de xīguā bù zěnme tián.	The water melons aren't very sweet today.

17.26 Further uses of 'kāi'

We have met **kāi** mostly in its basic meaning 'to open', 'to start', as in **kāishǐ**. Note these other uses:

kāi zhīpiào	to write a cheque
kāi yàofāng	to write out a prescription

New words

ànmó	massage
búyòng	there's no need

fāyán	inflammation
gǎnmào	influenza, flu
Hǎinán	Hainan (island off South China)
jiěkai	to undo
juéde	to feel
kāishuǐ	boiled water, boiling water
shàngyī	upper garments
shì biǎo	to take someone's temperature
tī	to kick
tī zúqiú	to play football/soccer
wèikǒu	appetite
xiāohuà	digestion
zhēnjiǔ	acupuncture (and moxibustion)
Zhōngyào	Chinese medicine

CONVERSATION 17C

A tourist with flu sees the doctor.

D : **Qǐng zuò, nǎr bù shūfu?**

Sit down, what's the problem?

T : **Tóuténg, késou, bízi bù tōng, juéde tèbié lèi, hǎoxiàng shi gǎnmào.**

My head aches, I've got a cough, my nose is blocked up, I feel extremely tired: I think it's flu.

D : **Shénme shíhou kāishǐ de?**

When did it start?

T : **Qiántiān wǎnshang tīwán zúqiú huílai.**

The night before last when I came back from playing football.

D : **Xiān shìshi biǎo ba.**

Let me take your temperature first.

T : **Fāshāo ma?**

Have I got a fever?

D : **Yǒu yìdiǎnr, 37 dù 4. Qǐng nǐ bǎ zuǐ zhāngkai. Ā-ā-ā .... Èn, hóulóng yǒu diǎnr fāyán. Xiāohuà zěnmeyàng?**

A little, 37.4°C. Please open your mouth. A-a-ah .... Hmm, your throat is a bit inflamed. How's your digestion?

T : **Hái hǎo, kěshi méi wèikǒu.**

It's OK, but I have no appetite.

D : **Qǐng nǐ bǎ shàngyī jiěkai, ràng wǒ tīngting ... méi shénme, jiù shi gǎnmào le.**

Please open up your upper clothing and let me listen ... Nothing much, it is only the flu.

T : **Dàifu, wǒ dàhòutiān děi qù Hǎinán, yòng zhēnjiǔ shì bu shi kěyǐ ràng gǎnmào kuài diǎnr hǎo?**

Doctor, in three days' time I have to go to Hainan: could acupuncture get flu cured quicker?

D : **Gǎnmào jiù shi xūyào duō xiūxi, zhēnjiǔ, ànmó yě méi shénme dà yòng, búguò kěyǐ ràng nǐ shūfu yìdiǎnr. Nǐ xiǎng shìshi ma?**

What flu needs is lots of rest, acupuncture or massage won't be much use, but they can make you feel a bit better. Would you like to try?

T : **Búyòng le.**

There's no need.

D : **Nà, wǒ gěi nǐ kāi ji zhǒng Zhōngyào, hòutiān zài lái kàn. Òu, bié wàng le duō hē kāishuǐ!**

Well then, I'll write you out some prescriptions for Chinese medicine, and you come back to see me the day after tomorrow. Oh, don't forget to drink plenty of boiled water!

Exercise 126
Translate into Chinese:

1. A: Will you please give this letter to Mr Wang.
   B: Yes, I will.

2. A: What time will the plane land in Hong Kong?
   B: I don't know. I'll go and ask.

3. A: Is he very busy today?
   B: Yes, he is so busy that he hasn't had his lunch [**wǔfàn** literally 'noon rice'] yet.

4. A: Did you find her?
   B: No, I had the address wrong.

5. A: Can you carry three suitcases by yourself?
   B: Of course I can.

6. A: What's the matter with her this morning?
   B: She doesn't feel very well. It was so hot last night that she only slept for two hours.

Chapter 18

THE HIGH LIFE

Throughout this book we have tried to make connections between new words and ones that you already know. It is a good way to build your vocabulary and understanding, and we hope you will find that it works for you. Famous, interesting and rich have even more in common in Chinese, you will find, than they do in English. And so that you can talk about the kind of wealth you deserve, we teach you here how to count beyond one thousand and on to the kind of figures you dream of.

Lots of useful little grammar patterns fill this chapter, and you will wonder how you have managed without them before. 'The more … the more …'; 'Apart from …'; 'I simply must …' all help to swell your ability to communicate, and they are simple to use. Perhaps not so easy is the little English word 'or'. It isn't till you learn Chinese that you realise that we use 'or' in more than one way, and that Chinese has a different word for each of them. This chapter explains it.

In case the prospect of so much new grammar does not excite you, we offer the joys of cooking and eating out, some serious shopping, and a 'wild night out' to finish up with.

(271) *18.1 Do whatever you like*

We met question words in their '-ever' forms in **14.2**. Here are some more examples where using question words twice gives the idea 'Do whatever you like':

Xǐhuan *shénme* jiù chī *shénme*.	Eat whatever is liked.
Xiǎng mǎi *něi ge* jiù mǎi *něi ge*.	Buy whichever is wanted.
Yīnggāi zhǎo *shéi* jiù zhǎo *shéi*.	Call on whoever ought to be called on.
Nǎr hǎowánr jiù qù *nǎr*.	Go wherever is good fun.
Nǐ yào *duōshao* wǒ jiù gěi (nǐ) *duōshao*.	I'll give you however much you want.

18.2 Foreigner

Wàiguó ('outside country') means 'foreign', and a **wàiguó rén** is a 'foreigner'. **Lǎo wài** ('old outside') is a rather informal version of the word: so **lǎo wài** is to **wàiguó rén** as 'Aussie' is to 'Australian'.

(272) 18.3 Adjectives with 'yǒu'

Remember **yǒu-yìsi** 'interesting' that you met in Chapter Fifteen? Here it is with some more of its friends to show how straightforward they are:

yǒu-yìsi	interesting, to be interesting [literally: 'have meaning']
yǒu-xìngqù	interested in, to be interested in [literally: 'have interest']
yǒu-míng	famous, to be famous [literally: 'have a name']
yǒu-qián	rich, to be rich [literally: 'have money']
yǒu-yòng	useful, to be useful [literally: 'have use']
yǒu-fúqi	lucky, to be lucky [literally: 'have good fortune']
yǒu-yánjiū	knowledgeable [literally: 'have research']

They are used in the same way as any other adjective, so you can put **hěn** or **zhēn** in front of them without difficulty, but just remember that in the negative you need to use **méi** not **bù**:

Zhè fùjìn zhù de dōu shi yǒu-qián de rén.	Everyone who lives hereabouts is wealthy.
Měi tiān shàng bān xià bān tài méi-yìsi le.	It's too too boring going to work and home again every day.

(273) 18.4 Culinary seasoning

táng 'sugar'	makes things	**tián** 'sweet'.
cù 'vinegar'	makes things	**suān** 'sour'.
yán 'salt'	makes things	**xián** 'salty'.
làjiāo 'chilli'	makes things	**là** 'peppery-hot'.
kǔguā 'bitter melon'	makes things	**kǔ** 'bitter'.

Exercise 127
How would you say it in Chinese?

1. Say that you can eat anything.
2. Tell the waiter that the fish is too salty.
3. Find out which wine your friend would like.
4. Ask the waiter for some chilli.

(274) 18.5   The more ... the better ...

Yuè...yuè... is used to give the meaning 'the more...the more':

Qǐng dàifu mǎshang lái, yuè kuài yuè hǎo.	Ask the doctor to come at once, the quicker the better.
Zhōngguó cài, wǒ yuè chī yuè xiǎng chī.	The more I eat Chinese food the more I want to eat it.

When only one idea is involved, as in 'gets more and more X', Chinese uses the pattern **yuè lái yuè** X ('the more time goes by the more X'):

Dōngxi yuè lái yuè guì le.	Things get more and more expensive.

Exercise 128
Translate into English:

1. **Qǐng nǐ míngtiān shàngwǔ lái, yuè zǎo yuè hǎo.**
2. **Wǒ yuè zháojí yuè bú huì shuō.**
3. **Wèishénme tā yuè chī yuè shòu?**
4. **Xué Zhōngwén de rén yuè lái yuè duō le.**

(275) 18.6   Cooking methods

Chǎo 'to stir fry' is a well-known Chinese cooking technique. Some standard stir-fried dishes are:

chǎo qīngcài/jīdīngr/ròupiànr ...	stir-fried green vegetables/diced chicken/sliced pork ...

Hóngshāo (literally 'red-cooked') is another technique based on braising in soy sauce (**jiàngyóu**):

| **hóngshāo jī / ròu / yú / dòufu ...** | red-cooked chicken/pork/fish/beancurd ... |

And here are some other common dishes:

làzi jīdīngr	diced chicken with chilli
tángcù páigu	sweet-and-sour spare ribs
suānlà tāng	sour-and-hot soup

18.7 Suit yourself

Suíbiàn has a range of meanings from 'easy-going' to 'please yourself' and 'at your convenience'. Note that sometimes the word can be split, as in the third example here:

> **Suíbiàn zuò, bié kèqi!**
> Please sit as you please, no need for politeness.

> **Nín suíbiàn gěi duōshao dōu xíng.**
> It's fine to give as much as you please.

> **A: Wǒmen shénme shíhou qù?**
> **B: Suí (nǐ) biàn.**
> A: What time shall we go?
> B: It's up to you.

Doubling up

You will hear **suíbiàn** a lot. 'Where would you like to eat tonight?' "**Suíbiàn, suíbiàn**" 'Oh, anywhere you please' comes the polite reply. Deference to others is typical of Chinese politeness. "**Nǐ xiān qǐng, nǐ xiān qǐng**" 'you go first please' comes automatically to people's lips as they approach a door together. Very commonly the phrases are doubled. Another example is "**Xièxie, xièxie**" 'Thank you'.

18.8 We here present

Wǒmen, as we know, means 'we', 'us'. There is another word **zánmen** which means 'we', 'us' but (unlike **wǒmen**) it always includes both the speaker and the person/s being spoken to.

18.9 'Lái' to cause to come

Lái of course means 'to come', but, as we saw in **12.1** and in Conversation 16A, it has also some extended meanings. In restaurants it is used for ordering:

> **Gěi wǒmen lái liǎng píng píjiǔ.**   Bring us two bottles of beer.

Alcohol

The excellence and variety of Chinese cuisine was never matched by similar sophistication in alcoholic drinks. There were some low strength fermented 'wines' made of rice, usually drunk warmed, and known as **huángjiǔ** 'yellow wine', but the accent was mostly on highly potent spirits distilled from other grains. Most famous is **máotái**, a clear spirit from Guizhou province, made from sorghum. American President Richard Nixon was introduced to it during his ground-breaking visit to China in 1972 and it suddenly acquired export status as a result. These fiery spirits go under the general name of **báijiǔ** and innocent foreigners have been known to be served it when they thought they had ordered 'white wine' — a rude shock! Wine made from grapes is called **pútáojiǔ** 'grape wine', and is now gaining in popularity, while beer (**píjiǔ** 'pilsner wine'), which was introduced by German merchants in the 19th century, is available everywhere in China. Of course over-indulgence in any of these products can make you **zuì** 'drunk'.

18.10 Formidable

Like the English word 'formidable' **lìhai** essentially means 'fearsome', 'terrible', but it can carry overtones of respect and admiration, and it can be applied to things as well as to people:

Zhèi ge rén tài lìhai le, **shéi dōu pà tā.**	This person is too tough, everyone's scared of him.
Jīntiān rè de lìhai, **kuài sìshí dù le.**	It's fearsomely hot today, nearly 40°C.

18.11 Despite

Bié kàn literally means 'Don't look at', and is used where English might say 'regardless of' or 'despite':

Bié kàn tā nàme yǒu-qián, **zhǐ yǒu yí tào xīzhuāng.**	Despite being so rich, he only has one suit.

(276) 18.12 Ain't it the truth!

In **16.5** we met **kě** meaning 'indeed', 'really'. It forms part of a common colloquial expression **Kě bú shì ma**, an emphatic way of saying 'That's just how it is!', 'Exactly!', 'Too right!', 'Not half!':

A: **Tā yú zuò de zhēn hǎo!**　　A: She cooks fish beautifully!
B: **Kě bú shì ma!**　　　　　　B: I couldn't agree more!

A: **Gōngzuò yuè lái yuè nán**　　A: It's harder and harder to
　　zhǎo le!　　　　　　　　　　find work!
B: **Kě bú shì ma!**　　　　　　B: You've said it!

(277) *New words*

bǎo	full, replete
diǎn cài	to order a (restaurant) meal
è	hungry, starving
gǎn	to dare
jiǎozi	filled dumplings
kuàizi	chopsticks
mǐfàn	(cooked) rice
xíguàn	custom; to be accustomed to

(278) CONVERSATION 18A

A Chinese host orders a meal for his foreign guest.

H : **Nǐ xǐhuan chī shénme jiù diǎn shénme, bié kèqi.**
Order whatever you like to eat, don't restrain yourself at all.

G : **Wǒ bú huì kèqi, kěshi wǒ zhèi ge 'lǎo wài' kànbudǒng càidān, háishi máfan nǐ ba.**
I don't even know how to be polite! But silly old foreigner that I am I can't read the menu, so I'd better trouble you.

H : **Zhèr de *làzi jīdīngr* hěn yǒu-míng, nǐ néng chī là de ma?**
The *diced chicken with chilli* here is very famous, can you take hot foods?

G : **Néng, wǒ ài chī là de, yuè là yuè hǎo.**
Yes, I love hot things, the hotter the better.

H : ***Tángcù páigu* zěnmeyàng?**
How about *sweet-and-sour spare ribs*?

G : **Hǎo jíle.**
Super.

H : **Zài lái yí ge _hóngshāo yú_, yí ge _chǎo qīngcài_, yí ge _suānlà tāng_ ...**

And then we'll have _red-cooked fish_, _stir-fried green vegetable_, _hot-and-sour soup_ ...

G : **Tài duō le ba?**

Isn't that too much?

H : **Bù duō. Nǐ xiǎng chī mǐfàn, háishi xiǎng chī jiǎozi?**

It's not a lot. Would you rather have rice or dumplings?

G : **Suíbiàn, dōu xíng. Zhōngwǔ méi chībǎo, wǒ kě zhēn è le.**

It doesn't matter, either will do. At lunch I didn't have enough and I'm really hungry now.

H : **Zánmen lái diǎnr báijiǔ, zěnmeyàng?**

Let's order a drop of _baijiu_, shall we?

G : **Báijiǔ tài lìhai le, wǒ kě bù gǎn hē. Yǐqián hēguo yí cì máotái, zuìle sān tiān.**

Baijiu's too strong, I just don't dare to drink it. I had some _maotai_ once, and I was drunk for three days.

H : **Nà jiù hē píjiǔ ba. Òu, duì le, nǐ xíguàn yòng kuàizi ma?**

In that case we'll have beer. Oh, by the way, are you used to using chopsticks?

G : **Méi wèntí, bié kàn wǒ Zhōngwén bù xíng, kuàizi yòng de hái kěyǐ. Zhōngguó cài bú yòng kuàizi bù hǎochī.**

No problem. Despite my poor Chinese, I'm not bad with chopsticks. Chinese food only tastes good with chopsticks.

H : **Kě bú shì ma!**

You're absolutely right!

⟨279⟩ _18.13 How terrific!_

Duō or **duōme** and the particle **a** enable you to 'exclaim' over an adjective:

Tiānqi duō hǎo a, chūqu wánrwanr ba.

How lovely the weather is! Let's go out (to enjoy ourselves).

Zhè cài zuò de duōme piàoliang a!

How beautifully this dish is cooked!

Exercise 129

Turn the sentences into exclamations, as in the example:

Lúndūn dōngxi guì becomes **Lúndūn dōngxi duōme guì a!**

1. **Tā Fǎyǔ shuō de hǎo.**
2. **Xué Zhōngwén bù róngyi.**
3. **Yàoshi wǒmen yǒu chuánzhēn jiù fāngbiàn le.**
4. **Kànjian hóngdēng bù tíng hěn wēixiǎn.**

18.14   What a shame!

Kěxī means 'it's too bad', 'what a pity':

Zhème hǎo de bīnguǎn, kěxī lí gōngchǎng tài jìn le.	Such a nice hotel, what a pity it's too close to the factory.
Zhème hǎo de bīnguǎn méi rén zhù, duōme kěxī a!	Such a nice hotel, what a shame that no one stays there.

18.15   Painting a painting

To paint is **huà** and a painting is **huàr**, so the Chinese and the English seem to echo each other:

Huà huàr.	To paint a painting.

18.16   'Duì' again

Note the use of the word **duì** ('towards') in the following cases where English uses 'in' or 'about':

Tā duì guójì wèntí hěn yǒu-yánjiū.	She's very knowledgeable about international problems.
Tā duì zuò Zhōngguó cài méi yǒu-xìngqù.	He has no interest in cooking Chinese food.

(280) 18.17   Large numbers

So far we have met numbers up into the hundreds only. The word for 'a thousand' is **qiān**. Beyond that, English counts in thousands ('ten thousand', 'a hundred thousand') but Chinese has a word **wàn** which means 'ten thousand' and it is this which is the base word for higher figures. Compare the two systems carefully — to get you used to the different base you may find it helpful to move the commas, as in the italicised column here:

1,000	**yìqiān**	*1000*
10,000	**yíwàn**	*1,0000*
100,000	**shíwàn**	*10,0000*
1,000,000	**yìbǎiwàn**	*100,0000*
10,000,000	**yìqiānwàn**	*1000,0000*
100,000,000	**yí (ge) yì**	*1,0000,0000*

(**Ge** is commonly inserted before **yì**, presumably to overcome the awkwardness of saying **yíyì**, but you may hear it after **sān, sì** etc as well.)

Exercise 130

Read off the following figures:

1. 1,500
2. 24,678
3. 186,395
4. 678,400,000
5. 1,154,260,000

18.18   Apologies

Duìbuqǐ is the common way of saying 'Sorry', and it will stand you in good stead. You can make it a little more heartfelt by adding **hěn** in front — **hěn duì buqǐ** 'I'm very sorry'. A more formal expression, equivalent perhaps to 'I very much regret that ...', is **fēicháng bàoqiàn**.

18.19   Haggling

The word for 'price' is **jiàqian**. In many markets and in some shops, bargaining for the price is still the practice, and the word for 'to bargain' is **jiǎng jià** (literally: 'talk price'):

Tā hěn huì jiǎng jià.   She's very good at bargaining.

18.20   Not even one measure

The simple sentence **Nǐ bú pàng** means 'You're not fat'. Much more emphatic is **Nǐ yìdiǎnr yě bú pàng** or (using **dōu** instead of **yě**) **Nǐ yìdiǎnr dōu bú pàng** ('You one bit even not fat'), i.e. 'You aren't even a bit fat':

Tā yí ge rén dōu bú rènshi.   She doesn't even know one person.

Wǒ yí cì Zhōngyào yě méi chīguo.   I haven't taken even one dose of Chinese medicine.

18.21 'Kāi' again

In **17.26** we met **kāi zhīpiào** 'to write a cheque'. **Kāi** is similarly used in **kāi zhèngmíng** 'to issue a certificate':

> **Bié wàngle qǐng yīyuàn gěi nǐ kāi ge zhèngmíng.**
> Don't forget to ask the hospital to issue you with a certificate.

18.22 Plastic acceptability

Xìnyòngkǎ are 'credit cards'; **shōu**, as you learned in Chapter Eleven, means 'to receive', 'to accept':

> **Nǐmen shōu bu shōu xìnyòngkǎ?**   Do you take credit cards?

(281) *New words*

fú	(measure for paintings)
Hè!	(exclamation of surprise or wonder)
héhuā	lotus flower
huàjiā	artist
nèiháng	expert, old hand
nóng	heavy (of colour)
shānshuǐ	scenery, landscape ['hills and water']
Wànlǐ Chángchéng	the (10,000 **lǐ**) Great Wall
Yìnxiàngpài	Impressionist school
yōuhuì	preferential, favourable
yúnhǎi	sea of clouds

(282) CONVERSATION 18B

A tourist buys a painting from a gallery salesperson.

S : **Nín kàn zhèi fú héhuā duō piàoliang a!**
See how beautiful this lotus flower painting is!

T : **Wǒ bǐjiào xǐhuan shānshuǐ ... Zhèi fú *Wànlǐ Chángchéng* huà de bú cuò. Kěxī yánsè tài nóng le.**
I rather prefer landscapes ... This *Great Wall* is painted rather well. What a pity that the colour is too heavy.

S : **Nín duì Zhōngguó huàr hěn yǒu-yánjiū a!**
You're very knowledgeable about Chinese paintings!

T : **Nǎli, zhǐ shi yǒu-xìngqù ... Hè, zhèi fú *Huángshān* hǎo a! Wánquán shi Yìnxiàngpài.**

Oh, I wouldn't say that, it's just that I'm interested ... Hey, this *Yellow Mountains* is good! It's completely Impressionist.

S : **Nín zhēn nèiháng!**

You're really expert!

T : *[Pointing at the price tag]* **Zhè shi jiàqian ma? Liǎngwàn liùqiān wǔ? Tài guì le ba!**

Is this the price? 26,500? That's terribly expensive!

S : **Yìdiǎnr yě bú guì. Zhèi wèi huàjiā hěn yǒu-míng. Nín kàn zhè yúnhǎi huà de duō hǎo a, hái zài dòng ne!**

It's not at all expensive. This artist is very famous. Look how well done the sea of clouds is, it's still moving!

T : **Néng piányi diǎnr ma? Dǎ ge bā zhé ba.**

Can you make it a bit cheaper? How about 20% off?

S : **Zhè ... Nín děngdeng, wǒ qù wèn yíxiàr jīnglǐ ...**

This ... er... If you'll wait a moment, I'll just go and ask the manager ...

[Two minutes later]

Jīnglǐ shuō rúguǒ nín zhēnde xǐhuan, wǒmen gěi nín jiǔ-zhé yōuhuì.

The manager says that if you really like it we'll give you a preferential price of 10% off.

T : **Bù néng zài shǎo le ma?**

Can you not make it even cheaper?

S : **Fēicháng bàoqiàn, píngcháng wǒmen shi bù jiǎng jià de.**

I'm very sorry, but normally we do not bargain at all.

T : **Dài chūjìng yǒu wèntí ma?**

Any problems with taking it out of the country?

S : **Méi wèntí. Nín fàngxīn, wǒmen gěi nín kāi zhèngmíng.**

No problem. Don't worry, we will issue you with a certificate.

T : **Nǐmen shōu bu shōu xìnyòngkǎ?**

Do you take credit cards?

S : **Shōu, shōu.**

Certainly we do.

18.23 Busy at

Mángzhe means 'busy at', 'busy with':

mángzhe xué Hànyǔ	busy studying Chinese
mángzhe kàn péngyou	busy visiting friends
mángzhe kāi huì	busy in meetings

(283) ## 18.24   Apart from ...

Chúle X **yǐwài** means 'Apart from X':

Wǒ de péngyou chúle nǐ yǐwài dōu qùguo Zhōngguó.	Apart from you, all my friends have been to China.
Chúle hóngshāoròu yǐwài tā hái xiǎng chī tángcù páigu.	He wants to have sweet-and-sour spare ribs as well as red-cooked pork.

18.25   'Shòu' to suffer

Shòu means 'to be at the receiving end of', 'to suffer'. **Shòu kǔ** is 'to suffer hardship', **shòu lèi** ['tired'] 'to be put to a lot of trouble', and **shòu huānyíng** is 'to be well received', 'to be welcomed', 'to be popular':

Zhōngguó cài zài Yīngguó hěn shòu huānyíng.	Chinese food is very popular in Britain.

Exercise 131
And how would you say these in Chinese?

1. Say that you are busy every day studying Chinese.
2. Ask what the most popular dish in this restaurant is.
3. Ask if your friend is interested in Chinese medicine.
4. Say that you aren't even a bit tired.

(284) ## 18.26   Verb + 'xiàqu'

Xiàqu literally and commonly means 'to go down', but it has an extended usage when added to a verb, meaning then 'to go on *verb*-ing':

Wǒ yǐjing bǎo le, zhēn de chībuxiàqù le.	I'm already full, I really can't eat any more.
Suīrán hěn nán, kěshi wǒ hái xiǎng xuéxiaqu.	Although it's very hard, I still want to go on studying it.
Gōngchǎng gěi de qián zhème shǎo, shéi dōu zuòbuxiàqù le.	The factory pays so little money, no-one can carry on working there.

(285) 18.27 Simply must again

In **12.25** you were introduced to the use of the double negative to convey the meaning of 'simply must'. There is one very common pattern used for this purpose: **fēi … bùkě** ('If you don't … it won't do'):

Gōng'ānjú de rén shuō,   The Public Security Bureau man says
wǒmen míngtiān fēi líkāi bùkě.   that we just have to leave tomorrow.

Wǒ fēi bǎ Hànyǔ xuéhǎo bùkě.   I simply must master Chinese.

Fēi* is an old word meaning 'not', and you met it in **fēicháng bàoqiàn** 'very much regret' (**18.18**). **Cháng** means 'ordinary' 'commonplace' and comes in another word you already know, **píngcháng** 'normally' 'usually' (Conversation 9A). So **fēicháng** means 'not ordinary' 'extraordinarily' and is often used in front of adjectives in the same way as **hěn** and **zhēn**;

Zhè pútáojiǔ fēicháng hǎo!   This wine is extraordinarily good drinking!

Exercise 132
Make it stronger!

Huángshān fēngjǐng nàme hǎo, <u>nǐ yīnggāi qù kànkan</u>.

>>> **Huángshān fēngjǐng nàme hǎo, <u>nǐ fēi qù kànkan bùkě</u>.**

1. **Nàme hǎochī de Běijīng kǎoyā, <u>wǒ yídìng yào chī</u>.** >>>
2. **Wǎnshang hěn lěng, <u>děi guānshang chuānghu</u>.** >>>
3. **Zhèi jiàn shì <u>bù néng bú gàosu tā</u>.** >>>
4. **Qǐng tāmen kāi zhèngmíng <u>děi gěi qián</u>.** >>>

18.28 Transliterations

Most languages accommodate foreign words in some way, often savaging the pronunciation in the process (think of what English does to 'Paris', ignoring its original 'Paree' sound). Chinese is not an exception, and there are lots of foreign borrowings:

Àolínpǐkè	Olympics
Dísīkē	Disco
Kǎlā-OK	Karaoke

18.29 Or

In statements 'or' is translated by **huòzhě**:

Qǐng nǐ míngtiān huòzhě hòutiān lái yíxiàr.	Please come over tomorrow or the day after.
Huòzhě nǐ lái, huòzhě wǒ qù, dōu kěyǐ.	Either you come or I'll go, either will do.

But you already know that in questions Chinese uses **háishi** for 'or?'. The following pairs should help you to sort out the difference:

A 1. **Nǐ míngtiān zǒu *huòzhě* hòutiān zǒu dōu kěyǐ.**
You can leave tomorrow *or* the day after.

2. **Nǐ shì míngtiān zǒu *háishi* hòutiān zǒu?**
Are you leaving tomorrow *or* the day after?

B 1. **Wáng xiǎojie shì Shànghǎi rén *háishi* Běijīng rén?**
Is Miss Wang from Shanghai *or* from Beijing?

2. **Wáng xiǎojie *huòzhě* shi Shànghǎi rén *huòzhě* shi Guǎngzhōu rén, kěndìng bú shi Běijīng rén.**
Miss Wang is from Shanghai *or* Guangzhou, certainly not from Beijing.

(286) *New words*

biéde	other
chàng gēr	to sing (songs)
diànshì	television
Zhōngyāng Diànshìtái	China Central Television (CCTV)
gùshi	a story, plot
huódòng	activity; to 'do something'
jiémù	programme
jiǔbā	a pub, wine bar
kū	to weep
liánxùjù	serial, soap opera
Niǎocháo	The Bird's Nest (nickname of the National Stadium built for the 2008 Beijing Olympics)
píndào	(television) channel
sànbù	to stroll, go for a walk
tán shēngyi	to talk/negotiate business
xiào	to laugh, to smile
yǎn	to act

yèjǐng	night scene
zǒng shi	always

CONVERSATION 18C

A foreign businessman and his Chinese friend plan 'a wild night out'.

C : **Lái Zhōngguó yǐhòu, cháng kàn diànshì ma?**

Since coming to China have you often watched television?

F : **Měi tiān mángzhe tán shēngyi, chúle xīnwén yǐwài, hěn shǎo kàn biéde jiémù.**

I'm busy every day talking business, apart from the news I rarely watch any other programmes.

C : **Zhōngyāngtái bā píndào de liánxùjù hěn shòu huānyíng, kànguo méi you?**

The serial on CCTV Channel 8 is very popular. Have you seen it?

F : **Kànguo liǎng cì jiù kànbuxiàqù le.**

I watched it twice, but couldn't go on watching it.

C : **Wèishénme? Gùshi yòu hǎo, yǎn de yòu hǎo. Wǒ měi tiān fēi kàn bùkě.**

Why not? The plots are good, and it's well acted. I just have to watch it every day.

F : **Wǒ jiù pà kàn rén kū, hǎoxiàng liánxùjù li zǒng shi yǒu rén zài kū.**

I just hate to see people cry, and it seems that in soap operas there are always people crying.

C : **Duì le, kū de shíhou shì bǐ xiào de shíhou duō.**

You're right, there's more crying than laughing.

F : **Shíjiān hái zǎo, zánmen chūqu huódònghuódòng ba.**

It's still early, let's go out and do something, shall we?

C : **Hǎo a. Qù Kǎlā-OK zěnmeyàng?**

Great. How about going to Karaoke?

F : **Wǒ duì chàng gēr kě yìdiǎnr xìngqù dōu méi yǒu.**

I haven't got the slightest interest in singing.

C : **Shàng jiǔbā huòzhě tiào dísīkē yě xíng a.**

To go to a bar or go disco-dancing would be alright too.

F : **Wǒ bù xiǎng qù rén duō de dìfang.**

I don't want to go where there are lots of people.

C : **Zhèr lí Àolínpǐkè gōngyuán bù yuǎn, zánmen qù nàr sànsanbù hǎo bu hǎo?**

It's not far from here to the Olympic Park. Let's go and stroll around there, what do you say?

F : **Hǎo a, wǒ zhèng xiǎng kànkan**   Good, I was wanting to have a look
    'Niǎocháo' de yèjǐng ne!   at The Bird's Nest by night!

Exercise 133

Translate into Chinese:

1. A: What would you like to eat?
   B: It's up to you. I'll eat whatever you order.

2. A: Have you got used to the weather here?
   B: Yes, I have. Now I feel the hotter it is the better.

3. A: What a beautiful park this is!
   B: You can say that again.

4. A: Are you interested in photography?
   B: No, not a bit.

5. A: What was the price of that Chinese painting you bought?
   B: I bargained with them for a long time and the final price
      was ¥18,500.

6. A: Why are you so busy practising *taichi* every day?
   B: I simply must master it before going back to Britain.

Chapter 19

HAPPY ENDINGS

Well, of course it is not really an ending. How could you stop now? If you have come this far, you are a stayer and will go on. And the world of Chinese characters is just about to open up to you ... How could you stop now? Oh, by the way, this chapter tells you how to ask just such a question.

There is plenty more to learn, that goes without saying, but you have a solid base in grammar and a great deal of essential vocabulary now. You should find that you can expand out into other topics that are of interest to you, and of course it is always so much easier to learn about things that interest you anyway.

We teach you how to say your goodbyes with the cheerful formality of a farewell party in Conversation 19B. For our part we raise our glasses in a toast to you in recognition of your stamina and hard work, and wish you well with your further excursions into Chinese — How could you stop now?

19.1   Within an inch of

Chà(yi)diǎnr means 'come very close to':

Jīntiān zǎochen wǒ chàdiǎnr méi gǎnshang huǒchē.	This morning I very nearly missed my train.
Chū guó nèi tiān tā chàdiǎnr wàngle dài hùzhào.	On the day he left the country he nearly forgot to take his passport.

Normally **chà(yi)diǎnr** is used when something is not entirely satisfactory, it's 'nearly there but not quite'. **Chàbuduō**, which you met in Chapter Ten, is not so judgemental: it means 'almost' 'more or less', but it just shows approximation, not that there is any failure or lack involved. So, in answer to the question **Nǐ zuòhǎole ma?**

    Hái chàyidiǎnr. would mean 'No, not quite there.' and

    Chàbuduō le. would mean 'Yes, more or less'.

⌒288 *19.2 The Passive*

Chinese does not use the formal passive construction as much as English does. Often what is a passive in English has no indication of the passive in Chinese, as you will see if you compare the following sentences where, despite the difference in English, the Chinese is the same in both cases:

Tā hái méi xǐ ne.	He still hasn't washed it. (active)
Xīzhuāng hái méi xǐ ne.	The suit still hasn't been washed. (passive)

Where the formal passive does occur, it is most commonly shown by the use of **bèi**. Sometimes **bèi** introduces the agent of the action (the person or thing carrying out the action):

Xìn bèi yóujú tuìhuilai le.	The letter was returned *by the Post Office.* (agent)

but sometimes the agent is not mentioned:

Xìn bèi tuìhuilai le.	The letter was returned.

Where the agent of the action is included, **bèi** may be replaced by **jiào** or **ràng**; and in these same cases **gěi** is sometimes inserted in front of the verb. So the passive pattern gives quite a few permutations:

Xìn bèi/jiào/ràng yóujú (gěi) tuìhuilai le.	The letter was returned by the Post Office.

A tip: when you do need to use the passive, you can make life simpler for yourself by sticking to **bèi**, because it works whether or not there is an agent.

Exercise 134
Translate into English:

1. **Xíngli yǐjing sòngdào nín de fángjiān le.**
2. **Chuánzhēn mǎshàng jiù fāchuqu.**
3. **Wǒ zhèi ge xiāngzi zài jīchǎng bèi jiǎnchá le sān cì.**
4. **Dàibiǎotuán bèi qǐngdào shí lóu qu le.**
5. **Diànshìjī jiào tā érzi gěi nònghuài le.**

19.3 To lose

Diū means 'to lose' 'to mislay':

Zhàoxiàngjī diū le, **zhǎobudào le.**   The camera is lost and can't be found.
Chēpiào yào náhǎo, bù néng diū.   You must hold tight to your ticket,
                                             you mustn't lose it.

19.4   *Leaving aside X, there's still Y*

X bù shuō, hái Y is the pattern for setting one consideration aside but being left with another:

Fángjiān tài rè bù shuō,   Forget about the fact that the room is
hái nàme zāng.   too hot, it's also so dirty.

Jiàqian guì bù shuō, hái hěn   As well as being high-priced, it's also
nán mǎidào.   hard to get hold of.

19.5   *Spending time or money*

Just as the one verb 'spend' works for both time and money in English, so there is one verb **huā** in Chinese which does the same:

Tā huāle yí ge xīngqī de   She spent a whole week packing her
shíjiān shōushi xíngli.   luggage.

Zhèi cì lǚxíng yígòng huāle   On this trip I spent ¥2000 altogether.
liǎngqiān kuài.

19.6   *Luckily*

'Fortunately', 'luckily', 'by good chance' can all be translated by **xìngkuī**:

Nǐ kàn yǔ zhème dà,   Look how hard it's raining,
xìngkuī wǒmen méi chūqu.   fortunately we didn't go out.

19.7   *It has to be said that...*

The adverb **yě** which we usually translate as 'also' sometimes is used to mean 'It has to be said that ...', 'Admittedly...':

Zhōngguó rén yě tài ài chī le.   It must be admitted that Chinese
                                             people are overfond of eating.

Suīrán tā hěn xiǎoxīn, kěshi yě   Although she is very careful, there are
yǒu chū shì de shíhou.   indeed times when she has accidents.

19.8 In no time at all

Yíxiàr means 'in no time at all', 'in a trice', 'all at once':

Tā zhīdao wèntí zài nǎr,	He knew where the problem lay,
yíxiàr jiù xiūhǎo le.	and had it mended in no time.

Four character phrases

The lilt of four syllables has great attraction to the Chinese ear, and there are so many thousands of 'four character' proverbs and popular sayings that huge dictionaries of them have been compiled. In the conversation below you will meet **yīn huò dé fú** [following disaster attaining fortune] 'Good luck coming out of misfortune'. And how about **yí rì qiān lǐ** [one day thousand miles] 'Making great progress'? Or **rén shān rén hǎi** [people mountain people sea] 'Teeming crowds'? Or **zuò chī shān kōng** [sit eat mountain void] 'Be idle and you will lose everything'? Being able to trot out a few will earn you admiration — they crop up all the time in people's speech and in writing, and no-one ever seems to tire of hearing them.

Exercise 135
How would you say these in Chinese?

1. Report to the police that your passport has been stolen.

2. Inform your colleague that it was yesterday that the new contract was received.

3. Ask your friend if his wallet has been found.

4. Tell your friend that the book she wants is sold out.

 New words

bèn	stupid
běnlái	originally; ought to be the case
chóngxīn	anew, afresh, all over again
dù jià	to spend one's holidays
Màngǔ	Bangkok
qiánbāor	wallet, purse
shēnqǐng	to apply for
tōu	to steal
xiǎotōur	thief

yīnwèi	because
zhuādào	to arrest, catch

(291) CONVERSATION 19A

A foreign resident returns from holiday and meets his Chinese friend.

C : **Dù jià huílai la?! Wánr de hǎo ba?**
You're back from holiday! Did you enjoy yourself?

F : **Bié tí le. Chàdiǎnr huíbulái le.**
Don't talk about it. I nearly couldn't get back.

C : **Zěnme le? Chūle shénme shì?**
What went wrong? What happened?

F : **Dào Màngǔ de dì-yī tiān, wǒ de hùzhào, qiánbāor jiù bèi tōu le.**
On the first day I got to Bangkok, my passport and wallet were stolen.

C : **Nà kě máfan le!**
You were in real trouble!

F : **Kě bú shì ma! Qián diūle bù shuō, hái děi chóngxīn shēnqǐng hùzhào, qiānzhèng, xìnyòngkǎ ...**
Too right! Forget the money I lost, but I also had to apply again for passport, visa, credit cards ...

C : **Huāle bù shǎo shíjiān ba?**
It must have cost you a lot of time.

F : **Běnlái bàn zhèi xiē shǒuxù zuì shǎo yě děi liǎng ge xīngqī. Xìngkuī dì-èr tiān jǐngchá jiù bǎ xiǎotōur zhuādào le.**
Normally it would take at least two weeks to go through the procedures. Luckily the police caught the thief the next day.

C : **Zhème kuài?**
So quickly?

F : **Nèi ge xiǎotōur yě tài bèn le, yòng wǒ de xìnyòngkǎ qù mǎi dōngxi, yíxiàr jiù bèi zhuādào le.**
That thief was really too stupid, he went shopping with my credit card and was caught in no time.

C : **Hùzhào, qiánbāor dōu zhǎodào le ma?**
Were your passport and wallet both found?

F : **Dōu zhǎodào le. Fàndiàn hái miǎnfèi zhāodài wǒ zhùle yí ge xīngqī, yīnwèi shi zài tāmen nàr diū de.**
Yes. And the hotel gave me a week's free stay because it was there that I lost them.

C : **Zhè zhēn shi 'yīn huò dé fú' a!**
This really is 'good luck coming out of misfortune'!

19.9 On the one hand... and on the other

Fāngmiàn means 'aspect' and **yì fāngmiàn ... yì fāngmiàn** give the sense of 'on the one hand ... and on the other':

Zhèi jiàn shì yì fāngmiàn shi yīnwèi tā bù xiǎoxīn, yì fāngmiàn yě shi yīnwèi tiānqi bù hǎo.

This thing happened because on the one hand he wasn't careful, and on the other the weather wasn't good.

Tā yì fāngmiàn xiǎng qù Zhōngguó, yì fāngmiàn yòu pà lǚxíng tài lèi.

On the one hand she wants to go to China, but on the other she is also afraid that the travelling will be too tiring.

19.10 Welcome and farewell

Huānyíng means 'to welcome' (see Chapter One), and its opposite 'to bid farewell' is **huānsòng**. (**Huān*** means 'joyous'.)

> ### Exercise 136
> *Give the opposites of the following:*
>
> 1. **gānjing**   2. **bǎo**   3. **xiào**   4. **fàngxīn**
> 5. **wàngle**   6. **qǐfēi**   7. **jìnkǒu**   8. **chū guó**
> 9. **tián**   10. **chūjìng**

19.11 On account of

Wèile means 'on account of', 'because of':

Tā xué Zhōngwén shi wèile qù Zhōngguó gōngzuò.

He's learning Chinese on account of going to China to work.

Wèile huàn qián, wǒ děngle sān ge xiǎoshí.

I waited three hours in order to change money.

(292) 19.12 Formal address

When talking formally to a group of people, such as when addressing a meeting, for example, the group is addressed as **gè wèi** ('everybody'):

Gè wèi dàibiǎo ...   "Delegates, ..."

Gè wèi péngyou …	"Dear friends, …"
Gè wèi guìbīn, gè wèi xiānsheng, gè wèi nǚshì … [**guìbīn** = 'honourable guest']	"Distinguished guests, ladies and gentlemen, …"
Nǚshìmen, xiānshengmen …	"Ladies and gentlemen, …"

(As we said in **4.3**, these plural forms using **men** cannot be used with measures, and you will not often come across them).

19.13 'Duō' and 'shǎo' as adverbs

Duō and **shǎo** can be used before verbs as adverbs meaning 'more' and 'less/fewer':

Chōu yān duì shēntǐ bù hǎo, nǐ yīnggāi shǎo chōu diǎnr.	Smoking is bad for your health, you should smoke less.
Tā shǎo gěile wǒ yì zhāng shí kuài de.	He gave me one ¥10 note short.
Méi shénme hǎo cài, qǐng nín duō chī diǎnr.	The food isn't very good, but please have some more.

19.14 Percentages

Percentages and fractions are both expressed in the same way:

bǎi fēn zhī shí	10%
bǎi fēn zhī liùshiwǔ	65%
bǎi fēn zhī sìshijiǔ diǎn bā	49.8%
wǔ fēn zhī yī	1/5
shí fēn zhī sān	3/10

Zhī* is actually an old Classical Chinese word that was used much as **de** is now, so **bǎi fēn zhī shíqī** is a logical construction 'seventeen of 100 parts', 17%. **Zhī** has survived in quite a number of other modern expressions. For

---

Politeness again

Oh, what a tangled web we weave when first we practise... politeness! Look what a mess that last example sentence has got the host into. Courtesy and modesty demand that he should never admit to serving good food. On the other hand, courtesy also says that he should encourage his guest to eat his fill. The result: encouragement to eat bad food! And that's politeness?! Well, of course no-one would dream of understanding it that way. It would be as unthinkable as saying 'I don't!' in response to 'How do you do?' Chinese and English both have their oddities!

instance, in the conversation you will see **Wǒmen zhījiān** 'between us' [literally: 'our space' 'what is between us']. And again:

Liǎng guó zhījiān de wèntí **yuè lái yuè duō.**	Problems between the two countries get greater and greater.

Exercise 137
Say it in Chinese:

1. 1/4   2. 1/25   3. 17%
4. 0.8%   5. 99.9%

19.15   The parties concerned

Here are a number of expressions which share the common element **fāng*** 'aspect', 'side', 'party':

wǒ fāng	my (our) side
nǐ fāng	your side
Rì fāng	the Japanese side
Zhōng fāng	the Chinese side
mǎi fāng	the buyers
mài fāng	the vendors
shuāng fāng	both sides

19.16   It is indeed so

To show strong agreement with something someone else has said, or to make a strong definitive statement the pattern **shi ... de** is used. Compare the following statements:

A	1. **Wǒ bú qù.**	I'm not going.
	2. **Wǒ shi bú qù de.**	I'm certainly not going.
B	1. **Zhǎo gōngzuò hěn kùnnan.**	It is very hard to find work.
	2. **Zhǎo gōngzuò shi hěn kùnnan de.**	It is indeed the case that work is hard to find.

(295) 19.17   Here's a toast to ...

Gānbēi of course means 'bottoms up' and is the standard way of toasting. 'To drink to ...' is **wèi ... gānbēi**:

Wèi wǒmen de yǒuyì gānbēi!	Let's drink to our friendship!
Wèi Zhōng-Yīng liǎng guó rénmín de yǒuyì gānbēi!	A toast to friendship between the peoples of China and Britain!

(296) *19.18 Good wishes*

Here is a useful list of expressions of good wishes:

zhù	to wish
zhù nǐ/gè wèi/dàjiā ...	I wish you/all of you/everybody ...
... shēntǐ jiànkāng	good health
... wànshì rúyì	satisfaction in all you do [**wànshì** = 10,000 matters]
... jiànkāng chángshòu	good health and long life (birthday greeting)
... shēngri kuàilè	birthday happiness
... Shèngdàn kuàilè	Happy Christmas
... Xīnnián kuàilè	Happy New Year
... yí lù píng'ān	*bon voyage!* [whole way peaceful safe]
... yí lù shùn fēng	*bon voyage!* [whole way following wind]

And talking of 'four character phrases', note how all of the above are just that. You can almost hear the inverted commas around them as you say them!

19.19 Style

Notice how in Conversation 19b the speakers drop into a semi-formal style, using resounding set phrases which add grandeur and colour to an occasion. **Zàizuò** is perhaps a good example: it is no more casual in Chinese than 'here present' is in English.

(297) *New words*

gǎnxiè	to thank, to be grateful to
hézuò	co-operation
huìtán	to hold formal talks
jiàzhí	value, worth

jīnhòu	henceforth
jìnyíbù	further, enhanced [literally: advance one step]
liǎojiě	to understand
qiāndìng	to sign (a treaty/contract)
qìngzhù	to celebrate
tōngguò	as a result of [literally:'having passed through']
xiāngxìn	to believe
xīnkǔ	hard work, toil
xìnxīn	confidence, belief
yànhuì	a feast, banquet
zēngjiā	to increase
zhàogù	consideration, care
zhídé	to be worth it
zǒngjīnglǐ	general manager

(298) *CONVERSATION 19B*

General Manager Wang hosts a celebration dinner for Mr Laker.

W : **Léikè xiānsheng, jīntiān de yànhuì yì fāngmiàn shi wèile qìngzhù zánmen qiāndìngle xīn hétong, yì fāngmiàn yě shi wèile huānsòng nín hé gè wèi Yīngguó péngyou. Dàjiā yídìng yào duō hē jǐ bēi!**

Mr Laker, today's banquet is on the one hand to celebrate our signing the new agreement, and on the other to bid farewell to you and all our British friends. We must all enjoy a few more glasses!

L : **Fēicháng gǎnxiè Wáng zǒngjīnglǐ. Zhèi cì huìtán suīrán shíjiān hěn cháng, kěshi hétong jiàzhí bǐ shàng cì zēngjiāle bǎi fēn zhī sānshí, dàjiā de xīnkǔ shi zhídé de.**

We are extremely grateful to General Manager Wang. Although the talks this time have taken a long while, the value of the contract has increased 30% over last time, and everyone's hard work has really been worth it.

W : **Tōngguò zhèi cì huìtán, wǒmen zhījiān yǒule jìnyíbù de liǎojiě, xiāngxìn xià cì huì zēngjiā de gèng duō.**

After this round of talks we have achieved a new level of understanding, and I believe that next time it will increase yet more.

L : **Wǒ duì shuāng fāng jīnhòu de hézuò shi yǒu xìnxīn de.**

I have great confidence in the future co-operation of our two sides.

W : **Lái, xiān wèi wǒmen de xīn hétong gān yì bēi!**

Come on, let's first drink a toast to our new contract!

L and party: **Gānbēi!**

Cheers!

L : **Wǒ hái yào tèbié gǎnxiè Zhōngguó péngyou duì wǒmen de zhāodài hé zhàogù, wǒ jìng dàjiā yì bēi, zhù gè wèi shēntǐ jiànkāng, wànshì rúyì. Gānbēi!**

I would especially like to thank our Chinese friends for their hospitality and care, and I drink a toast to you all, and wish you good health and success in all you do. Cheers!

W and party: **Gānbēi!**

Cheers!

W : **Míngtiān shàngwǔ zàizuò de Yīngguó péngyou jiù yào huí guó le, lái, zài lái yì bēi, wǒmen yìqǐ zhù tāmen 'Yí lù shùn fēng'! Gānbēi!**

Tomorrow morning our British friends here will be returning home, so, come on, let's have another glass and wish them '*Bon voyage!*' Cheers!

19.20 *Making fun*

The expression **kāi wánxiào** means 'to make a joke' or 'to poke fun' or 'to take the mickey', so it can be either wholly pleasant or perhaps a little hurtful:

Tā hěn xǐhuan kāi wánxiào.

She loves making jokes.

Tā shi gēn nǐ kāi wánxiào de, bié zháojí.

He's just making fun of you, don't worry.

⌢299⌣ 19.21 *How could that be?*

Zěnme huì ... ne? is a useful way to express incredulity or great surprise:

Xiàtiān zěnme huì xià xuě ne?

How could it be snowing in summertime?

Sìchuān rén zěnme huì bú ài chī là de ne?

How could a Sichuanese not like spicy food?

Exercise 138

Convert to 'How could it be?', as in this example:

Măgē Bōluó shi Xībānyá rén.
>> **Măgē Bōluó zěnme huì shi Xībānyá rén ne?**

1. Yì nián yǒu sānbǎi liùshiliù tiān. >>
2. Yīngguó rén bù hē xiàwǔ chá. >>
3. Zuò huǒchē bǐ zuò fēijī wēixiǎn. >>
4. Chī Zhōngguó cài róngyi pàng. >>

⑩ 19.22   *Never ever*

In **11.12** you met **cónglái**, 'all along', 'always', 'at any time'. There it was used with **méi** and **-guo** to mean 'has never at any time':

Wǒ cónglái méi pèngjianguo zhème bèn de rén.	I have never met such a stupid person.
Tā cónglái méi kànguo Zhōngwén bào.	He has never read a Chinese newspaper.

And note how this contrasts with **cónglái**'s use with **bù**, when it means 'never does':

Tā cónglái bú kàn Zhōngwén bào.	He never reads a Chinese newspaper.

Exercise 139   *Often and never*

Answer the questions in 'I have never done it before' style:

Tā cháng chī Zhōngguó cài. Nǐ ne?
>> **Wǒ cónglái méi chīguo Zhōngguó cài.**

1. Tā cháng qù Zhōngguó. Nǐ ne? >>
2. Tā cháng yòng Zhōngwén xiě xìn. Nǐ ne? >>
3. Wǒ chángcháng pèngjian zhèi zhǒng shì. Nǐ ne? >>
4. Tā zǒng shi bù xiǎoxīn, cháng diū dōngxi. Nǐ ne? >>

19.23   From time to time

As you saw in **7.14**, **yǒu shíhou** or **yǒude shíhou** means 'sometimes', 'from time to time', 'now and then'. Like other adverbs of time it comes before the verb:

Tā yǒu shíhou xǐhuan yígerén chūqu sànbù.	She sometimes likes to go out for a stroll on her own.
Xué wàiyǔ yǒu shíhou juéde róngyi, yǒu shíhou juéde kùnnan.	Learning a foreign language sometimes seems easy, and at others hard.

(301) *New words*

Hànzì	Chinese characters
jiǎng	to expound, explain, speak
jīchǔ	foundation, basis
kàn shū	to read
kè	a lesson
pīnyīn	to spell out sounds
Hànyǔ pīnyīn	Hanyu pinyin (the official Chinese system of Romanisation used in this book)
rèn zì or **shí zì**	to recognize characters
shèngxia	to remain over
zhēnzhèng	true, real

(302) *CONVERSATION 19C*

A reader of this book talks to a Chinese friend.

F :	**Zhèi běn shū kuài xuéwán le ba?**	You'll soon have finished studying this book, won't you?
R :	**Kuài le. Zhǐ shèngxia zuì hòu yí kè le.**	Soon. There only remains the last lesson.
F :	**Nǐ xiànzài yígòng rènshi duōshao Hànzì le?**	How many characters do you know altogether now?
R :	**Yí ge dōu bú rènshi.**	I don't know even one.
F :	**Bié kāi wánxiào le, nǐ Hànyǔ shuō de zhème liúlì, zěnme huì bú rènshi Hànzì ne?**	Don't pull my leg, how could you not know any characters when you speak Chinese so fluently?
R :	**Shì zhēnde. Wǒ shi yòng Hànyǔ pīnyīn xué de, cónglái**	It's the truth. I learned through Hanyu Pinyin, I've never learned

méi xuéguo Hànzì. Zhèi běn
shū shuō yīnggāi xiān xué shuō
huà, zài xué rèn zì kàn shū.

any Chinese characters. This book
says that learning to speak should
come before learning how to
recognize characters and read.

F : **Bú rènshi Hànzì, duō bù
fāngbiàn a!**

Not to know characters! How
inconvenient that must be!

R : **Shì a, yǒu shíhou dàole cèsuǒ
ménkǒur dōu bù gǎn jìnqu.**

Yes, sometimes even when I get to
the door of the toilets I daren't go in.

F : **Wèishénme?**

Why is that?

R : **Yīnwèi bú rènshi mén shang
xiě de shi náncèsuǒ háishi
nǚcèsuǒ.**

Because I don't know whether
what is written on the door is Men's
Toilet or Women's Toilet.

F : **Nà nǐ dǎsuan shénme shíhou
kāishǐ xué ne?**

So, when do you intend to start
learning?

R : **Xiànzài wǒ de kǒuyǔ yǒule
diǎnr jīchǔ, mǎshang jiù kěyǐ
kāishǐ le. Nǐ kàn, xià yí kè
jiǎng de jiù shi Hànzì.**

Now that I have acquired a certain
foundation of the spoken language,
I can start immediately. Look, what
the next lesson talks about is in fact
characters.

F : **Tài hǎo le, xuéle Hànzì cái
néng zhēnzhèng liǎojiě
Zhōngwén!**

Excellent. You cannot truly
understand Chinese until you have
learned characters!

Exercise 140
Translate into Chinese:

1. A: How long did you wait for your visa?
   B: It usually takes about one week, but fortunately I knew people
   in the Embassy, so I got it at once.

2. A: How come you are not wearing a suit today?
   B: Don't even mention it — all my clothes have been stolen.

3. A: Have car imports increased this year?
   B: Yes, they have increased by 7.5%.

4. A: There are too many people on the road, will you please drive a bit
   slower?
   B: Don't worry, I have never had an accident while driving.

5. A: It says in the paper that more than 70% of men students are smokers.
   B: How could there be so many?

6. A: Why do you want to study Chinese?
   B: For one thing, I am very interested in learning foreign languages,
   and for another, I would like to have a real understanding of China.

Chapter 20

WRITING

This last short chapter comes with a health warning — Chinese characters are addictive! They will not do much to help your speaking of the language, but they increase your understanding a great deal. They help you to sort out the connections and dissimilarities between words which are pronounced the same. They point to interesting derivations, to ways in which Chinese culture thinks, to depths of meaning that the mechanical representation of words in a phonetic writing system cannot plumb. Trying to explain why they are so addictive is like trying to describe colour to someone blind from birth.

Literacy was never so challenging in English, nor so frustrating, nor so rewarding, nor so infuriating, nor so exhilarating, nor so special, nor so … but what's the use? Just try some, and we know you will receive the enlightenment that we lack means to communicate to you in words. But remember, you will never be the same again.

You have been warned!

20.1 How Chinese characters were created

Chinese characters have been created in various ways over the millennia, but the earliest ones were simple pictures of objects:

日 **rì** 'sun' ☉
月 **yuè** 'moon' ☽
山 **shān** 'mountain', 'hill' ᗜ
木 **mù** 'a tree', 'wood' was a simple sketch of a tree ✶
人 **rén** 'person', 'Man' derives clearly enough from a picture of a man ⟩
目 **mù** 'eye' ⬮

Some abstract ideas could be indicated by an extension of the picture principle:

上 **shàng** 'above' and 下 **xià** 'below' derived from ⌣ and ⌢
一 **yī** 'one', 二 **èr** 'two', and 三 **sān** 'three'

A further extension was the 'logical' one, where new characters were logically put together from existing ones:

明 **míng** 'bright', formed by putting the sun 日 and the moon 月 together.

旦 **dàn** 'dawn', shown by a picture of the sun 日 rising above the horizon.

尖 **jiān** 'sharp' 'pointed', consists of 小 'small' above 大 'big'.

信 **xìn** 'trust', 'belief', composed of 'a person' 人 and his 'word' 言.

从 **cóng** 'to follow', shows one man 人 behind another.

Over time, as writing materials and fashions changed, these original pictures became stylised in different ways. Here are some simple characters showing how they have developed from the oldest forms on the left to the regular modern forms on the right:

'child' 子 **zǐ**

'water' 水 **shuǐ**

'tiger' 虎 **hǔ**

'silk' 丝 **sī**

'fruit' 果 **guǒ**

The most common way of forming characters has been to build them from a meaningful 'radical' element and a sound-indicating 'phonetic' element. The characters for types of tree and things made of wood usually contain the 'wood radical' 木, the same character which started out as a picture of a tree.

For example, 松 **sōng** is a 'pine tree', 棍 **gùn** is a 'stick', 柴 **chái** is 'firewood', and 森 **sēn** is a 'forest'. 氵 represents 'water' (the full character for which is 水 **shuǐ**) and appears in characters for liquids, so 河 **hé** is a 'river', 油 **yóu** is 'oil', and 汗 **hàn** is 'sweat'. There are many other radical elements, such as 钅 for metals (full character 金), 车 for vehicles, 石 for minerals, 艹 for plants (full character 草), 鱼 for fish, and 虫 for insects.

The 'phonetic' element is added to the 'radical' to give a pronunciation guide. The character 工 means 'work' and is pronounced **gōng**: it appears in a number of other characters where it gives a clue to pronunciation — 功 means 'merit', 攻 means 'to attack', and both of these characters are pronounced **gōng**. Alas, there are also some characters which contain 工 but which are not pronounced **gōng** , even if they had originally been read that way, (江 for instance, is nowadays pronounced **jiāng**, while 红 is pronounced **hóng**), and there are many more characters which are pronounced **gōng** but which do not contain 工, so you cannot put too much faith in these pronunciation guides. Still, they are a useful aid to character learning, and the 'radical + phonetic' system is still the method used to create new characters today. For instance, the character which was devised for 'lithium' is 锂 **lǐ**, that is, a metal 钅 that sounds like **lǐ** 里 (**lǐ**- thium).

There are dozens of words pronounced **shì**, but they are easily distinguished from each other when written down in characters. Here are a few of them :

是 to be	事 business	市 market
士 scholar	室 room	视 to see
试 to try	示 to show	世 a generation

The first advantage of characters, then, is that they serve to make clear what in speech can be quite muddling. The second advantage is that Chinese people who can read and write all use the same writing system, regardless of which kind of Chinese they speak. A Cantonese speaker is unintelligible to a Shanghainese listener, and vice versa, but when they write things down they understand each other perfectly because they both use standard written Chinese which does not take account of their different pronunciations and dialect peculiarities. So the written language allows China to have communication and unity where there might otherwise be misunderstanding and division.

20.2   Organising characters.

Looking up words in English dictionaries is very simple — we have an alphabet which has a fixed order, and we organise our words in that same order. Chinese has no alphabet, and therefore has no such obvious way of organising a dictionary, and of course it is not possible to know how an unfamiliar character should be pronounced just by looking at it. So other ways had to be found. Some dictionaries are arranged by rhyme, some by topic in much the same way as a Thesaurus, some by very complicated numerical systems arbitrarily assigned to characters. Some recent dictionaries have used romanisation and been arranged in alphabetical order, but the most frequently used method has been to arrange characters by their radical elements. In the late 17th century a table of 214 radicals was compiled and all characters were classified under one or other of the 214, which were in a set order like the twenty-six letters of the ABC.

To look up a character in a dictionary, you start by identifying the radical and then count the number of additional pen strokes used in writing the character. To find the character 城 you first decide that the left-hand side (土 'earth') is the radical, then look that up in the chart of radicals and find that it is the 32nd of the 214, then count the additional strokes in the remainder of the character (成), finding that there are six of them. So the character (it is pronounced **chéng** and means 'city') will be found in the sixth subsection of the 32nd section of the dictionary, along with a few other characters which also have six strokes added to the earth radical. Maybe not simple, but it works.

One of the reforms carried out during the first two decades after the foundation of the People's Republic of China in 1949 was the simplification of the Chinese script. The idea was not entirely a revolutionary one. For speed and ease of writing, many characters had over the ages acquired simpler variant forms, and quite a lot of these now became adopted as the recognised formal versions. For the most part, simplification consisted of cutting down the number of strokes used to write complex characters:

錢	**qián**	'money'	simplified to 钱
國	**guó**	'country'	became 国
視	**shì**	'to see'	slightly cut down to 视

Some of the simplifications were much more swingeing:

邊	**biān**	'side'	pared right down to 边
聽	**tīng**	'to listen'	unrecognisably reduced to 听
龍	**lóng**	'dragon'	slimmed down to 龙

The simplified characters could not easily be forced into the 214 categories, and new radical tables had to be devised. Unfortunately each new dictionary that has been published since seems to have followed a different table, so that the old standard was not replaced by anything so universal, and dictionary-searching has tended to become more rather than less complicated accordingly. The old 'full form' (non-simplified) characters are still used in Hong Kong, in Taiwan, and among most of the Overseas Chinese communities.

Until the early 20th century, Chinese was written from top to bottom and from the right to the left of the page, so that the writer started at the top right-hand corner of what would be the last page in a western book, wrote in a column down to the bottom, then started at the top again, and so on until he finished the page at the bottom left-hand corner. Another result of the reforms was that nowadays it is becoming much more common to write across the page from left to right, starting at what all western writers would agree to be the front of the book. Newspapers sometimes mix the two systems, having some text reading across and some down, and publishers have by no means ceased to print in the traditional top-to-bottom/right-to-left mode for all books.

In print, each character, however complicated or simple, takes up the same space on the page. You can think of characters as being written in squares all of the same size. Handwriting rarely has such neat or boring uniformity, and stylish writers delight in varying the size, strength and impact of their characters. Many different types of script have been developed over the centuries (much as English can be written in block capitals, or in 'joined-up' long-hand, or in Gothic calligraphic style), and this variety is reflected in the different fonts which are available to the printer. Here is a small selection of printed forms of the traditional non-simplified character for **dōng** 'east', the one on the end of the row being closely modelled on what is perhaps the most popular standard handwritten form:

東　東　東　**東**　**東**　東

There is a set order for writing the strokes of a character, most of them starting at the top left hand corner and working downwards and to the right, ending usually in the bottom right hand corner of the imaginary square. This is the order for writing the simplified form of **dōng**:

一　七　车　车　东　(5 strokes altogether)

and **zhōng** 'middle':

丶　冂　口　中　(just 4 strokes)

个 **ge**, the measure word for people and many other objects, is very simple:

丿 人 个 (3 strokes)

南 **nán** 'south':

一 十 𠂇 内 内 㐄 㐄 南 南 (9 strokes)

国 **guó** 'country' is a little trickier:

丨 门 冂 冋 囯 国 国 国 (8 strokes)

你 **nǐ** 'you' is split into a left and a right side:

丿 亻 亻 价 你 你 你 (7 strokes)

20.3 *Some useful characters*

We cannot possibly hope to teach you to read and write in this book, but it is not too hard to introduce a few characters which are frequently met with and which are useful for everyday life in China. Remember that each character is meaningful and read as one syllable of speech. Let's start with a very important pair:

男	**nán**	man, male
女	**nǚ**	woman, female
男厕 (所)	**náncè(suǒ)**	men's toilet
女厕 (所)	**nǚcè(suǒ)**	women's toilet
有人	**yǒu rén**	occupied
无人	**wú rén**	vacant
推	**tuī**	push
拉	**lā**	pull
开	**kāi**	open
关	**guān**	closed
出口	**chūkǒu**	exit
入口	**rùkǒu**	entrance
不准	**bù zhǔn...**	not permitted to ...
不准停车	**Bù zhǔn tíng chē**	No parking

禁止吸烟	**Jìnzhǐ xī yān**	No smoking ...
禁止…	**jìnzhǐ...**	forbidden to ...
游客止步	**Yóukè zhǐ bù**	Out of bounds to visitors
出入请下车	**Chū-rù qǐng xià chē**	Please dismount at the gate
一 二 三	**yī, èr, sān**	one, two, three
四 五 六	**sì, wǔ, liù**	four, five, six
七 八 九	**qī, bā, jiǔ**	seven, eight, nine
十 百 千	**shí, bǎi, qiān**	10; 100; 1,000
万 亿	**wàn, yì**	10,000; 100,000,000
元	**yuán**	dollar, yuan
角	**jiǎo**	dime, ten cents
分	**fēn**	cent
人民币	**Rénmínbì**	Renminbi
公斤	**gōngjīn**	kilogram
公里	**gōnglǐ**	kilometre
东南西北	**dōng nán xī běi**	east, south, west, north
北京	**Běijīng**	Beijing (Peking)
成都	**Chéngdū**	Chengdu
重庆	**Chóngqìng**	Chongqing (Chungking)
广州	**Guǎngzhōu**	Guangzhou (Canton)
桂林	**Guìlín**	Guilin
南京	**Nánjīng**	Nanjing (Nanking)
上海	**Shànghǎi**	Shanghai
台北	**Táiběi**	Taipei
台湾	**Táiwān**	Taiwan
天津	**Tiānjīn**	Tianjin (Tientsin)
西安	**Xī'ān**	Xian
香港	**Xiānggǎng**	Hong Kong
中国	**Zhōngguó**	China
派出所	**pàichūsuǒ**	police station
公用电话	**gōngyòng diànhuà**	public telephone
邮局	**yóujú**	Post Office
银行	**yínháng**	bank
中国银行	**Zhōngguó Yínháng**	The Bank of China

外币兑换	**wàibì duìhuàn**	foreign exchange
医院	**yīyuàn**	hospital
人民医院	**Rénmín Yīyuàn**	The People's Hospital
火车(站)	**huǒchē(zhàn)**	train (station)
地铁(站)	**dìtiě (zhàn)**	subway/underground (station)
售票处	**shòupiàochù**	ticket office
公共汽车(站)	**gōnggòngqìchē(zhàn)**	bus (station/stop)
出租汽车(站)	**chūzūqìchē(zhàn)**	taxi (rank/station)
机场	**jīchǎng**	airport
首都机场	**Shǒudū Jīchǎng**	Capital Airport
饭店	**fàndiàn**	hotel
北京饭店	**Běijīng Fàndiàn**	The Peking Hotel
百货商店	**bǎihuò shāngdiàn**	department store
营业时间	**yíngyè shíjiān**	hours of business
收款台	**shōukuǎntái**	cashier's desk

Exercise 141

Just for fun, see if you can translate the following from characters into English:

1. 金鱼　　2. 龙虎山　　3. 北京市　　4. 西安站

5. 上海饭店　6. 台湾水果　7. 广州游客　　8. 男厕所无人

9. 首都医院　10. 中国银行　11. 你是中国人　12. 禁止石油出口

13. 美国车大　　　　　　14. 人民币三亿八千六百五十万元

15. 游客是不是香港人?

If you are going to take your learning of Chinese beyond what this book has to teach you, you will certainly need to study characters in earnest. This chapter has just been a 'taster' — if you would like to learn systematically how to read and write, try the *Character Text for Colloquial Chinese* by P. C. T'ung. It is available in two versions, one in full form and one in simplified characters. You may order from the following email address: pctung@hotmail.co.uk.

KEY TO EXERCISES

Chapter Two

1. Identifying countries:

    1. Holland   2. Denmark   3. India   4. Ireland
    5. Mexico   6. Malaysia   7. Scotland   8. Russia

2. True or False?

    1. True.
    2. False. Zhou Enlai was born in Jiangsu province.
    3. True.
    4. False. Shaw was born in Dublin.
    5. False. Picasso was Spanish.

3. Introduce yourself:

    1. **Wǒ shi … .**
    2. **Wǒ xìng … , míngzi jiào … .**
    3. **Wǒ shi … rén.**
    4. **Wǒ shi … rén.**

4. Changing statements into questions:

    1. **Tā shi Běijīng rén ma?**
    2. **Tā shi Ài'ěrlán rén ma?**
    3. **Tā xìng Lǐ ma?**
    4. **Tā jiào Wáng Zhōng ma?**

    [Note that it would be possible to use **ba** instead of **ma** in all these examples, so there are two correct answers to each.]

5. Say it in Chinese:

    1. **Wǒ shi Jiānádà rén.**
    2. **Wǒ bú shi Lúndūn rén.**
    3. **Wǒ (míngzi) bú jiào** Tony.
    4. **Zhè shi Zhōu Jūn xiānsheng.**

6. Read aloud and translate into English:

   1. We are all friends.
   2. They are all called Wang.
   3. Are you German too?
   4. I'm British. They are all British too.

7. Say it in Chinese:

   1. **Nà shi wǒ fūren.**
   2. **Zhè bú shi wǒ de míngzi.**
   3. **Zhè shi wǒ de péngyou, Lǐ Dàwěi.**
   4. **Nà shi tā de míngpiàn.**

9. Translate into Chinese:

   1. **Wǒ xìng Lǐ. Wǒ shi Yīngguó rén.**
   2. **Nǐ shi Běijīng rén ma?**
   3. **Wǒmen dōu jiào tā Lǎo Wáng.**
   4. **Tā fūren yě shi Měiguó rén.**
   5. **Zhè bú shi wǒ de míngpiàn.**
   6. **Tā de péngyou dōu shi Xiānggǎng rén.**

Chapter Three

10. Questions for answers:

    1. **Tā xìng shénme?**
    2. **Tā jiào shénme míngzi?**
    3. **Tā shi něi guó rén?**
    4. **Nà shi shénme?**
    5. **Tā shi shéi?**

11. Ask in Chinese:

    1. **Zhè shi shénme?**
    2. **Tā shi shéi?**
    3. **Tā shi shéi de péngyou?**
    4. **Tā shi něi guó rén?**

12. Ask in Chinese:

    1. **Tā shi Àodàlìyà Huáqiáo ma?**
    2. **Tā bú shi nǐ de péngyou ma?**

3. **Zhè bú shi nǐ de hùzhào ma?**

4. **Tāmen bù dōu shi Yīngguó rén ma?**

13. Fill in adverbs:

1. **yě**
2. **yě**
3. **dōu**
4. **jiù**
5. **yě, dōu**

14. Phone numbers:

1. **yāo-líng-sì**
2. **jiǔ-jiǔ-jiǔ**
3. **líng-yāo-sān-èr-bā   qī-wǔ-liù-èr-liù-yāo**
4. **líng-èr-líng   qī-èr-sān-sì   wǔ-liù-bā-jiǔ**
5. **líng-yāo-bā-liù-wǔ   wǔ-sān-sān   liù-sì-qī-èr**

15. Say it in Chinese:

1. **Nǐ jiā duōshao / jǐ hào?** or **Nǐ jiā de hàomǎ shi duōshao?**
2. **Tā fùqin wǔshisān suì.**
3. **Nǐ de hùzhào hàomǎ shi duōshao?**
4. **Wǒ de shǒujī hàomǎ shi líng-qī-jiǔ-bā   wǔ-jiǔ-yāo   bā-sān-jiǔ-èr.**

16. Say it in Chinese:

1. **Wǒ bù zhīdao.**
2. **Wǒ bù zhīdao tā shi shéi.**
3. **Wǒ zhīdao Wáng xiānsheng de shǒujī hàomǎ.**
4. **Qǐng jiē yāo-líng-sì-liù (fángjiān).**

18. Translate into Chinese:

1. A: **Tā xìng shénme?** B: **Tā xìng Wáng.**
2. A: **Nǐ de diànhuà hàomǎ shi duōshao? / Nǐ de diànhuà duōshao hào?**
   B: **Líng-yāo-èr-yāo   sì-bā-liù   wǔ-qī-sān-jiǔ.**
3. A: **Zhè shi shéi de hùzhào?** B: **(Shi) wǒ péngyou de.**
4. A: **Nǐ zhīdao tā shi něi guó rén ma?** B: **Zhīdao, tā shi Fǎguó rén.**
5. A: **Wáng jīnglǐ shi Shànghǎi rén ma?** B: **Bú shi, tā shi Rìběn Huáqiáo.**
6. A: **Wéi, shi Zhāng xiānsheng ma?** B: **Shì. Nín shi ...?**

Chapter Four

19 Fill in the blanks.

1. **ge**   2. **bēi**   3. **jiān**   4. — (no measure word is needed)   5. **ge** or **wèi**

20. Say it in Chinese:

1. **Wǒmen dōu yǒu hùzhào.**
2. **Tā méi yǒu shǒujī.**
3. **Wǒmen yào zhù liǎng tiān.**
4. **Nà shi wèishēngjiān ma?**

21. Change into negatives.

1. **Wǒ bù xiǎng zhù Běijīng Fàndiàn.**
2. **Tāmen dōu méi yǒu hùzhào.**
3. **Nǐmen bú yào shuāngrénfáng ma?**
4. **Nín méi yǒu míngpiàn ma?**
5. **Wǒmen de fángjiān dōu bú dài wèishēngjiān.**

22. At the café:

1. **Qǐng zuò.**
2. **Nǐ xiǎng hē shénme?**
3. **Wǒmen yào liǎng bēi hóng chá.**
4. **Nǐmen yǒu diǎnxin ma?**

23. What do they mean?

1. There's no phone in my room.
2. There are two bathrooms on the third floor.
3. Are there any Chinese companies in London?
4. At their place there's tea and coffee too.

24. Make choice-type questions.

1. **Tā shi bu shi Běijīng rén?**
2. **Tā yǒu mei yǒu Zhōngguó péngyou?**
3. **Tā xiǎng bu xiǎng hē hóngchá?**
4. **Tā rèn(shi) bu rènshi Dèng Xiǎopíng?**
5. **Nàr rè bu re?**

25. Ask for permission:

1. **Wǒ kě bu kěyǐ chōu yān?**

2. Wǒ kě bu kěyǐ zuò zhèr?

3. Wǒ kě bu kěyǐ hē bēi píjiǔ?

4. Wǒ kě bu kěyǐ xiūxi xiūxi?

27. Translate into Chinese.

1. A: **Nǐmen yǒu liǎng jiān dānrénfáng ma?**
   B: **Méi yǒu. Wǒmen zhǐ yǒu yì jiān shuāngrénfáng.**

2. A: **Nín zhù jǐ tiān?**
   B: **Wǔ tiān.**

3. A: **Nǐmen xiǎng hē shénme?**
   B: **Liǎng bēi chá, yì bēi kāfēi.**

4. A: **Wǒmen de fángjiān tài rè le!**
   B: **Nín xiǎng huàn yì jiān ma?**

5. A: **Zhèr zhǔn hē jiǔ ma?**
   B: **Duìbuqǐ, bù zhǔn. Hē jiǔ, chōu yān dōu bù zhǔn.**

6. A: **Nàr de fēngjǐng piàoliang ma?**
   B: **Piàoliang. Nàr de rén yě piàoliang.**

Chapter Five

28. Say it in Chinese:

1. **Nǐ jiā zài nǎr?**

2. **Wǒ de fángjiān zài sì lóu, bú zài shí lóu.**

3. **Wáng xiáojie zài Shànghǎi ma?**

4. **Wǒ bù zhīdao nǐ de shǒujī zài nǎr.**

29. Say it in Chinese:

1. **Lǐ xiānsheng zài ma?**

2. **Wáng xiáojie zài jiā ma?**

3. **Wèishēngjiān zài yī lóu.**

4. **Tā zài lǐtou.**

5. **Kāfēitīng zài zuǒbianr.**

6. **Běijīng Fàndiàn jiù zài qiántou.**

30. Tell the prices.

1. **Wǔ máo (qián).**

2. **Yí kuài èr (máo).**

3. **Shíbā kuài.**

4. **Sìshiwǔ kuài wǔ (máo).**

5. **Liùshiqī kuài sān (máo).**
6. **Jiǔshijiǔ kuài jiǔ máo jiǔ.**

31. Fill blanks with question words.

1. **shéi**
2. **jǐ**
3. **nǎr**
4. **shénme**
5. **duōshao**
6. **nǎr**

32. Tell the relative locations.

1. **xībianr**
2. **dōngbianr**
3. **nánbianr**
4. **běibianr**
5. **nánbianr** or **dōngnánbianr**

34. Translate into Chinese.

1. A: **Wéi, Wáng xiānsheng zài ma?**
   B: **Duìbuqǐ, tā bú zài.**
2. A: **Tāmen dōu zài nǎr?**
   B: **Tāmen dōu zài kāfēitīng.**
3. A: **Qǐng wèn, cèsuǒ zài nǎr?**
   B: **Zài èr lóu.**
4. A: **Zhèi ge cháhú duōshao qián?**
   B: **Shíliù kuài wǔ.**
5. A: **Tā jiā zài nǎr?**
   B: **Zài gōngyuán (de) dōngbianr.**
6. A: **Kànkan nín de lǚyóutú kěyǐ ma?**
   B: **Kěyǐ, nǐ kàn ba.**

Chapter Six

35. Give directions in Chinese.

1. **Wǎng qián zǒu.**
2. **Wǎng dōng guǎi.**
3. **Wǎng zuǒ guǎi.**
4. **Qiántou bù zhǔn wǎng yòu guǎi.**

5. **Qù gōngyuán.**

36. A taste of **le**

1. He has gone/went to Shanghai.
2. Miss Li has arrived in Beijing.
3. They all know it now.
4. She has gone/went to the park.
5. Have you looked at the tourist map?

37. Practice with measure words

1. **ge / wèi**   2. **ge / jiān**   3. **bēi**
4. **tiáo**   5. **zhāng**   6. **kuài**

38. Words into pattern

1. **Wǒ xǐhuan mǎi dōngxi, wǒ xiǎng qù bǎihuò dàlóu.**
2. **Wǒ xǐhuan hē chá, wǒ xiǎng qù kāfēitīng.**
3. **Wǒ xǐhuan rè de dìfang, wǒ xiǎng qù Xībānyá.**
4. **Wǒ xǐhuan kàn fēngjǐng, wǒ xiǎng qù Guìlín.**

[Guilin is in Guangxi Province, and the city and its surrounding scenery are renowned for their beauty.]

39. Translate into Chinese

1. **hē chá de rén**
2. **mài bíyānhú de dìfang**
3. **tā xiǎng qù de gōngyuán**
4. **qù Tiān'ānmén de gōnggòngqìchē**
5. **zuò qìchē de rén**

40. Give the Chinese equivalents:

1. **Tāmen hē de kāfēi hěn guì.**
2. **Zhè bú shi wǒ yào mǎi de lǚyóutú.**
3. **Tā yào qù de dìfang hěn yuǎn.**
4. **Xiǎng qù Zhōngguó de rén tài duō le.**

41. Translate into English

1. I want to go to the department store to buy something.
2. He wants to come to England as a tourist.
3. I am thinking of going to the north to see friends.
4. Would you like to go to the park to relax?

5. I would like to go to the antiques market to have a look around.

42. Guesswork

1. **Rè shuǐ**   2. **Xīzhàn**   3. **Yuǎndōng Gōngsī**
4. **Chē yàoshi**   5. **Zhōngshānmén**
6. **Bíyānhú méi yǒu shìchǎng**

44. Translate into Chinese

1. A: **Qǐng wèn, huǒchēzhàn zài nǎr?**
   B: **Nǐ kàn, jiù zài nàr. Jiù zài nèi ge dà fàndiàn hòutou.**
2. A: **Tóngzhì, qǐngwèn, qù gǔdǒng shìchǎng zěnme zǒu?**
   B: **Hěn yuǎn. Wǒ yě bù zhīdao zěnme zǒu.**
3. A: **Qǐng wèn, zhè chē dào Tiān'ānmén ma?**
   B: **Dào. Hái yǒu liǎng zhàn.**
4. A: **Tāmen dōu qù Zhōngguó le ma?**
   B: **Dōu qù le.**
5. A: **Zhè fùjìn yǒu yínháng ma?**
   B: **Yǒu, jiù zài nèi ge dàlóu lǐtou.**
6. A: **Wǒ yào qù (fēi)jīchǎng.**
   B: **Nǐ shi zuò gōnggòngqìchē (qu) háishi zuò chūzūchē (qu)?**

Chapter Seven

45. Say it in Chinese

1. **Yī-bā-sì'-èr nián sì yuè èrshibā hào/rì**
2. **Yī-jiǔ-yī-yī nián shí yuè shí rì/hào**
3. **Èr-líng-líng-yī nián jiǔ yuè shíyī hào/rì**
4. **Èr-líng-líng-bā nián bā yuè bā hào/rì**
5. **Èr-líng-èr-wǔ nián yī yuè sānshiyī hào/rì**

46. Put into English

1. She has already left for China.
2. I have already bought that thing.
3. We already know each other.
4. The train has already arrived.
5. Today is the fifth already.

47. Translate into Chinese

1. **Piàoliang de dōngxi dōu hěn guì.**
2. **Zhè bú shi qù jīchǎng de lù.**
3. **Fùjìn yǒu méi you kěyǐ huàn qián de yínháng?**
4. **Wǒ yǒu hěn duō xǐhuan hē jiǔ de péngyou.**

48. Give a quick answer

1. **Míngtiān liù hào.**
2. **Jīntiān xīngqīsì.**
3. **Hòutiān èrshisān hào.**
4. **Jīntiān shí yuè èr hào.**

49. Tell the time in Chinese

1. **Jiǔ diǎn zhōng.**
2. **Liǎng diǎn bàn.**
3. **Bā diǎn wǔ fēn.**
4. **Sì diǎn sān kè.**

50 . Answer the questions

1. **Shàngwǔ shí diǎn.**
2. **Xiàwǔ sì diǎn yí kè.**
3. **Zhōngwǔ shí'èr diǎn sìshibā fēn.**
4. **Wǎnshang qī diǎn bàn.**

51. Translate into English

1. I have a friend who is from Hong Kong.
2. He wants to invite me to go for a drink.
3. She asks/asked me how much money I have.
4. I know an Overseas Chinese who owns ten Chinese restaurants.

53. Translate into Chinese

1. A: **Nǐ shénme shíhou qù Rìběn?** B: **Jiǔ yuè wǔ hào/rì.**
2. A: **Tā xīngqīliù lái ma?** B: **Bù lái, tā xīngqītiān lái.**
3. A: **Qǐng wèn, xiànzài jǐ diǎn le?** B: **Shí diǎn shí fēn.**
4. A: **Xīngqīliù nǐ jǐ diǎn zhōng xià bān?** B: **Shí'èr diǎn bàn.**
5. A: **Nǐ rènshi Huáyuán Gōngsī de Lǐ jīnglǐ ma?**
   B: **Bú rènshi, kěshi wǒ yǒu ge hǎo péngyou rènshi tā.**
6. A: **Huǒchē jǐ diǎn zhōng dào?** B: **Yǐjing dào le.**

Chapter Eight

54. Simple comparisons

1. **Shǒudū Fàndiàn bǐ Huáyuán Fàndiàn dà.**
2. **Píjiǔ bǐ kuàngquánshuǐ guì.**
3. **Shānshang bǐ shānxia lěng.**
4. **Lóushang de zhōng bǐ lóuxia de (zhōng) kuài.**

55. Durations of time

1. to stay for three weeks
2. to have Chinese food for two years
3. to be on duty/working for eight hours
4. to be on a plane for 15 hours
5. to ride a bike for twenty minutes

56. Change of state

1. **... tā méi (yǒu) qián le.**
2. **... tā bù xiǎng chī le.**
3. **... bù máng le.**
4. **... bù jǐ le.**

57. Translate into English

1. The weather isn't good there, and things are expensive too.
2. On the mountain the scenery is beautiful and the weather is cool.
3. The Capital Hotel is well-situated and its rooms are large.
4. The Dahua Restaurant is a long way away but its roast duck is excellent.

58. Add a bit of colour

1. **hóng**   2. **hóng** or **bái**   3. **hēi**   4. **lán**

60. Translate into Chinese

1. A: **Jiānádà dōngtiān zěnmeyàng?**
   B: **Lěng jíle.**
2. A: **Xiānggǎng sān yuè hěn nuǎnhuo ma?**
   B: **Hěn nuǎnhuo, bǐ Shànghǎi nuǎnhuo.**
3. A: **Nǐ (de) péngyou dài yǎnjìngr ma?**
   B: **Tā bú dài.**
4. A: **Nǐ chuān jǐ hàor de?**
   B: **Wǒ bù zhīdao. Kěnéng shi sìshí'èr hàor.**

5. A: Nǐ xǐhuan shénme yánsè de?
   B: Wǒ xǐhuan huáng de.
6. A: Nǐ zěnme bù xiǎng qù le?
   B: Wǒ de qián bú gòu.

Chapter Nine

61. Add information:

1. Tā yào zuò fēijī qù Zhōngguó.
2. Qǐng nǐ bié zài zhèr chōu yān.
3. Qǐng nǐ gěi wǒ mǎi píng píjiǔ.
4. Nǐ kěyǐ tì wǒmen qǐng Wáng Xiānsheng lái ma?

62. Make a comparison:

1. Shànghǎi bǐ Běijīng nuǎnhuo yìdiǎnr.
2. Tiān'ānmén bǐ Shǒudū Jùchǎng jìn duōle.
3. Lǎo Lǐ de biǎo bǐ huǒchēzhàn de zhōng kuài yìdiǎnr.
4. Zuò fēijī qù bǐ zuò huǒchē qù kuài duōle.

63. All the same:

1. Bíyānhú gēn diànzǐ biǎo yíyàng guì.
2. Tiān'ānmén gēn Bǎihuò Dàlóu yíyàng yuǎn.
3. Zuò chē qù gēn qí chē qù yíyàng kuài.
4. Xiǎo Wáng gēn Xiǎo Lǐ yíyàng pàng.

64. What are they doing now?:

1. Tāmen zài xiūxi ne.
2. Tāmen zài tiào wǔ ne.
3. Tāmen zài lóuxia hē jiǔ ne.
4. Tāmen kàn tiānqi yùbào ne.
5. Tāmen méi (yǒu) zài chōu yān.

65. Say it in Chinese:

1. chōu yān de rén
2. chī sù de rén/bù chī ròu de rén
3. ài hē chá de rén
4. xiǎng qù Zhōngguó de rén/xiǎng dào Zhōngguó qù de rén
5. zǎochen dǎ tàijíquán de rén

66. Needy-verb sentences:

    1. Smoking is not allowed on the bus.

    2. Eating is not permitted here.

    3. Don't talk while (you're) eating.

    4. Who does the cooking for you?

68. Translate into Chinese:

    1. **Qǐng nǐ tì wǒ mǎi yí ge.**
       Hǎo. Wǒ xiǎng hóng de zuì hǎo.

    2. **Nǐmen liǎng ge rén yíyàng gāo ma?**
       Bù, tā bǐ wǒ gāo yìdiǎnr.

    3. **Wǒmen qǐng tā chī kǎoyā hǎo bu hao?**
       Bù xíng. Tā shi chīsùde.

    4. **Tā zài gànmá ne?**
       Tā zài xiūxi ne.

    5. **Wǒ xiǎng xué tàijíquán; nǐ kěyǐ tì wǒ zhǎo wèi lǎoshī ma?**
       Méi wèntí.

    6. **Nǐ jīntiān shàng wǎng le ma?**
       Wǒ de diànnǎo chū wèntí le, bù néng shàng wǎng le.

Chapter Ten

69. Where is he?:

    1. He isn't here; he's gone to the park.

    2. He's not at home; he's gone to the (company) office.

    3. He didn't come to work; he went shopping.

    4. Has he also gone for a drink?

70. 'Already' and 'Not yet':

    1. a) **Yǐjing chī le.**   b) **Hái méi (chī) ne.**

    2. a) **Yǐjing lái le.**   b) **Hái méi (lái) ne.**

    3. a) **Yǐjing jié le.**   b) **Hái méi (jié) ne.**

    4. a) **Yǐjing mǎi le.**   b) **Hái méi (mǎi) ne.**

71. Shift of emphasis:

    1. A: Were you drinking yesterday?
       B: Yes.
       A: How many bottles did you have?

2. A: Did you go to see friends?
   B: Yes.
   A: How many did you see?

3. A: Did you go to Japan?
   B: Yes.
   A: How many days did you stay there?

4. A: Have you bought any snuff bottles?
   B: Yes.
   A: How many have you bought?

5. A: Have you done your *taichi*?
   B: Yes.
   A: How many minutes did you do?

73. Say it in Chinese:

   1. yí (ge) xīngqī yí cì
   2. yí ge yuè liǎng cì
   3. yì nián sān tàng
   4. yì tiān sì zhēn

74. Say it in Chinese:

   1. Wǒ shàng xīngqī mǎile yī ge xīn shǒujī.
   2. Nǐ qùnián qùle jǐ cì/tàng Àodàlìyà?
   3. Nǐ xíngli shōushihǎo le ma?
   4. Wǒ zuótiān gěi tā dǎle sān cì diànhuà.

76. Translate into Chinese:

   1. A: Wéi, wǒ kěyǐ gēn Lǐ xiānsheng shuō huà ma?
      B: Duìbuqǐ, tā yǐjing huí guó le.
   2. A: Zuótiān nǐ dǎ le duōshao ge diànhuà?
      B: Yígòng dǎle yìbǎi èrshisān ge.
   3. A: Bàoshang yǒu shénme xīnwén?
      B: Bàoshang shuō jīnnián yǒu hěn duō rén yào chū guó.
   4. A: Nǐ chīwán le ma?
      B: Hái méi ne. Wǒ hēwán tāng jiù lái.
   5. A: Tā fāshāo le ma?
      B: Sānshijiǔ dù. Wǒmen zhǎo dàifu lái ba?
   6. A: Nǐmen cháng chī Zhōngguó fàn ma?
      B: Cháng chī. Chàbuduō yí ge yuè liǎng cì.

Chapter Eleven

77. Answer the questions:

1. **Qùguo.**
2. **Zhùguo** (Probably).
3. **Qùguo.**
4. **Méi shuōguo.** (We presume!)

78. **Guo** or **le**?

1. **-guo**   2. **-guo**   3. **-guo**   4. **-le**

79. Fill in the blanks:

1. **wán** or **hǎo**
2. **wán**
3. **hǎo**
4. **wán**
5. **dào**

80. Guided answers:

1. **Shi yī-jiǔ-bā-liù nián shí yuè qù de.**
2. **Shi zài Xiānggǎng mǎi de.**
3. **Tā shi zuò fēijī lái de.**
4. **Tā shi qùnián qī yuè zǒu de.**
5. **Shi Wáng xiáojie zuò de.**

81. Translate into English:

1. He has been living in Shanghai for three years.
2. We have been studying Chinese for two years.
3. She has already bought ten fish.
4. He has already been talking for five hours.
5. I have already taken 200 photos.

82. Translate into English:

1. After arriving in Shanghai I will certainly phone you. [Having arrived in Shanghai ...]
2. They left after taking a photograph/after having their photos taken. [Having had their photos taken ...]
3. When I've changed some money I'll go shopping.
4. After work you must come back home.

5. Once he's on the aircraft he goes to sleep.

83. Revision. Jumbled sentences:

   1. c.b.a.d.

   2. b.c.a.d.

   3. c.b.d.a.

   4. b.c.a.d.

   5. d.b.a.c.

84. Translate into Chinese:

   1. A: **Nǐ xuéle jǐ nián (de) Yīngwén/Yīngyǔ le?**
      B: **Chàbuduō shínián le, kěshi wǒ hái bú huì shuō.**

   2. A: **Nǐ shénme shíhou dǎ tàijíquán?**
      B: **Shuì jiào yǐqián.**

   3. A: **Nǐ qùguo Rìběn ma?**
      B: **Qùguo, wǒ yǐqián měi nián qù yí tàng/cì.**

   4. A: **Shì nǐ zuò háishi tā zuò?**
      B: **Wǒmen liǎng ge rén dōu bú huì zuò.**

   5. A: **Tā lái kāi huì ma?**
      B: **Bù lái. Tā dǎ diànhuà jiào wǒ gàosu nǐ tā bù néng lái.**

   6. A: **Jīntiān méi yǒu gōnggòngqìchē, nǐ shi zěnme lái de?**
      B: **Wǒ shi zuò chūzūqìche lai de/Wǒ shi dǎ dī lai de.**

Chapter Twelve

85. Add information:

   1. **Xué de hěn kuài.**

   2. **Zuò de hǎo jíle.**

   3. **Shuì de bú tài hǎo.**

   4. **Zhào de hěn piàoliang.**

86. Answer the questions:

   1. **Guǎngzhōu jīntiān sìshi'èr dù.**

   2. **Nèi ge fàndiàn yǒu sān bǎi liùshi ge fángjiān.**

   3. **Tā yào qù sān ge yuè.**

   4. **Tā wǔ suì le.**

87. What's going on?

   1. Who is sitting outside the door?

2. What is she wearing?

3. Whose air ticket is he holding?

4. He is waiting for you.

5. She looks very thin.

88. Translate into Chinese:

1. **Tā zhōngxué bìyè yǐhòu jiù dào Měiguó qu le.**

2. **Wǒ yǐwéi Lǎo Lǐ yě zài nǐmen xuéxiào jiāo shū.**

3. **Tā yǐjing tiàole sān ge xiǎoshí de wǔ le.**

4. **Shéi shuō Xiǎo Zhāng yào gēn Wáng xiáojie jiéhūn?**

89. Fill in the result verbs:

1. **jiàn** or **dào**

2. **wán**

3. **wán**

4. **dào**

90. Translate into English:

1. (having) studied for 3 years   didn't study for 3 years

2. (having) listened for 2 days   didn't listen for 2 days

3. (having) practised for 3 months   didn't practise for 3 months

4. (having) rained for 5 weeks   didn't rain for 5 weeks

91. Make sentences:

1. **Lǎo Wáng bǐ Xiǎo Lǐ dà liǎng hàor.**

2. **Tā de biǎo bǐ nǐ de (biǎo) kuài wǔ fēn zhōng.**

3. **Tā bǐ tā érzi duō wǔshí ge.**

4. **Jī bǐ yú guì sān kuài qián.**

92. Translate into Chinese:

1. A: **Tā jīntiān zǎoshang kànzhe hěn lèi.**
   B: **Shì a, tā zuótiān wǎnshang méi shuìhǎo/shuì de bù hǎo.**

2. A: **Tā (zuò) yú zuò de hǎo ma?**
   B: **Tā bù cháng zuò yú, wǒ lái ba.**

3. A: **Nǐ Zhōngguó huà/Hànyǔ shuō de tài hǎo le.**
   B: **Náli, wǒ cháng shuōcuò.**

4. A: **Tā shǒu shang názhe shénme ne?**
   B: **Yídìng shi tāde hùzhào.**

5. A: **Wǒmen sān ge yuè méi chī jī le.**
   B: **Hǎo, wǒ mǎshang qù mǎi yì zhī.**

6. A: **Něi jiàn T-xùshān guì? Huáng de háishi lán de?**
   B: **Lán de bǐ huáng de guì liǎng kuài qián.**

Chapter Thirteen

93. Translate into English:

    1. How do I get to the station?

    2. How do you cook this dish?

    3. How is this thing used?

    4. How do you open the toilet door?

    5. How do you say 'Cheers!' in Chinese?

    6. How do you dial direct to Beijing?

94. Finish sentences:

    1. **hē jiǔ ne.**

    2. **shuì jiào ne.**

    3. **mǎi dōngxi ne.**

    4. **xué Zhōngwén/Hànyǔ ne.**

95. Fill in the blanks:

    1. **qu**

    2. **lai**

    3. **lai**

    4. **qu**

96. Translate into English:

    1. This fish isn't real, it's made of potato.

    2. She says this 100 yuan note is a forgery.

    3. Last night's dishes were all the most expensive ones.

    4. That car he bought is a red one.

97. Could you help?

    1. Do you think you could help by calling a taxi for us?

    2. Can you help me find a *taiji* teacher?

    3. Can you take a photograph for us please?

    4. Could I trouble you to ask if Old Wang is in for me?

98. Lodging a complaint:

1. The room is too noisy, there is no way I can get to sleep.
2. The food has all gone cold, there's no way we can eat it.
3. There's no water in the toilet, we can't use it.
4. There are too many people smoking, we can't eat.

99. Translate into Chinese:

1. A: **Wǒ kěyǐ zhíbō Yīngguó ma?**
   B: **Dāngrán kěyǐ.**
2. A: **Máfan nǐ sòng wǒ dào huǒchēzhàn hǎo ma?**
   B: **Méi wèntí**, **shàng chē ba!**
3. A: **Wǒmen yídìng děi qǐng tāmen chī dùn fàn ma?**
   B: **Kěyǐ bù qǐng.** *or* **Bù qǐng yě kěyǐ.**
4. A: **Wǒmen shénme shíhou qù Rìběn?**
   B: **Yàoshi qiānzhèng méi wèntí, wǒmen xià ge yuè jiù kěyǐ qù.**
5. A: **Wáng xiáojie zài nǎr ne?**
   B: **Tā zhèngzài fā chuánzhēn ne.**
6. A: **Xièxie nǐ bāngmáng.**
   B: **Bú kèqi.**

Chapter Fourteen

100. Translate into English:

1. The bank is to the east of the hotel.
2. The business centre is just opposite the cafe.
3. The men's toilet is behind the western restaurant.
4. My passport is on top of the tourist map on your right.
5. That photograph is in the passport which he is holding in his hand.

101. True or false?

1. False.
2. True.
3. False.
4. True.

102. Fill in the blanks:

1. **lai**
2. **shangqu**

3. **xialai**

4. **shang**

103. Place where/place whither:

1. You can write it in your room./Your address can be written on the luggage.

2. She gave birth to a daughter in China./Her daughter was born in China.

3. He often practises *taiji* in the park./The rain falling on him made him very uncomfortable.

4. Where shall we fill in the forms?/Where should I fill in my name?

104. **Jiù** v **cái**:

1. **jiù**

2. **cái**

3. **cái**

4. **jiù**

5. **cái**

105. Translate into Chinese:

1. A: **Guójì Zhǎnlǎn Zhōngxīn zài nǎr?**
   B: **Jiù zài Xīnhuá Fàndiàn duì miàn.**

2. A: **Nǐ jiā lí huǒchēzhàn (yǒu) duō yuǎn?**
   B: **Wǒ xiǎng chàbuduō (yǒu) wǔ gōnglǐ.**

3. A: **Nǐ yǒu tā de Běijīng dìzhǐ ma?**
   B: **Yǒu, jiù zài zhèr: Běijīng 100826, Yǒngdìng Lù èrshijiǔ hào, sān lóu.**

4. A: **Tā shi shénme shíhou huí Shànghǎi qu de?**
   B: **Tā yì shōudào nǐ de yóujiàn jiù huíqu le.**

5. A: **Wáng xiānsheng shuō méi fázi.**
   B: **Gàosu tā nǐ shi wǒ de péngyou: tā yídìng huì bāngmáng.**

6. A: **Lǐ xiáojie, wǒ kěyǐ zuòzài nǐ pángbiānr ma?**
   B: **Dāngrán kěyǐ, kěshi wǒ mǎshang jiù děi zǒu.**

Chapter Fifteen

106. Answer the questions:

1. **Wǒmen gěile tā qián, tā jiù qù le.**

2. **Tā kànle xīnwén jiù zǒu.**

3. **Wǒ jìle xìn jiù qù (kàn tā).**

4. **Tā dǎle tàijíquán jiù chī zǎofàn.**

107. Fill in the blanks:

    1. **shéi…shéi**

    2. **shénme…shénme** <u>or</u> **duōshao…duōshao**

    3. **zěnme…zěnme**

    4. **jǐ…jǐ**

108. Translate into Chinese:

    1. **Zhōngguó cài hǎo chī kěshi bù hǎo zuò.**

    2. **Tā jiā zài shānli, hěn bù hǎo zhǎo.**

    3. **Yì zhī kǎoyā gòu shí ge rén chī ma?**

    4. **Zhèi jù huà hěn hǎo xué.**

109. Translate into English:

    1. The earliest he could arrive would be tomorrow.

    2. His house is at least 20 minutes walk from the bus stop.

    3. It won't get hotter than 40° in Beijing in August.

    4. Letters from China take at least a week.

110. Advice:

    1. **Nǐ háishi bié chōu le ba.**

    2. **Wǒmen háishi míngtiān zuò ba.**

    3. **Nǐ háishi zuò huǒchē qù ba.**

    4. **Wǒmen háishi fā chuánzhēn gěi tā ba.**

111. New situation **le**:

    1. What's happened to his hand?

    2. She's ill and can no longer come.

    3. How come you haven't bought a ticket? Sorry, I forgot.

    4. The lift is out of order. Let's walk up.

112. Translate into Chinese:

    1. A: **Qǐng wèn, zhè fùjìn yǒu yóujú ma?**
       B: **Yǒu, Xīnhuá Lù shang jiù yǒu yí ge.**

    2. A: **Jì Ōuzhōu de hángkōng míngxìnpiàn duōshao qián?**
       B: **Guójì hángkōng míngxìnpiàn dōu shi sì kuài wǔ.**

    3. A: **Qǐng wèn, zuì jìn de yínháng zài nǎr?**
       B: **Dào hónglǜdēng wǎng yòu guǎi, yínháng jiù zài dì-èr ge lùkǒur.**

    4. A: **Nǐmen de diànhuà zěnme le?**
       B: **Wǒ yě bù zhīdao wèishénme, kěshi xiànzài zhǐ néng dǎjìnlái,**
         bù néng dǎchūqù.

5. A: **Chuánzhēnjī huài le ma?**
   B: **Yǐjing huài le liǎng tiān le.**
6. A: **Wǒmen zǒu něi tiáo lù qù?**
   B: **Háishi zǒu dà lù ba; wǎnshang xiǎo lù bù hǎo zǒu.**

Chapter Sixteen

113. Answer the questions:

   1. **Wǒ něi ge dōu xiǎng mǎi.**
   2. **Nǎr dōu yǒu Zhōngguó fànguǎnr.**
   3. **Wǒ shénme shíhou dōu yǒu gōngfu.**
   4. **Wǒ shéi dōu méi qù kàn.**

114. Fill in the blanks:

   1. **bu**   2. **de**   3. **bu**   4. **de**

115. Opposites:

1. **huài**	2. **shǎo**	3. **bái**	4. **xiǎo**	5. **rè**
6. **shòu**	7. **wǎn**	8. **màn**	9. **cuò**	10. **jìn**
11. **guì**	12. **nán (kùnnan)**	13. **liángkuai**		
14. **hòutou**	15. **yòubian**			

116. Fill in the blanks:

   1. **buwán**
   2. **buqǐ**
   3. **bujiàn**
   4. **bují**
   5. **dedào**

117. Using *verb-adj-(yi)diǎnr*:

   1. **Qǐng nǐ shuōmàn yìdiǎnr.**
   2. **Qǐng nǐ màipiányi diǎnr.**
   3. **Qǐng nǐ láizǎo diǎnr.**
   4. **Qǐng nǐ zuòhǎo diǎnr.**

118. Translate into English:

   1. If someone is talking upstairs, can it be heard downstairs?
   2. In America can one buy books in Chinese?
   3. He can't eat a large water melon all on his own.
   4. Don't worry, I certainly can't forget this matter.

119. Translate into Chinese:

    1. A: **Xiāngjiāo zěnme mài?**
       B: **Liǎng kuài liù yì jīn, liǎng jīn wǔ kuài.**

    2. A: **Shuǐguǒ dōu guì le ma?**
       B: **Shì a, píngguǒ xiànzài mài sān kuài èr yì jīn, bǐ qùnián guì le sān bèi.**

    3. A: **Nǐ zuò huǒchē qù kǒngpà láibují le.**
       B: **Méi fázi, wǒ mǎibuqǐ fēijī piào** (*or* **zuòbuqǐ fēijī**).

    4. A: **Yàoshi wǒmen gǎnbushàng liù diǎn sìshiwǔ de huǒchē zěnme bàn?**
       B: **Bié zháojí, liù diǎn wǔshiwǔ hái yǒu yì bān.**

    5. A: **Fēijī jiù yào qǐfēi le, qǐng kuài yìdiǎnr.**
       B: **Nǐ shuō shénme? Qǐng nǐ shuōmàn yìdiǎnr.**

    6. A: **Jīnnián xiàtiān nǐ qù nǎr?**
       B: **Nǎr piányi wǒ qù nǎr.**

Chapter Seventeen

120. Translate into English:

    1. He has already given me the money.
    2. May I put the luggage over here?
    3. Who has taken my camera?
    4. Will you please take this upstairs?

121. Translate into English:

    1. What about the large size? Try it on and see.
    2. Which is the best method? Let's all think about it and see.
    3. I forget where I put it. I'll go and look for it.
    4. When will the train arrive? Can you go and ask, please?

122. Fusing together:

    1. **Tā lèi de zǒubudòng le.**
    2. **Yǔ dà de wǒmen chūbuqù le.**
    3. **Zhōngguó cài hǎo chī de shéi dōu xiǎng chī.**
    4. **Tā de xiāngzi dà de shí ge rén dōu bānbudòng.**

123. Fill in the blanks:

    1. **bàn**   2. **fā**   3. **jiǎo**   4. **shuā**   5. **chū**

124. Not quite opposite:

    1. **Zuótiān yǒu diǎnr lěng.**

2. Nàr de dōngxi yǒu diǎnr guì.

3. Gōngyuán wàitou yǒu diǎnr chǎo.

4. Tā àiren de yīfu yǒu diǎnr zāng.

5. Zài guówài lǚxíng yǒu diǎnr kùnnan.

125. Fill in blanks:

1. wán   2. gānjing   3. xia   4. hǎo

126. Translate into Chinese:

1. A: Qǐng nǐ bǎ zhèi fēng xìn gěi Wáng xiānsheng.
   B: Hǎo.

2. A: Fēijī shénme shíhou zài Xiānggǎng jiàngluò?
   B: Bù zhīdao. Wǒ qù wènwen kàn.

3. A: Tā jīntiān hěn máng ma?
   B: Hěn máng, máng de hái méi chī wǔfàn ne.

4. A: Nǐ zhǎodào tā le ma?
   B: Méi yǒu, wǒ bǎ tā de dìzhǐ nòngcuò le.

5. A: Nǐ yígerén nádeliǎo sān ge xiāngzi ma?
   B: Dāngrán nádeliǎo.

6. A: Tā jīntiān zǎochen zěnme le?
   B: Yǒu diǎnr bù shūfu. Zuótiān wǎnshang rè de tā
      zhǐ shuìle liǎng ge xiǎoshí.

Chapter Eighteen

127. How to say it

1. Wǒ shénme dōu néng chī.

2. Zhè yú tài xián le.

3. Nǐ xiǎng hē shénme jiǔ?

4. Qǐng gěi wǒ diǎnr làjiāo.

128. Translate into English:

1. Please come tomorrow morning. The earlier the better.

2. The more I worry the less I can speak.

3. Why is it that the more he eats the skinnier he gets?

4. There are more and more people who study Chinese.

129. Turn into exclamations:

1. Tā Fǎyǔ shuō de duō hǎo a!

2. Xué Zhōngwén duōme bù róngyi a!
3. Yàoshi wǒmen yǒu chuánzhēn duōme fāngbiàn a!
4. Kànjian hóngdēng bù tíng duō wēixiǎn a!

130. Numbers:

1. Yìqiān wǔ(bǎi).
2. Liǎngwàn sìqiān liùbǎi qīshibā.
3. Shíbāwàn liùqiān sānbǎi jiǔshiwǔ.
4. Liùyì qīqiān bābǎi sìshiwàn.
5. Shíyīyì wǔqiān sìbǎi èrshiliùwàn.

131. And how do you say these?

1. Wǒ měi tiān mángzhe xué Hànyǔ.
2. Zhèi ge fànguǎnr shénme cài zuì shòu huānyíng?
3. Nǐ duì Zhōngyī yǒu-xìngqù ma?
4. Wǒ yìdiǎnr yě bú lèi.

132. Make it stronger!

1. wǒ fēi chī bù kě.
2. fēi guānshang chuānghu bù kě.
3. fēi gàosu tā bù kě.
4. fēi gěi qián bù kě.

133. Translate into Chinese:

1. A: Nǐ xiǎng chī shénme?
   B: Suí nǐ biàn, nǐ diǎn shénme wǒ jiù chī shénme.
2. A: Nǐ xíguàn zhèr de tiānqi le ma?
   B: Xíguàn le, xiànzài wǒ juéde yuè rè yuè hǎo.
3. A: Zhèi ge gōngyuánr duō piàoliang a!
   B: Kě bú shì ma!
4. A: Nǐ duì zhào xiàng yǒu-xìngqù ma?
   B: Yìdiǎnr yě méi yǒu.
5. A: Nǐ mǎi de nèi fú Zhōngguó huàr jiàqian shi duōshao?
   B: Wǒ gēn tāmen jiǎng jià jiǎngle hěn jiǔ, zuì hòu shi yíwàn bāqiān wǔ.
6. A: Nǐ wèishénme měi tiān dōu zài mángzhe liàn tàijíquán?
   B: Wǒ huí Yīngguó yǐqián fēi (bǎ tàijíquán) xuéhuì bù kě.

Chapter Nineteen

134. Translate into English:

1. The luggage has already been sent to your room.
2. The fax will be sent straight away.
3. This suitcase of mine was checked three times at the airport.
4. The delegation has been invited to go to the tenth floor.
5. The television was broken by his son.

135. How would you say it?

1. Wǒ de hùzhào bèi tōu le.
2. Xīn hétong shi zuótiān shōudào de.
3. Nǐ de qiánbāor zhǎodào le ma?/zhǎodào le méi you?
4. Nǐ yào de nèi běn shū màiwán le.

136. Opposites:

1. zāng   2. è   3. kū   4. zháojí   5. jìde
6. jiàngluò   7. chūkǒu   8. huí guó   9. kǔ   10. rùjìng

137. Say it in Chinese:

1. sì fēn zhī yī
2. èrshiwǔ fēn zhī yī
3. bǎi fēn zhī shíqī
4. bǎi fēn zhī líng diǎn bā
5. bǎi fēn zhī jiǔshijiǔ diǎn jiǔ

138. How could it be?

1. Yì nián zěnme huì yǒu sānbǎi liùshiliù tiān ne?
2. Yīngguó rén zěnme huì bù hē xiàwǔ chá ne?
3. Zuò huǒchē zěnme huì bǐ zuò fēijī wēixiǎn ne?
4. Chī Zhōngguó cài zěnme huì róngyi pàng ne?

139. Often and never:

1. Wǒ cónglái méi qùguo Zhōngguó.
2. Wǒ cónglái méi yòng Zhōngwén xiěguo xìn.
3. Wǒ cónglái méi pèngjiànguo zhèi zhǒng shì.
4. Wǒ zǒngshi hěn xiǎoxīn, cónglái méi diūguo dōngxi.

140. Translate into Chinese:

1. A: **Nǐ de qiānzhèng děngle duō jiǔ?**
   B: **Píngcháng chàbuduō yào yí ge xīngqi, xìngkuī wǒ rènshi dàshǐguǎn de rén, yíxiàr jiù nádào le.**

2. A: **Nǐ jīntiān zěnme méi chuān xīzhuāng?**
   B: **Bié tí le, wǒ de yīfu quán bèi tōu le.**

3. A: **Jīnnián qìchē jìnkǒu zēngjiā le ma?**
   B: **Zēngjiā le, zēngjiāle bǎi fēn zhī qī diǎn wǔ.**

4. A: **Lù shang rén tài duō, qǐng nǐ kāimàn diǎnr.**
   B: **Nín fàngxīn, wǒ kāi chē cónglái méi chūguo shì.**

5. A: **Bàoshang shuō bǎi fēn zhī qīshí de nán xuésheng dōu chōu yān.**
   B: **Zěnme huì yǒu zhème duō ne?**

6. A: **Nǐ wèishénme yào xué Zhōngwén?**
   B: **Yì fāngmiàn shì wǒ duì wàiyǔ yǒu-xìngqù, yì fāngmiàn shì wǒ xiǎng zhēnzhèng liǎojiě Zhōngguó.**

Chapter Twenty

141. Translate from characters

1. **Jīnyú**	Goldfish
2. **Lónghǔ Shān**	Dragon & Tiger Mountain
3. **Běijīng Shì**	Beijing Municipality
4. **Xī'ān Zhàn**	Xi'an Station
5. **Shànghǎi Fàndiàn**	Shanghai Hotel
6. **Táiwān shuǐguǒ**	Taiwan fruit
7. **Guǎngzhōu yóukè**	Tourists from Guangzhou
8. **Náncèsuǒ wú rén.**	The men's toilet is vacant.
9. **Shǒudū Yīyuàn**	The Capital Hospital
10. **Zhōngguó Yínháng**	The Bank of China
11. **Nǐ shi Zhōngguó rén.**	You are Chinese.
12. **Jìnzhǐ shíyóu chūkǒu.**	It is forbidden to export petroleum.
13. **Měiguó chē dà.**	American cars are large.
14. **Rénmínbì sānyì bāqiān liùbǎi wǔshiwàn yuán.**	¥386,500,000 RMB.
15. **Yóukè shi bu shi Xiānggǎng rén?**	Are the tourists from Hong Kong?

CHINESE-ENGLISH WORD-LIST

Numbers refer to the chapter in which an item first appears.

a	(final particle) 3	bǎo	full, replete 18
ài	to love, to love to 8	bào	a newspaper 10
Ài'ěrlán	Ireland 2	bào shang	in the newspaper 10
àiren	spouse 10	bàoqiàn	to regret 18
Āiyā!	Ouch! Oh dear! 13	bēi	(measure: cup of) 4
ānjìng	quiet 17	běi	north 5
ānpái	to arrange, arrangement 7	Běijīng	Beijing (Peking) 2
ànmó	massage 17	bèi	multiple 16
Àodàlìyà	Australia 2	bèi	(forms passive) 19
Àozhōu	Australia 15	běn	(measure for books) 15
Àolínpǐkè	Olympics 18	běndì	native 15
		běnlái	originally 19
bā	eight 3	bèn	stupid 19
bǎ	to grasp 17	bǐ	compared with 8; 'ratio' 13
ba	(final particle) 2	bǐjiào	rather, comparatively 4
bàba	dad, father 3	bǐ	a pen 14
bái	white 8	bì xìng	my humble surname 2
báijiǔ	Chinese spirit 18	biànfàn	a simple meal, pot-luck 14
báitiān	in daylight 15	-bianr	side 5
bǎi	hundred 10	biǎo	a watch 7
bǎi fēn zhī	per cent 19	biǎoshì	to show/express feelings 13
bǎihuò dàlóu	department store 5	bié	don't 4
bǎihuò gōngsī	department store 5	biéde	other 18
bān	shift, work 7;	biékàn	despite 18
	scheduled service 16	bié tí le	don't even mention it 17
bān	to move 14	bìng	illness, disease 10
bān jiā	to move house 14	bìng le	to become ill 10
bǎn	printing block; edition 15	bīnguǎn	guest-house, hotel 11
bàn	half 7	bìyè	to graduate 12
bàn	to manage, handle, deal with 13	bízi	nose 17
bànbuchéng	cannot do successfully 16	bíyānhú	snuff bottle 5
bàndechéng	can do successfully 16	bō	to dial 13
bàn shǒuxù	to carry out a procedure 15	bō hàomǎ	to dial a number 13
bāng	to help 13	bù	not 2
bāngmáng	to help 13	búbì	no need to 9
bāo	guaranteed 16	búcuò	not bad (very good) 9
bāoguǒ	parcel 15	bú èr jià	'only one price' 16
bāoguǒdān	parcel form 15	búguò	but, however 11

bù hǎo yìsi	embarrassed; I'm sorry 1	
bú kèqi	impolite; don't be polite 6	
bù shūfu	uncomfortable; unwell, off-colour 10	
bù tóng	different 16	
búxiè	don't mention it 1	
bù xíng	it's no good, it won't do 9	
bú yào	don't 4	
bú yàojǐn	unimportant; it doesn't matter 10	
búyòng	there's no need 17	
bú zài le	deceased 14	
bù	ministry, government department 11	
bùzhǎng	head of a ministry 12	
cái	merely 11; only then 14	
cài	vegetable; food; cuisine 9	
càidān	menu 9	
cānjiā	to take part in 11	
cāntīng	restaurant 7	
céng	layer, storey, floor 14	
cèsuǒ	toilet, washroom 5	
chá	to examine, to check 9	
chá	tea 4	
cháhú	teapot 5	
chàbuduō	almost, more or less 10	
chà(yi)diǎnr	come very close to 19	
cháng	long 8	
Chángchéng	the Great Wall 10	
chángshòu	long life 19	
chángtú	long-distance 13	
cháng	often 8	
chángcháng	often 12	
cháng	to taste 9	
chàng gēr	to sing songs 18	
chāopiào	banknote 13	
chǎo	noisy 4	
chǎo	to stir fry 18	
chē	wheeled vehicle 6	
chēcì	train number 7	
chēng	to weigh 15	
chéng	a defensive wall 11	
Chénghuáng	City God 5	
chéngli	in town 11	
chéngwài	outside the city 11	
Chéngdū	Chengdu (city) 7	
chī	to eat 4	
chībuqǐ	cannot afford to eat 16	
chīdeqǐ	can afford to eat 16	

chī fàn	to have a meal, to eat 7
chīsùde	a vegetarian 9
chī yào	to take medicine 10
chóngxīn	anew, afresh 19
Chóngqìng	Chungking (city) 7
chōu yān	to smoke 4
chū	to put out, to develop, to emit 7
chūbǎn	to publish 15
chū chāi	to go away on business 12
chū guó	to go abroad 10
chūjìng	to leave the country 11
chūkǒu	export 16
chū máobìng	to go wrong 14
chūmén	to set out from home 17
chūqu	to go out 9
chūshēng	to be born 7
chū shì	to have an accident 14
chū wèntí	to develop a problem 7
chūzū	for hire, to let 15
chūzū(qì)chē	taxi 6
chù*	office 13
chuān	to wear 8
chuānshang	to put on (clothes) 8
chuānghu	window 17
chuánzhēn	fax 13
chuánzhēnjī	fax machine 13
chuī	to blow 17
chúle … yǐwài	apart from … 18
chūntiān	spring 16
cì	(verbal measure) time, occurrence 6
cóng	from 6
cónglái	always, at any time, ever 11
cù	vinegar 18
cuò	error, wrong 12
dǎ	to hit 10
dǎ dī	to take a taxi 8
dǎ diànhuà	to make a phone call 10
dǎ lánqiú	to play basket-ball 8
dǎ lǐngdài	to wear a tie 17
dǎ quán	to box 10
dǎsuan	to intend to, plan to 7
dǎ tàijíquán	to do taiji 9
dǎ yú	to catch fish 10
dǎ yǔmáoqiú	to play badminton 9
dǎ zhékòu	to give a discount 16
dǎ zhēn	to have/give an injection 10
dǎ zì	to type 10

dà	big 6		diàotóu	to turn around 6
dàhòutiān	day after day after tomorrow 17		dìfang	a place, location 5
dàjiā	everybody 1		dìtiě	subway, underground 6
dà jiǎn jià	'sale' 16		dìtú	a map 5
dàlù	main road 6		dìxià	basement, lower ground floor 5
dàqiántiān	day before day before yesterday 17		dìzhǐ	an address 14
			dísīkē	discotheque 18
dàrén	adult, grown-up 8		diū	to lose 19
dàshǐ	ambassador 15		dōng	east 5
dàshǐguǎn	embassy 15		dōngběi	northeast 5
dàxué	university 11		dōngnán	southeast 5
dài	bring with, carry 4		Dōngnányà	Southeast Asia 15
dài	to wear (accessories) 8		dōngxi	thing 5
dàibiǎo	to represent; a representative 11		Dōngyà	East Asia 15
dàibiǎotuán	delegation 13		dǒng	to understand 11
dàifu	a doctor 10		dòng	to move 16
dān/dānzi	bill, form, list 15		dōngtiān	winter 8
dānrénfáng	single room 4		dōu	all, both 2; even 12; already 16
dāng	to be in the role of 12			
dāngrán	of course 11		dòufu	beancurd, tofu 9
Dānmài	Denmark 2		dù	(measure: degrees) 8
dǎo chē	to change trains etc 6		dù jià	to spend holidays 19
dào	to arrive; to 6		duǎn	short (length) 14
dàoqī	to expire, reach time limit 7		duǎnxìn	a note, text message 14
dàobǎn	pirated edition 15		duàn	(measure: section) 16
dāying	to respond, agree to 17		duànliàn	to exercise 9
de	(possessive) 2; (link) 5		duì	correct 6; about 18
de	in such a way that 12, 17		duìbuqǐ	sorry; excuse me; pardon me 1
Déguó	Germany 2		duìdeqǐ	to be worthy 16
Déwén	German language 3		duì le	that's right 13
Déyǔ	German language 11		duìmiàn	opposite 14
děi	must; require 6		duì X	
děng	to wait, to wait for 8		yǒu-xìngqù	interested in X 18
děng … zài …	let's first … 11		duì X	
Dèng	(surname) 2		yǒu-yánjiū	knowledgeable about X 18
dì-	(prefix for ordinal numbers) 15		dùn	(measure for meals) 13
diǎn	dot, hour 7		duō	many, much 12; how? 12
diǎn cài	to order (in restaurant) 18		duōle	a lot more 9
diǎnxin	pastries, snacks 4		duō(me)	how … ! 18
diàn	electricity, electric 3		duōshao?	how many? how much? 3
diànchí	battery 10		dùzi	stomach, belly 10
diànhuà	phone 3		dùziténg	stomach ache 17
diànnǎo	computer 7			
diànshì	television 18		è	hungry, starving 18
diàntī	lift, elevator 4		Ēi	Hey! 2
diànyóu dìzhǐ	email address 14		Éluósī	Russia 2
diànzǐ	electron, electronic 9		èr	two 3
diànzǐ biǎo	quartz watch 9		ěrduo	ears 17
diànzǐ jìsuànjī	computer 9		érzi	son 12
diànzǐ yóujiàn	email message 9			

fā	to send out, emit 13
fā chuánzhēn	send a fax 13
fā duǎnxìn	send a text message 14
fāshāo	to have a fever 10
fāyán	inflammation 17
fā yóujiàn	send an email 13
Fǎguó	France 2
Fǎguó cài	French food 9
Fǎyǔ	French language 11
fázi	way, method 13
fàn	cooked rice; a meal 7
fàndiàn	hotel 3
fànguǎnr	restaurant (not part of institution) 7
fāng*	side, party 19
fāngbiàn	convenient 9
fāngmiàn	aspect, side 19
fāngxiàng	direction 15
fáng	room 4
fángjiān	a room 3
fángzi	house 9
fàng	to put in/on, to place 11
fàngxīn	don't worry 16
fēi … bùkě	simply must 18
fēicháng	extraordinarily 18
fēicháng bàoqiàn	very much regret 18
Fēizhōu	Africa 10
fēijī	aircraft 6
fēijīchǎng	airport 6
fēijīpiào	air ticket 16
fēn	a cent 5; a minute 7
fèn	(measure for newspapers, documents) 13
fēng	wind, breeze 17
fēngjǐng	scenery 4
fēng	(measure for letters) 14
fú	(measure for paintings) 18
"Fú"*	"Good Luck" 8
fúqi	good fortune 8
fù	to pay 7
fù*	assistant-, vice-, deputy- 12
fùdàibiǎo	assistant representative 12
fùjúzhǎng	deputy bureau chief 12
Fùdàn Dàxué	Fudan University 14
fùjìn	nearby 5
fùqin	father 3
fūren	wife; Mrs. 2

gǎn	to dare 18
gǎn	to catch up with 16
gǎnbushàng	can't catch up 16
gānbēi!	bottoms up! cheers! 1
gānjing	clean 17
gānxǐ	dry-cleaning 17
gāng + verb	to have just … 10
gànmá?	doing what? Why on earth? 9
gǎnmào	influenza, 'flu 17
gǎnxiè	to be grateful to 19
gāo	high, tall 8
gāo'ěrfū (qiú)	golf 7
gāofēng	peak 16
gāofēng shíjiān	peak time 16
gāoxìng	happy, delighted 12
gàosu	to tell, inform 11
ge	(measure for people etc) 4
gēge	elder brother 14
gěi	for 9; to 14
gēn	with 9
gèng	even more 8
gè wèi	everybody 19
gèzi	build, stature 8
Gōng'ānjú	Public Security Bureau. Police 12
gōnggòng qìchē	bus 6
gōngjīn	kilogram 12
gōnglǐ	kilometre 14
gōngsī	company 3
gōngyuán	a park 5
gōngchǎng	factory 17
gōngfu	free time, available time 12
gōngzuò	to work; work 11
Gōngxǐ!	Congratulations! 1
Gōngxǐ fācái!	Happy New Year! 1
gòu	enough 8
guǎi	to turn 6
guān mén	to shut the door 7
Guǎngdōng cài	Cantonese food 9
Guǎngdōng huà	Cantonese language 11
Guǎngzhōu	Guangzhou (Canton) (city) 8
guāngpán	CD, DVD, CD ROM 15
gǔdǒng	antiques 5
guì	honourable 2; expensive 5
guìbīn	distinguished guest 19
guìxìng?	What is your surname? 2
guīdìng	to stipulate, lay down 13
Guìlín	Guilin (city) 6

guó	country, state 2
Guó Háng	Air China 17
guójì	international 13
guójì diànhuà	international phonecall 13
guónèi	inland 14
guówài	abroad 14
guò	to cross over 15
- guo	(verb-ending) to have had the experience 11
gùshi	story, plot 18
hái	still, yet 6; even more so 9; in addition 13
hái kěyǐ	passable 12
háishi	for preference 6
háishi... ba	it would be better if 8
Hǎinán	Hainan Island 17
háizi	a child 10
hángbān	airline flight 16
hángkōng	aviation; airmail 15
hángkōng gōngsī	airline company 16
hángzhànlóu	airport terminal building 11
Hànrén	Chinese people 11
Hànyǔ	Chinese language 11
Hànyǔ pīnyīn	official romanisation system 19
Hànzì	Chinese characters 19
hǎo	good, fine, well, OK 1; very 12
hǎochī	delicious, tasty 11
hǎo ji ge	quite a few 14
hǎo jiǔ bú jiàn	long time no see 12
hǎokàn	attractive, good-looking, pretty 9
hǎo le	then it'll be OK 16
hǎotīng	good to hear, nice-sounding 11
hǎowánr	good fun, amusing 5
hǎoxiàng	seems like 9
hào	number 4; day of month 7
hàomǎ	number 3
hàor	size 8
hē	to drink 4
hē jiǔ	to drink (alcohol) 9
hé	and 15
Hé	(surname) 2
Hè!	Wow! Gosh! 18
héhuā	lotus flower 18
Hélán	Holland 2
hēi	black 8
hěn	very 4
hétong	a contract 16
hézuò	co-operation 19

hóng	red 4
hóngchá	black tea 4
hóngdēng	red light 15
hónglùdēng	traffic lights 15
hóngshāo	'red-cooked' 18
Hóng Shízì Huì	Red Cross 15
hòu	thick 17
hóulóngténg	sore throat 17
hòutou	behind 5
hòulúnr	rear wheel(s) 15
hòunián	the year after next 7
hòutiān	day after tomorrow 7
huā	to spend 19
huà	speech 3
huàjù	a play 6
huà huàr	to paint a painting 18
huàjiā	an artist 18
huài	bad, evil 15
huài le	rotten, broken down 15
huàn	to change, exchange 4
huàn chē	change (trains etc) 6
huàn qián	to change money 6
huáng	yellow 8
huángdēng	amber light 15
huángjiǔ	rice wine 18
Huángshān	the Yellow Mountains 18
huánjìng	surroundings, environment 9
huānsòng	to bid farewell 19
huānyíng	welcome 1
Huānyíng guānglín	We welcome your custom 1
Huáqiáo	Overseas Chinese 3
Huáyǔ	Chinese language 11
huī	grey 17
huí	to return 10
huí guó	to return from abroad 10
huí jiā	to return home 10
huì	a meeting 7; to know how to 11; 'future possibility' 14
huìtán	to hold formal talks 19
hùliánwǎng	internet 9
huǒchē	railway train 6
huǒchēzhàn	railway station 6
huódòng	activity, to 'do something' 18
huòzhě	or 18
hūrán	suddenly 15
hùzhào	passport 3

jī	chicken 9
jīdīngr	diced chicken 18
jǐ	crowded, packed 8
jǐ?	how many? 3
jì	to post, to mail 14
ji	few, several 11
jiā	family, home 3; (measure for shops/businesses) 7
jiā yóu!	come on! play up! 1
Jiānádà	Canada 2
jiǎchāo	counterfeit note 13
jiān	(measure for rooms) 4
jiàn	to see 7
jiàn	(measure for items of clothing) 8
jiǎnchá	to check, examine 11
jiǎng	to speak, lecture 19
jiǎng jià	to bargain 18
jiàngluò	to land (aircraft) 17
jiàngyóu	soy sauce 18
jiànkāng	good health 19
jiànmiàn	to meet face to face 9
jiànzhù	structure, building 11
jiào	to call; be called 2; (forms passive) 19
jiāo fèi	pay charges 5
jiāo shū	to teach 12
jiàoshòu	professor 14
jiāoyìhuì	trade fair 11
jiǎozi	filled dumplings 18
jiàqian	price 18
jiàzhí	value, worth 19
jīchǎng	airport 6
jīchǔ	foundation, basis 19
jìde	to remember 17
jìzhě	a reporter 10
jiē	to connect 3; to answer, receive 5; pick up, meet 7
jiēdào	to receive 14
jiē	street 5
jiéguǒ	result 14
jiéhūn	to marry 12
jié zhàng	to settle the bill 8
jiěkai	to undo 17
jiémù	(television) programme 18
jièshào	to introduce 12
jìjié	season 16
-jíle	exceedingly 7
jīn	catty 16
jìn	close, near 5

jìn	enter 11
jìn chéng	to go into town 11
jìn - chū	in and out 14
jìnkǒu	import 16
jìnyíbù	enhanced 19
jìng	to respect, salute, toast 12
jǐngchá	policeman 15
jīngjì	economics 14
Jīngjì Tèqū	Special Economic Zone (SEZ) 14
jīnglǐ	manager 3
jīnhòu	henceforth 19
jīnnián	this year 7
jīntiān	today 7
jì'niànpǐn	souvenir, memento 15
jìsuànjī	computer 9
jiǔ	a long while 11
jiǔ	alcoholic drink 4
jiǔbā	pub, wine bar 18
jiǔbēi	wine glass 12
jiǔ	nine 3
jiù	old (of inanimate things) 13
jiù	just 3; at once 6
jiù hǎo le	I wish; that's what matters 11
jiù shi	That's just what it is 3
jiù mìng a!	Help! 1
jìxù	to continue 17
jú*	bureau, office 12
júzhǎng	bureau chief 12
jù	(measure for speech: phrase, sentence) 11
jù*	huge, enormous 11
jùchǎng	theatre 6
juéde	to feel 17
kǎ	a card 10
kǎlā-OK	karaoke 18
kāfēi	coffee 4
kāfēitīng	café 5
kāi	to drive 6; to open 7
kāi chē	to drive a car 14
kāidào	to drive to 6
kāi huì	to hold/attend a meeting 7
kāi mén	to open the door 7
kāishǐ	to begin 17
kāishuǐ	boiled/boiling water 17
kāi wánxiào	to make fun, to joke 19
kāi yàofāng	write out a prescription 17
kāi zhèngmíng	to issue a certificate 18
kāi zhīpiào	write a cheque 17

kàn	to look at 5
kàn bào	to read the newspaper 10
kànbujiàn	cannot see 16
kàndejiàn	can see 16
kànjian	to see 12
kàn shū	to read 19
kǎo yā	roast duck 7
kě	(adverb for stressing) 16
Kě bú shì ma!	Too right! 18
Kěkǒu Kělè	Coca Cola 4
kěnéng	maybe 5
kěshi	but 3
kěxī	what a pity 18
kěyǐ	may, can 4
kěyǐ bù	alright not to 9
kè	quarter hour 7
kè	a lesson 19
kěndìng	sure to 16
kèqi	polite 6
késou	cough, to cough 17
kǒngpà	I'm afraid 14
kōngqì	air 9
kōngtiáo	air-conditioning 8
kǒuyīn	accent 14
kǒuyǔ	oral, spoken language 9
kū	to weep 18
kǔ	bitter 18
kǔguā	bitter melon 18
kuài	fast, quick 7; soon 11
kuàichē	fast train 7
kuàilè	happy 19
kuài	dollar, buck, yuan 5
kuàizi	chopsticks 18
kuàngquánshuǐ	mineral water 4
kùnnan	difficult, difficulty 16
la	= **le** + **a** 15
là	peppery-hot 18
làjiāo	chilli 18
làzi jīdīngr	diced chicken with chilli 18
lái	to come 6; cause to come 18
láibují	not be in time for 16
láidejí	be in time for 16
lán	blue 8
lánqiú	basket-ball 8
lánqiúduì	basket-ball team 8
lǎo	old 2
lǎoshī	teacher 9
lǎo tàitai	old lady, old woman 9
lǎo wài	foreigner 18

le	'excessive' 4;
	(final particle: new state) 6;
	(verb-ending) 10, 11
lèi	tired, weary 8
lei	(final particle: with pleasure) 11
lěng	cold 8
lí	separated from (by distance) 14;
	(by time) 16
Lǐ	(surname) 2
lǐ	Chinese mile 16
liànxí	to practise 9
liàn qìgōng	to practice *qigong* 9
liǎng	two 4
liàng	(measure for wheeled
	vehicles) 8
liángkuai	pleasantly cool 8
liánxùjù	serial, soap opera 18
liǎojiě	to understand 19
liáotiānr	to chat 9
lìhai	formidable, tough 18
líng	zero 3
lǐngdài	necktie 17
lǐngdǎo	to lead; leadership, leader 13
lǐtou	inside 5
liù	six 3
liúlì	fluent 12
liúxia	to leave behind 14
lóng	a dragon 11
lóu	building, floor 4
lóushang	upstairs 8
lóuxia	downstairs 8
lù	road 6; bus line 6
lùkǒur	road junction 15
lǜ	green 8
lǜdēng	green light 15
Lúgōu Qiáo	Marco Polo Bridge 15
Lúndūn	London 3
lùnwén	academic paper, essay 14
lúnzi	a wheel 15
Luómǎ	Rome 14
lǚxíng	to travel 6
lǚxíng zhīpiào	travellers cheque 6
lǚyóu	tourism, to tour 5
lǚyóujú	tourist bureau 12
lǚyóutú	tourist map 5
lǚyóutuán	tour group 13
mǎ	horse 8
mǎlù	major road 15
mǎshang	at once 6

ma	(final particle: question) 2
ma!	(final particle: obviously) 16
máfan	trouble, to trouble, troublesome 13
mǎi	to buy 5
mǎibudào	cannot be bought 16
mǎibuqǐ	unable to afford 16
Mǎi dān!	Bill, please! 15
mǎidedào	can be bought 16
mǎideqǐ	able to afford 16
mǎifāng	purchasers 19
mài	to sell 5
màifāng	vendors 19
Màidāngláo	Macdonald's restaurant 7
Mǎláixīyà	Malaysia 2
māma	mum, mother 3
mǎn	full 16
màn	slow 12
máng	busy 7
máng shénme?	busy doing what? 14
mángzhe	busy at 18
Màngǔ	Bangkok 19
máo	(surname) 2; 10 cents, dime 5
máobìng	defect, fault 14
máotái	Maotai sorghum spirit 18
màozi	hat, cap 11
méi	not to have 4
méi fázi	there's no way 13
méi guānxi	not at all 1
méi shìr	it's nothing 1
méi xiǎngdào	didn't expect 11
méi-yìsi	uninteresting 15
měi	each, every 10
Měiguó	USA 2
Měiqiáo	American expatriates 3
Měiyuán	American dollars 6
Měizhōu	America 15
miàn*	face 12
miǎnfèi	free of charge 17
miào	temple 5
mǐfàn	(cooked) rice 18
míngnián	next year 7
míngtiān	tomorrow 7
míngxìnpiàn	postcard 15
míngzi	name 2
míngdān	name list 15
míngpiàn	namecard 2
míxìn	superstition 16
Mòxīgē	Mexico 2
mǔqin	mother 3

ná	to take 12
Nà	Well then; In that case 6
nà	that 2
nǎli	where? How could that be? 12
nàme	so, so much as that 8
nán	difficult 16
nán	south 5
Nán (fāng) Háng (kōng Gōngsī)	Southern Airlines 16
nán de	male 8
nánshì	gentleman 8
nǎr	where? 5
nàr	there 4
ne	(final particle) 'And how about…' 5
něi?	which? 3
nèi	that 5
nèiháng	expert, old hand 18
néng	to be able, can 10
Ǹg	Mm; oh yes! 9
nǐ	you 1
nǐ fāng	your side 19
Nǐ hǎo	Hello! 1
nǐmen	you (plural) 2
nián	year 4
niàn shū	to study 12
Niǎocháo	The Bird's Nest 18
nín	you (polite) 1
Nín guì xìng?	What is your surname? 2
niúnǎi	(cow's) milk 4
nóng	heavy (of colour) 18
nòng	to play with; make, get 17
nǚ de	female 8
nǚ'ér	daughter 12
nǚshì	woman, lady, madam; Ms 8
nǚwáng	queen 11
nuǎnhuo	warm 8
Òu	Oh! 3
Oūyuán	Euro (Ā) 6
Ōuzhōu	Europe 10
pà	to fear, be afraid 4
pài	to dispatch, deploy 13
pái(zi)/páir	brand 17
páijià	exchange rate 13
páigu	spare ribs 18
pàng	fat (of people) 8
pèngjian	to bump into, meet 12

péngyou	friend 2	quán	completely 10
piān	(measure for writings) 14		
piànr	(measure: tablet) 10	ràng	to allow, to cause 17;
piányi	cheap 15		(forms passive) 19
piào	ticket 6	rè	hot 4
piàoliang	beautiful 4	rén	person, man 2
píjiŭ	beer 4	rénmín	the people 6
píndào	(television) channel 18	Rénmínbì	RMB Chinese currency 6
píng	(measure: bottle of) 4	rénrén	everybody 9
píngcháng	normally, usually 9	rén shān rén	
píngyóu	surface mail 15	hăi	teeming crowds 19
píngguŏ	apple 16	rénxíng	
pīnyīn	to spell out sounds 19	héngdào	pedestrian crossing 15
pò	damaged, broken, torn 13	rènshi	to recognise, know 3
pútáojiŭ	grape wine 18	rèn zì	to be literate 19
Pŭtōnghuà	'Universal Language',	rì	sun; day 7
	Mandarin 11	Rìběn	Japan 2
		Rìběn huà	Japanese language 11
qī	seven 3	róngyi	easy 11
qí	to straddle, ride (horse, bike) 8	ròu	meat (usually pork) 9
qiān	a thousand 18	ròupiànr	sliced pork 18
qiān	to sign 16	rùjìngkă	immigration card 11
qiāndìng	to sign (contract) 19		
qiānzhèng	a visa 7	sān	three 3
qián	money 5	sànbù	to go for a stroll 18
qiánbāor	purse, wallet 19	săosao	elder brother's wife 14
qiăn	light (colour) 17	shàng	to board 6; to go to 10
qiánlúnr	front wheel(s) 15	shàng bān	to go to work 7
qiánnián	the year before last 7	shàng cì	last time 6
qiántiān	day before yesterday 7	shàng (ge) yuè	last month 8
qiántou	in front 5	Shànghăi	Shanghai 2
qìchē	motor vehicle 6	shàng kè	to go to class 9
qĭfēi	to take off (aircraft) 16	shàngtou	on top, over, above 5
qìgōng	qigong exercises 9	shàng wăng	to go on the internet 8
qĭng	please; will you please 1;	shàngwŭ	a.m. 7
	to invite 7	shàng-xià	up and down 14
qĭngtiě	invitation card 13	shàng xīngqī	last week 8
Qĭng wèn	Please may I ask 5	shàngyī	upper garments 17
Qĭng zuò	Please take a seat 1	shāngdiàn	store, shop 7
qīngcài	green vegetable 18	shāngwù	commercial, business 13
qīngchu	clear 9	shānli	in the mountains 15
qìngzhù	to celebrate 19	shānshang	on top of the hill 8
qípáo	cheongsam 12	shānshuĭ	scenery, landscape 18
qíshí	actually, in fact 11	shānxia	at the bottom of the hill 8
qiú	a ball 7	shăo	few 9
qiūtiān	autumn, fall 16	shéi?	who? 1
qū	district 14	shéi de?	whose? 3
qŭ	to take, to withdraw 13	shèjì	to design 11
qù	to go 5	shēn	deep (colour) 17
qùnián	last year 7	shēng	to be born, to give birth to 14

shēng háizi	to give birth to a child 10	
shēngrì	birthday 19	
shēngyi	business 18	
shěng	province 14	
Shèngdàn	Christmas 19	
shèngxia	to remain over 19	
shénme?	what? what kind of? 2	
shénme dìfang?	where? 7	
shénme rén?	what person? Who? 7	
shénme shì?	what matter? What's up? 7	
shénme shíhou?	when? 7	
shēnqǐng	to apply for 19	
shēntǐ	body; health 12	
Shēnzhèn	Shenzhen (Shamchun) 12	
shí	ten 3	
shízìlùkǒur	crossroads 15	
shì	to be 2	
shì	it is the case that 6	
Shìde	Yes Sir! 14	
shì	business, matter, affair 4	
shì	to try 17	
shì biǎo	to take temperature 17	
shìshi	to try, have a try 15	
shì	city, municipality 14	
shìchǎng	a market 5	
shīfu	master, maestro, chief 5	
shíhou	time 7	
shíjiān	time 7	
shí zì	to be literate 19	
shōu	to receive, accept 11	
shōuhǎo	keep, look after 11	
shōushi	to pack, put in order 10	
shóu	familiar with 16	
shǒu	hand 12	
shǒujī	mobile phone, cell-phone 3	
shǒushang	in the hand 12	
shǒuxù	procedure 15	
shòu	slim, thin, skinny 8	
shòu	to suffer 18	
shòu huānyíng	to be popular 18	
shòu kǔ	to suffer hardship 18	
shòu lèi	to be put to a lot of trouble 18	
shǒudū	capital city 6	
shū	a book 12	
shūdiàn	bookstore 15	
shú	familiar with 16	
shǔ	to count 13	
shuākǎ	swipe card 7	
shuāngfāng	both sides 19	
shuāngrén fáng	double room 4	

shūfu	comfortable 10
shuǐ	water 4
shuǐguǒ	fruit 16
shuǐxǐ	laundry 17
shuì jiào	to sleep 10
shùnzhe	following 15
shuō	to speak, to say 9
shuōdào	to mention 9
shuōdìng	to settle, to agree on 13
shuō huà	to speak 9
sǐ	to die 14
sì	four 3
Sìchuān cài	Sichuan (Szechwan) food 9
sòng	to escort, see someone to 11; to send, deliver 13
suān	sour 18
suānlà tāng	sour & hot soup 18
suàn	to calculate 16
suàn le	forget it! 16
sùcài	vegetarian food 9
sùcàiguǎnr	vegetarian restaurant 9
Sūgélán	Scotland 2
suì	year of age 3
suíbiàn	please yourself 18
suīrán	although 9
suǒyǒu de	all 16
tā	he, she, it 2
tāmen	they, them 2
tài	too, too much 4
tàijíquán	*taiji* 9
tàitai	Mrs. 9
tán	to talk, chat 18
tán shēngyi	to talk business 18
tāng	soup 10
táng	sugar 4
tángcù páigu	sweet & sour spare ribs 18
Táng	(surname) 14
tàng	(verbal measure: a trip, a time) 10
tào	(measure: suit of, set of) 17
tǎoyàn	annoying 16
tèbié	special, especially 7
tèbié kuàichē	an express 7
tè-dà	extra-large 8
tèkuài	an express 7
Tèqū	special zone, Special Administrative Region 14
téng	sore, painful, ache; to be painful 10

tī	to kick 17	
tī zúqiú	to play football/soccer 17	
tí	to lift up 17	
tíkuǎnjī	ATM 13	
tí yìjiàn	to give an opinion 14	
tì	on behalf of 9	
tiān	day; sky, heaven 4, 8	
Tiān'ānmén	Tiananmen 6	
tiānqì	weather 8	
tiānqì yùbào	weather forecast 8	
tiāntiān	every day 9	
tián	sweet 18	
tián biǎo	to fill in a form 4	
tiāo	to choose 16	
tiáo	(measure for long flexible things) 6	
tiáojiàn	condition, conditions 14	
tiào wǔ	to dance 9	
tiē	to stick, to paste 15	
tīng	to listen to, to heed 11	
tīngjiàn	to hear 12	
tīngshuō	it is said that, I've heard that 11	
tíng	to stop 17	
tíng diàn	power cut 17	
tíng shuǐ	water shut-off 17	
tōng	to get through, to communicate 17	
tōngguò	as a result of 19	
tōngzhī	to inform, to let know 14	
tóngxué	fellow student 12	
tóngzhì	comrade 6	
tōu	to steal 19	
tóufa	hair (on the head) 8	
tóuténg	to have a headache 10	
tù	to vomit 10	
tuán*	a group 13	
tǔdòur	potato 9	
tuì	retreat, return 14	
tuìhuílai	return to sender 14	
T-xùshān	T-shirt 8	
wài	outside, foreign 2	
wàibì	foreign currency 13	
wàidì	non-native 15	
wàiguó	foreign country 2	
wàiguó rén	foreigner 2	
wàiqiáo	aliens 3	
wàishìchù	foreign affairs office 13	
wàitou	outside 5	
wàiyǔ	foreign language 11	

wán	to end, to finish 10	
wánquán	completely 10	
wǎn	(measure for 'bowl of'); a bowl 10	
wǎn	late 7	
wǎndiǎn	behind time 11	
wǎnshang	in the evening 7	
Wǎnshang hǎo	Good evening 2	
wàn	ten thousand 18	
Wànlǐ Chángchéng	the Great Wall 18	
wàn shì rú yì	satisfaction in all you do 19	
Wáng	(surname) 2	
wǎng	towards 6	
wǎng huí zǒu	to turn back 15	
wàng	to forget 10	
wàngbuliǎo	unforgettable 16	
wǎngyǒu	internet friend 9	
wǎngzhǐ	website 14	
wánr	to play, amuse oneself 8	
Wéi	Hello**!** (on phone) 1	
wèi	(measure: polite for people) 4	
wèizi	seat, place 16	
wèidao	flavour 9	
wèikǒu	appetite 17	
wèile	on account of 19	
wèishénme?	why? 7	
wèishēngjiān	bathroom, toilet 4	
wēixiǎn	danger, dangerous 16	
wèn	to ask a question 5	
wèntí	a question, problem 7	
wénhuà	culture 11	
Wénhuàbù	Culture Ministry 11	
wénjiàn	document 13	
wǒ	I, me 1	
wǒ fāng	my/our side 19	
wǒmen	we, us 2	
Wú	(surname) 2	
wǔ	five 3	
wǔfàn	lunch 17	
xī	west 5	
Xībānyá	Spain 2	
xīběi	northwest 5	
xīcān	Western food 13	
xīcāntīng	Western food restaurant 13	
xīguā	water melon 16	
xī'nán	southwest 5	
xīzhuāng	(western-style) suit 17	
xǐ	to wash 17	

xǐ shǒu	to wash the hands, go to the toilet 17	**xíguàn**	custom; accustomed to 18
xǐshǒujiān	the toilet 17	**xǐhuan**	to like, be fond of 5
xǐ tóu	to wash the hair 17	**xīn**	new 14
xǐ yī(fu)	to wash clothes 17	**Xīnjiāng**	Xinjiang (Autonomous Region) 16
xǐyījī	washing machine 17	**Xīnnián**	New Year 19
xǐzǎo	to have a bath 17	**xīnwén**	(media) news 10
xià	to disembark 6	**xìn**	letter 14
xià bān	to finish work 7	**xìnxīn**	confidence 19
xià cì	next time 6	**xìnyòngkǎ**	credit card 18
xià (ge) yuè	next month 8	**xíng**	OK, alright, will do 9
-xiàqu	to go on doing 18	**xíngli**	luggage 10
xiàtou	under, below 5	**xìng**	surname; to be surnamed 2
xiàwǔ	p.m. 7	**xìngkuī**	luckily 19
xià xīngqī	next week 8	**xīngqī**	week 7
xià xuě	to snow 8	**xīngqīrì/tiān**	Sunday 7
xià yǔ	to rain 8	**Xīngbākè**	Starbucks 14
xiān	first 4	**xìngqù**	interest 18
xiān…zài…	first…next… 13	**xīnkǔ**	hard work 19
xiānsheng	Mr., sir 2	**xiū/xiūlǐ**	to mend, repair 15
xián	salty 18	**xiūxi**	to rest; to shut 4, 7
xiǎng	to think; would like to 4	**xīwàng**	hope, to hope 14
xiǎngdào	to imagine, think of 11	**xué**	to learn 9
xiàng	like, to resemble 11	**xuésheng**	student 12
Xiānggǎng	Hong Kong 2	**xuéxiào**	a school 12
xiāngjiāo	banana 16	**xūyào**	to need, to need to 13
Xiāngshān	Xiangshan county 6		
xiāngxìn	to believe 19	**yā(zi) or yā***	duck 9
xiāngzi	a case, box 17	**yān**	smoke; a cigarette 4
xiànzài	now 7	**yán**	salt 18
xiànchāo	ready money, banknote 13	**yǎn**	to act 18
xiànjīn	cash, ready money 6	**yàngzi**	appearance 9
xiǎo	small, little 2	**yànhuì**	a banquet 19
xiǎojie	Miss, young lady 2	**yǎnjing**	eyes 17
xiǎoshí	hour 7	**yǎnjìngr**	glasses, spectacles 8
xiǎotōur	a thief 19	**yánjiū**	research, to research 14
xiǎoxīn	Watch out! 1; careful 15	**yánsè**	colour 8
xiǎoxué	primary school 11	**yāo**	one (on phone) 3
xiào	to laugh, smile 18	**yào**	medicine 10
xiāohuà	digestion 17	**yàofāng**	a prescription 17
xiāoxi	news, tidings 10	**yàopiànr**	(medicinal) tablet 10
xiàtiān	summer 16	**yào**	to want 4
xiē	(measure: plural/uncountable nouns) 9	**yàojǐn**	important 10
		yàoshi	if 13
xiě	to write 14	**yāoqǐng**	to invite 11
xiě xìn	write a letter 14	**yāoqǐngxìn**	letter of invitation 11
xiè	to have diarrhoea 10	**yàoshi**	a key 5
xiè dùzi	to have diarrhoea 10	**yáténg**	toothache 17
xièyào	a laxative 10	**Yàzhōu**	Asia 15
xièxie	thank you 1	**yě**	also 2

yèjǐng	night scene 18	
yī	one 3	
yìdiǎnr	a bit more 9	
yídìng	certainly 8	
yì fāngmiàn …	on the one hand…	
yì fāngmiàn …	on the other … 19	
yígerén	on one's own 9	
yígòng	altogether 10	
yíhuìr	a little while 8	
yì … jiù	as soon as 14	
yí lù píng ān	bon voyage 19	
yí lù shùn fēng	bon voyage 19	
yìqǐ	together 14	
yí rì qiān lǐ	making great progress 19	
yíxiàr	a bit; once 9;	
	in no time at all 19	
yìxiē	some, a few 9	
yíyàng	the same 9	
yìzhí	directly, straight 6;	
	(time) all along 11	
yì	100 million 18	
Yìdàlì	Italy 2	
yìjiàn	idea, opinion 14	
yìsi	meaning 8; token of	
	appreciation 13	
yīfu	clothes 17	
yǐhòu	after, afterwards 11	
yǐqián	before, formerly 11	
yǐwéi	to think, thought wrongly 12	
yǐjing	already 7	
yīmèi'ér	email 9	
Yìndù	India 2	
Yìnxiàngpài	Impressionist school 18	
yīnggāi	ought to, should 5	
Yīngguó	U.K., Britain 2	
Yīngbàng	Sterling 6	
Yīngháng	British Airways 16	
Yīngqiáo	British expatriates 3	
Yīngwén	English language 3	
Yīngwénbǎn	English edition 15	
Yīngyǔ	English language 11	
yínháng	bank 6	
yīntèwǎng	internet 9	
yīnwèi	because 19	
yīn huò dé fú	good luck from misfortune 19	
yīyuàn	hospital 10	
yòng	to use 9	
yòng … zuò de	made of … 9	
yǒu	to have; there is/are 4	
yǒude	some 7	

yǒu(de) shíhou	sometimes 7, 19	
yǒu-fúqi	lucky 18	
yǒu máobìng	to be faulty, to be ill 14	
yǒu-míng	famous 18	
yǒu-qián	rich 18	
yǒu-xìngqù	interested in 18	
yǒu-yánjiū	knowledgeable 18	
yǒu (yi)diǎnr	a bit 17	
yǒu-yìsi	interesting 15	
yǒu-yòng	useful 18	
yòu	furthermore, yet again 9	
yòu …yòu …	both … and … 17	
yóubiān	postcode, zipcode 14	
yóufèi	postage 15	
yóujiàn	email 13	
yóujú	Post Office 14	
yóupiào	postage stamp 15	
yóuzhèng		
biānmǎ	postcode, zipcode 14	
yòubianr	right 5	
yōuhuì	preferential, favourable 18	
yǒuyì	friendship 19	
yóuyǒng	to swim 5	
yóuyǒngchí	swimming-pool 5	
yú	fish 9	
yǔ*	language 11	
yuán	Yuan, ¥ 5	
yuǎn	far, distant 5	
yuè	month 7	
yuè … yuè …	the more … the more … 18	
yǔmáoqiú	badminton 9	
yùndòng	to take exercise; sport; activity 9	
yùnqi	luck 16	
yúnhǎi	sea of clouds 18	
zài	again 1; and then 11	
zàijiàn	goodbye 1	
zài	to be at, in, on 5	
zàizuò	here present 19	
zāng	dirty 13	
zánmen	we (present) 18	
zǎo	good morning; early 1	
zǎochen	in the morning 9	
zǎofàn	breakfast 10	
zǎojiù	long since 14	
zǎoshang	in the morning 7	
zǎoshang hǎo	good morning 1	
zēngjiā	to increase 19	
zěnme?	how? how come? 6, 8	
zěnme bàn?	what's to be done? 13	

zěnme huì ...?	how could it be...? 19	Zhōngcān	Chinese food 13
zěnme le	what's the matter? 15	Zhōngcāntīng	Chinese restaurant 13
zěnmeyàng	what's it like? how's things? 7	Zhōngguó	China 2
zhàn	station, stop, stand 6	Zhōngguó huà	Chinese language 11
zhāng	(surname) 2; (measure for flat sheet-like things) 6	Zhōngshān	Sun Yat-sen 6
zhāngkai	to stretch open 17	Zhōngwén	Chinese language 3
zhǎng	to rise (prices or water) 16	zhōngwǔ	noon 7
zhǎng*	head (of office etc) 12	zhōngxīn	a centre 13
zhàng	account 8	zhōngxué	secondary school 11
zhàngdān	the bill 8	Zhōngyāngtái	China Central Television 18
zhǎnlǎn	to exhibit 14	Zhōngyào	Chinese medicine 17
zhǎo	to look for: give change 6	zhōng	clock 7
Zháo huǒ la!	Fire! 1	zhǒng	(measure: kind, sort, type) 15
zháojí	anxious, worried, in a rush 11	Zhōu	(surname) 2
zhāodài	to serve, entertain 17	zhù	to live, to stay 4
zhāodàihuì	a reception 17	zhù	to be stationed in 15
zhàogù	consideration, care 19	zhù	to wish 19
zhàopiàn	a photograph 10	zhuādào	to catch, arrest 19
zhào xiàng	to take a photograph 4	zhuàn	to revolve 15
zhàoxiàngjī	camera 10	zhuàngshang	to crash into 16
zhè	this 2	zhǔn	to permit, to be permitted 4
zhème	so, so much as this 8	zhǔnbèi	to prepare, to get ready 10
-zhe	(verb ending) 'prolonged action' 12	zì	a Chinese character 8
zhèi	this 5	zìdòng	automatic 13
zhèi cì	this time 6	zìdòng tíkuǎn jī	automatic telling machine (ATM) 13
zhēn	a needle 10; (measure for injections) 10	zìjǐ	self, oneself 9
zhēnjiǔ	acupuncture 17	zìxíngchē	bicycle 8
zhēn(de)	true, real; truly, really 8	zǒngjī	switchboard, "Operator" 13
zhēn shi	truly, really 11	zǒngjīnglǐ	general manager 19
zhēnzhèng	true, real 19	zǒng shi	always 18
zhèng xiǎng	just about to, just thinking of 14	zǒu	to walk, go, leave 6
zhèng yào	just about to 14	zǒubudòng	can't get moving 16
zhèngzài	just –ing 13	zǒu lù	to walk 6
zhèngmíng	a certificate 18	zū	to rent, hire 15
zhèr	here 4	zuǐ	mouth, jaws 17
zhī	(measure for stick-like objects) 4	zuì	most 9
zhī	(measure for most animals) 10	zuì shǎo	at least 15
zhǐ	only 4	zuìjìn	recently 12
zhǐyào	provided that, so long as 9	zuì	drunk, tipsy 18
zhíbō	direct dial 13	zuò	to make 9
zhíjiē	directly 13	zuòbuwán	cannot finish doing 16
zhīdao	to know 3	zuòdewán	can finish doing 16
zhídé	to be worth 19	zuò fàn	to cook 9
zhījiān	between 19	zuò	to sit 1; travel by 6
zhīpiào	a cheque 7	zuò chī shān kōng	be idle and lose all 19
zhìshǎo	at least 12	zuǒbianr	left 5
zhōng	middle, centre 2	zuótiān	yesterday 7

INDEX

Use this index to find information quickly in the book. To help you locate points that you want to refresh your memory on, grammar notes are listed under the headings they bear in the text. In addition you will find grammatical categories such as 'adverbs', 'final particles' and 'measures' listed, as well as general topics like 'names', 'numbers' and 'telephoning', and key words like 'also', 'even' and 'sorry'.

References are to **Chapter and Note *(e.g. 11.3)*; Chapter and Conversation *(11B)*;** Chapter and Boxed Text *(11.box)*; the **Introduction *(Intro.)*,** and the **Exercises *(Ex.79)*.**